LARRY MILLSON

BALLPARK FIGURES

THE BLUE JAYS AND
THE BUSINESS OF BASEBALL

McCLELLAND AND STEWART

Canadian Cataloguing in Publication Data

Millson, Larry
Ballpark figures

ISBN 0-7710-5876-4

1. Toronto Blue Jays (Baseball Team).   2. Sports
franchises – Ontario – Toronto.   I. Title.

GV875.T6M54 1987   796.357′64′09713541   C87-093700-6

A Peter Livingston Book

DESIGN: RICHARD MILLER

Printed and Bound in Canada by
John Deyell Co.

McClelland and Stewart
The Canadian Publishers
481 University Avenue
Toronto   M5G 2E9

CONTENTS

FIRST   The Game Within the Game   7

SECOND   Doing it on the Road   36

THIRD   Back to the Drawing Board   66

FOURTH   Chasing the Dream   95

FIFTH   Selling the Sizzle   120

SIXTH   They Call Us the KGB   147

SEVENTH   Cultivating the Future Down on the Farm   177

EIGHTH   The Latin Connection   208

NINTH   Spring Training – Land of Hope and Story   234

TENTH   The Name of the Game is Hardball   262

TO MY FAMILY
Diane, Cara, Suzi, Isobel and Eaton

F I R S T

THE GAME
WITHIN THE GAME

IN WINTER, from beneath the huge right-field scoreboard – a silent sentry 41 feet high and 131 feet long – the stadium stood empty and and cold. Snow blew in on the icy winds off Lake Ontario by the light stanchions towering over the grey and blue concrete slabs that rise from the visiting team's dugout. The snow piled in corners of the grandstand, formed latticework patterns among the field-level chairs, lashed in jagged streaks across the too-green Monsanto turf – 160,000 square feet of it when the football field is included to form the largest splash of ersatz grass in North America.

A sorry imitation of a baseball park in season, the illusion fails altogether when the field is stripped of its blue outfield fences. The outfield barriers are removable panels of chain link fence, six feet wide and 12 feet high, which for the first eight feet have a blue vinyl covering over the one-inch foam rubber padding – thicker around the supporting posts. When the fences are not being battered by baseballs or enduring crashing outfielders, they are loaded onto flat-bed trailers for storage beneath the grandstand. The dirt sliding pits around each base and home plate have been covered with spare patches of artificial turf for the winter. Hay was used one year, which meant the ground crew was raking hayseeds from the dirt all the next season. No game today, though the aisle directly behind home plate would make a terrific toboggan run.

It is the American stereotype of a baseball stadium in Canada, only slightly more wintry looking than in the final innings of that improbable first game on April 7, 1977, when the newly hatched Toronto Blue Jays defeated the Chicago White Sox, 9–5, and the few shivering fans left of the Exhibition Stadium crowd of 44,649 began an absurd but euphoric chant: ''We're number one.''

It would take nine seasons before the chant could be taken seriously, when the Blue Jays won the 1985 American League East on a bleak afternoon when it rained, not snowed. And all that time, an engraved plaque showing Toronto undefeated at 1–0 and tied for first in the Eastern Division after that snowswept opening day in 1977 was on display in a trophy case in the lobby of the club's executive offices beneath the stadium seats. Sharing space with a growing collection of memorabilia, including one team-autographed baseball for each season the Blue Jays have played, the plaque is an engraving of the standing as sent out by Broadcast News that had Toronto topping the standing above Cleveland and New York, who also were 1–0. It was presented to the Blue Jays by radio station CKOC in Kitchener.

The Blue Jays, of course, at a competitive disadvantage as an expansion team, would soon be snowed under after Doug Ault's two-home-run heroics on opening day; but even during that first season it became obvious that the Blue Jays were winners. Despite the opening-day blizzard, despite 108 losses, despite a makeshift stadium conceded to be the worst in major-league baseball, the new Blue Jays attracted 1,701,052 fans to the home park that first season, the highest attendance achieved by a first-year major-league expansion team.

That is the business of baseball: the game within the game. It means stayin' alive, surviving, being competitive, and if all goes well – a happy confluence of good weather, talent, courage, savvy, luck – turning a profit. Some years it means coming within a couple of hundred thousand dollars of making a profit, breaking even. At the very least, it means avoiding bankruptcy, which is no cinch when players' salaries alone have risen from a 1977 team total of $850,000 to $13.3 million in 1986. All in U.S. funds. The risk is greater because the Blue Jays are a Canadian team: three-quarters of income is in Canadian dollars, while two-thirds of expenses are in U.S. dollars. When the Canadian dollar falls a penny against the U.S. dollar, it costs the Blue Jays $285,000 for the season; even in the good years the dollar descrepancy can kill what should have been a profit. But if the expenses have gone up, so has the value of the team to its ownership, a curious mixture of a brewery based in London, Ontario, an introverted, sports-minded business-man from Montreal, and a bank based in Toronto.

Labatt's Breweries and R. Howard Webster each own a 45 per cent share; the Canadian Imperial Bank of Commerce owns 10 per cent. They bought the expansion franchise for $7 million in 1976, when the dollar was nearly at par. *Fortune* magazine listed the value of the franchise in the $36-to-$40-million range in the summer of 1986. But the same *Fortune* article valued the New York Mets – purchased for $21 million in 1981 – at between $56 and $60 million. Yet the team was appraised at $100 million when Nelson Doubleday, Jr., sold his publishing company but kept the baseball club at year's end.

Other estimates put the Blue Jays higher than *Fortune* does. In 1985, Roger Noll of Stanford University was commissioned by the players' association to review the books of major-league baseball teams during negotiations for a new basic agreement with the owners. Noll, an eco-nomics professor, said the Blue Jays would be worth $40 to $45 million (U.S.).

The Blue Jay partnership was created in late 1975 to purchase the ailing San Francisco Giants. The sale fell through in March, 1976, with the success of a last-ditch attempt to keep the team in that city. Labatt's, trying to improve its market share in the important Metro-politan Toronto area, believed that even the pursuit of a major-league baseball team would enhance its image. In 1975 the brewery had tried to buy the Cleveland Indians and then the Baltimore Orioles. Webster, who always has had an interest in sports and twice was an intercolle-giate golf champion, had tried to buy the San Diego Padres in the early seventies so that he could move them to Toronto. Now he threw in his lot with the brewery. The bank was included because it dealt with both major partners and thus could provide a bridge between two unfamiliar partners. It could also act as a tiebreaker in board decisions, a role it has never played. For the brewery and, to a lesser extent, for the bank, there was the incalculable benefit of having given Toronto a major-league baseball team, one that developed into a winner at that.

By business standards, a baseball team is not big – the Blue Jays were projecting expenditures of about $42 million in 1987 – but it has an extremely high profile and businessmen do not like to look foolish. If they are perceived to be running the baseball team poorly, it can raise doubts about how they must run their other, less visible businesses. A major-league baseball team in Canada, with the sharp decline of the Canadian dollar compared to the U.S. dollar in the past 10 years and the sharp increase in salaries, has become no better than a break-even business. A baseball team is primarily a people business – better than 70 per cent of the expenses are salaries. And the business of baseball is baseball – almost 75 per cent of the Blue Jays' 1986 budget was directed at the baseball operation.

"It's about as simple as running a McDonald's franchise, and it's about as difficult a business as a law partnership because all you're dealing with is people," says Paul Beeston, the Blue Jays' executive vice-president for business. "And if you can find any type of magic formula of how you handle people, then you've got the ultra-simple business. It's all people and that's the toughest thing in the world to manage. There is no great magic formula for how to manage people.

"Managing a successful business basically is managing inventory and receivables . . . we don't have that, we're dealing with people. The whole thing is people and personalities. So it can be very, very complex."

Increased player salaries, which are the product of success on the field, a Canadian dollar that was struggling to remain above the 70-cent level in relation to its U.S. counterpart, and a limited supply of good, top-priced seats in a makeshift stadium that makes it difficult to capitalize on a winning team, conspired in 1986 to create the the Blue Jays' first major loss – $3 million – despite near record attendance. It could have been worse. Actually, the Blue Jays had budgeted for a $5-million loss for 1986, but that was based on a conservative 2.2 million in attendance, which the team exceeded by 200,000. Despite winning the American League East in 1985 and setting a club record home attendance of 2,468,925 – second in the league to the California Angels who play in a favourable climate and in one of the best and biggest stadiums in baseball – the Blue Jays lost about $130,000 in 1985, which the club considered a break-even season. They had budgeted for a $4-million loss in 1985, but that was based on another conservative home attendance estimate of two million. In baseball it is never wise to predict how good the weather will be or how close the pennant races will be. Besides,

1985 was a strike year for the major-league players, but this time it was a short-lived one, two days, compared to the 50-day siege of 1981. Still, if there had not been the excellent attendance of the last week-end of the 1985 season when the Blue Jays clinched the division against the Yankees, and if the American League playoffs had not gone the full seven games, the team would have lost more than $2 million. The playoffs alone were worth about $2 million in revenue. Obviously, the business skills of the franchise's management were being tested. In this game within the game, there is no off-season; in fact, it is most demanding *after* the World Series, when the players have headed home to hunt, fish, lift weights, or rest up before playing winter baseball in Latin America.

As the snow drifted in on the blue and green playground of spring, summer, and fall, the private boxes and the media facilities high above home plate looked like an isolated research bunker somewhere on the barren coast of Labrador. Yet in the administrative offices facing the lake and beneath the stands, the lights were on and the telephones were ringing. Business as usual: contracts to be negotiated, players to be promoted and demoted, and free agents to be pondered; trades to be mulled, college and high school players to be assessed, winter leagues in Latin America to be observed, minor-league teams to be assembled, and arbitrations to be arranged; equipment and uniforms to be ordered, hotels and airplanes to be reserved, tickets to be priced and printed (and in the winter of 1986–87, a computerized ticket system to be installed), and insurance premiums to be examined; a media guide to be prepared (and sometimes altered just before deadline because of a trade); calls to be taken from news-starved reporters, and baseball scouts to be called across the United States and Canada, Puerto Rico, Dominican Republic, Venezuela, Mexico, Korea, Taiwan, Guam, even Australia.

In the cramped office of marketing director Paul Markle, the big board on the wall is blocked off for the months of April until September. Already all the appropriate days had been marked in, starting with calendar day, April 6, which also was opening day against the Cleveland Indians, all the way to fan appreciation day on September 27. With winter firing its first salvo, it wasn't as far away as it seemed.

GORD ASH is the administrator of player personnel for the Blue Jays. His office, in the administration wing below the third-base seats, is

11

across an entrance way from that of Pat Gillick, who spins the Blue Jays' revolving door as the fast-lane general manager or, as he is officially known, the executive vice-president of baseball for the club. Like Gillick, Ash has a board that covers nearly an entire wall of his office listing the name of every player under the control of the Blue Jays, starting with the major-league club through the six farm teams. Fitted into the slots of the black board are plastic letters: blue for the team names, red for the players on the major-league roster, white for the rest of the players. White symbols indicate whether a player hits or pitches left-handed, or bats from either side of the plate. The board in Ash's office, but not in Gillick's, has a yellow symbol beside the name of each player on the bonus plan, by which the players receive $1,000 for reaching Double A, $1,500 for reaching Triple A, and $5,000 for reaching the major leagues. A green symbol indicates the players who need visas to play in the United States. Also listed are players whose professional baseball rights are controlled by the Blue Jays: injured players, those placed with a team outside the organization, playing another sport, or in another country. Danny Ainge, a guard for the Boston Celtics of the National Basketball Association who last played with the Blue Jays in 1981, was still one of four on the board as "voluntarily retired." Korean pitcher Dong-Won Choi, who signed a Blue Jay contract in 1981 but decided not to come to North America, appears as one of seven on the restricted list. On a grey, snowy day in December, the board listed 178 players under Blue Jay control, a number that would increase slightly as the winter progressed.

Ash is known as a detail man for the high foreheads in the front office as they make the big deals involving trades, contract negotiations, free-agent acquisitions, and player promotions and demotions. Ash does the preparatory paperwork and informs public relations director Howie Starkman – and often the players involved – of developments. Another responsiblity is negotiating the contracts of the major-leaguers of lesser seniority and all the minor-leaguers except the players in Latin America, who are handled by Gillick's trusted Dominican lieutenant, Epy Guerrero. Ash is deeply involved also in establishing the Blue Jays' working arrangements with minor-league teams. "There's a lot of paperwork to baseball," Ash said. "There's paper for every contract you produce, paper for every time a player moves. And there's a lot of movement, especially in the minor leagues."

One of Ash's favourite days is the U.S. Thanksgiving in November. The offices of the agents and of the U.S. teams are closed, allowing him to make inroads into the paper mountain. "When I told my dad I was going to get a job with the ball club, he said, 'That's fine, but what are you going to do in the winter?' That's the common perception, that we're busy from April to October and twiddle our thumbs for the rest of the year. It's really the reverse. We're busiest through the off-season. During the season, it's day-to-day maintenance.''

Ash is a big, balding, laconic man in his mid-thirties, with an air of quiet authority, the sort of beefy fellow Hollywood would cast as a homeplate umpire. In fact, one of the pictures on his wall in his office is a big print of the Norman Rockwell 1949 magazine cover of the umpire holding out his hand, testing for rain. Ash is built like a football lineman, which he was in high school. He sometimes leaves his office, walks down the polished concrete corridor beneath the stands into the players' training room, and works out, alone, on the Nautilus machine. Above the desk in his office, there's a small brass basketball hoop with the matching ball nestled in the netting. On the same wall is a picture of the 1981 American League All-Star team. Ash left it in the visitors' clubhouse during the 1982 season so that the players in the picture could autograph it. Most did, but one who did not was Rod Carew. On his crammed bookshelf, a row of black binders called the "dead file" contains the records of players no longer with the organization, including various salary information. There's a set of blue binders with the records and salaries and other pertinent information of the players still in the organization and another set of blue binders with scouting expense reports. A conversation in the office often is interrupted by a telephone call. It could be a player representative, or a minor-league trainer, or a scout.

Ash has a good forthright way of explaining the complex rules governing the game within the game, rules that sometimes confound those who play it. When he digs out from the avalanche of paperwork and relaxes, Ash likes to listen to classical music on CBC-FM and to read the newspapers. He likes newspapers. Sharing the wall with the Rockwell print and a framed picture of the 1926 Toronto Maple Leaf baseball team, which he found years ago during cleanup beneath the north grandstand at Exhibition Stadium, there is a framed page from *The Toronto Star* proclaiming the Blue Jays' first win with a blue headline: "The Birth Of The Blue Jays." At home, Ash has a copy of the last *Toronto Telegram*, published in October, 1971, and the first *Toronto Sun*, which came out the next day. He also has a copy of the *Globe and Mail* from 1968 with the green front-page headline: "Man on Moon."

When he's away on business, often to minor-league cities where airports and hotels are not conveniently located, Ash misses the Toronto newspapers. Those, and his wife and two children with whom he lives in Richmond Hill, are now in a house instead of a townhouse so that there is a garage for the bicycles and he can turn up the volume on Handel's *Messiah*.

In many ways, Ash typifies the loyalty and continuity the Blue Jays cultivate in the front office and on the field. He is Toronto-born and attended Vaughan Road Collegiate and York University, contemplating a career as a teacher. By the time Ash graduated, however, the market for teachers had shrivelled and he took a job in a bank, went through the officer-in-training program, and became a branch administrator. When the Blue Jays came to town in 1977, Ash figured that working for a major-league baseball team would be a lot more interesting than banking. (Coincidentally, the bank he worked for was the Canadian Imperial Bank of Commerce.) When one of his friends got a part-time job selling tickets at the stadium, Ash decided to give it a try. It so happens that ticket manager George Holm, a rotund fellow with a beard and pet cats named Buck and Ernie, favoured hiring school teachers or bank workers as ticket sellers because they were used to dealing with numbers and people.

"It was kind of neat, because by about the second inning, when you finished selling tickets, you could go in and watch the game," Ash said.

In February, 1978, Ash joined the ticket office full time. Nine months later, he moved over to the club's operations department. For a year, he worked on the field with the ground crew, drawing chalk lines on the diamond, raking the dirt, installing the pitcher's rubber, and hauling out the tarpaulin when it rained. Most of Ash's pre-game field manicuring involved working on the pitcher's mound. He loved it. He became the supervisor of the ground crew, then assistant to the director of operations, Ken Erskine, which involves supervising security, ushers, and the ground crew. In 1984 Ash moved to the player development department to fill the vacancy left by Elliott Wahle's departure to become the president of the Canadian division of Toys R Us.

Like most people who come to work for a baseball team from the outside, Ash had anticipated a certain glamour in his new job. It soon passes. "For the first two weeks in 1978 I thought I was in a different world," Ash said. "That wears off very quickly, but it's still a better environment than most. When I was working at the bank, I'd get up in the morning and think, 'Well, I have to go to work again.' Now when I get up, I *want* to go to work. It's really not like a job at all.''

Baseball's front-office people must work in the off-season with several deadlines in mind, which in 1986–87 included the following dates.

- November 11 (15 days after the Word Series) – last day for players to declare free agency or to demand a trade;
- November 12 – the last day to promote players to the 40-man major-league rosters;
- December 1 – the last day to demote a player from the major-league roster until the major-league, or Rule 5, draft;
- December 5-12 – winter meetings in Hollywood, Florida;
- December 7 – deadline for former team to offer salary arbitration to players declaring free agency;
- December 8 – major-league draft, where players with three years' professional service not protected on the major-league roster can be claimed for $50,000 (such players must be kept on the selecting team's roster for the following season or offered back to the original team for half price before a demotion to the minors);
- December 9 – Triple A draft, $12,000 for players not protected on Triple A rosters; Double A draft, $4,000 for players not protected on Double A rosters;
- December 19 – last day for free agents to accept salary arbitration from former club, thus keeping their rights to try free agency again after the season (those who don't accept arbitration waive free agency rights for five years);
- December 20 – last date to tender contracts to players, with those not offered contracts becoming free agents;
- January 8 – former teams must sign free agents who rejected arbitration or lose right to sign player until May 1;
- January 5–15 – period in which players with more than three years of major-league service and fewer than six can file for salary arbitration;
- January 19 – players filing for arbitration and their teams must submit salary figures;
- February 1–20 – arbitration hearings: arbitrator hears arguments and must choose either figure (negotiations can continue up until the hearing);

- February 25 – Blue Jay pitchers and catchers report to spring training;
- February 28 – all Blue Jay players report to spring training;
- March 11 – last day for team to renew an unsigned player's contract for any figure, but with a maximum cut of 20 per cent.

The selections for the final few spots on the 40-man roster can be a cerebral juggling act, and every year it gets more difficult, as better players are produced in the Blue Jay farm system. It was not always so difficult in the early years when the organization was thin. "Usually, we could do it pretty quick," said Pat Gillick, who has been involved with this process since the team's beginning.

By 1985, that had changed. "We had some guys that we felt queasy about leaving unprotected," Gillick said. Even then, the Blue Jays thought 1986 would be their most difficult year yet in which to determine the 40-man roster. It was.

There are calculated risks, such as leaving some gifted ballplayers unprotected, perhaps late developers, hoping they won't be noticed. There is the devious legerdemain of trying to "hide" a player with talent. It can be like dressing your kid sister in burlap, in the hope she won't be seduced by the town masher.

It is an ongoing process. Once the June amateur draft is out of the way, eastern scouting supervisor Bob Engle and western scouting supervisor Wayne Morgan, a Saskatoon native, will have seen and made reports on the players on all six Blue Jay farm teams. Veteran scout and vice-president Al LaMacchia, who has been with the Jays since the beginning, and the club's two special assignment scouts, Moose Johnson and Gord Lakey, will have seen the Jays' Double A and Triple A teams. Bob Mattick, a long-time scout and vice-president who has also been with the club since the start, runs the minor-league system and is familiar with its talent. And Dave Yoakum, the advance scout during the season who observes the Jays' next opponent and reports his findings to manager Jimy Williams, knows the American League talent.

These scouts, Gillick, Williams, and the major-league coaches – Al Widmar, Cito Gaston, John Sullivan, Billy Smith, and John McLaren – met the day after the 1986 season ended. Such things as trades, acquiring free agents, how players in the organization figure in the next year's plans, and determining the 40-man roster were discussed for two and a half days. During the first day's meetings, catcher Buck

Martinez, just before he was to catch a plane to Boston to do radio work on the American League playoffs, was told he did not figure in the team's plans for 1987. He expected it. Designated hitter Cliff Johnson already knew the option for his 1987 contract would not be picked up; his contract, signed with the Texas Rangers when he was a free agent in December, 1984, stipulated that he be told by October 1. His deal with the Rangers gave him a $250,000 signing bonus, $600,000 per year in 1985 and 1986 ($300,000 of it deferred each year with interest), with $650,000 if the club picked up his option for 1987. Johnson received a buyout of $250,000 (deferred with interest) if the club did not pick up the 1987 option.

While Ash sits in on these brain-storming sessions, he does not pretend to have the baseball knowledge and experience to make player assessment decisions. The input comes from the scouts, the coaches, and the manager.

Gillick is a former scout; when a scout talks, he listens. The day before the deadline for promoting players to the 40-man roster, Gillick makes one final conference-call poll of his scouts. Gillick lives on the telephone and he is considered a good listener. He must make the final decisions but consults, and acts upon, the opinions of the people he hires. They appreciate it.

Even during the World Series, their thoughts had been on next year. The Toronto contingent attended the middle three games in Boston; at the party in the Boston Sheraton, the night before the first game in Boston, the third game of the series, the Blue Jay contingent was seated together discussing a trade even as the band packed up for the night. Gillick and Williams then flew to the West Coast to talk to some players about their prospects with the team. One of them was Garth Iorg, who lives in Arcata, California. They met him at the airport in San Francisco, went to a restaurant, and told him that Kelly Gruber was going to be given a full shot at the third-base job in 1987. Iorg, 32, one of the original Blue Jays selected in the expansion draft of 1976, appreciated the gesture. During the chat with Gillick and Williams, he was asked how he felt about the move and if he wanted them to try to arrange a trade. Iorg likes the Toronto organization, but if it meant playing more he said he would like the trade. But if he was going to spend most of his time on the bench, he wanted to do it in Toronto.

Two and a half hours before the 2 p.m. deadline on November 12, the final day for promoting players to the 40-man roster before the

Rule 5 draft, Ash signed outfielder Ron Shepherd to a major-league contract. Then the Blue Jays demoted him to their Triple A team in Syracuse. The 26-year-old Shepherd had been with the Blue Jay organization since 1979 and the rules allow a player with seven years in the minor leagues, who is not protected on the major-league roster or signed to a contract, to become a free agent. By signing Shepherd, the Blue Jays were able to remove him from the 40-man roster, clear him through waivers, and assign him to Syracuse without the risk of losing him as a free agent. Thus, they could promote another outfielder, Lou Thornton, to the roster. The Blue Jays had made a similar move with right-handed pitcher Colin McLaughlin earlier in the fall.

If the Blue Jays had simply given Shepherd his release to open a roster spot, they could not have used him on the major-league team until May 15 even if they had re-signed him to a minor-league contract. Shepherd, like McLaughlin, would be invited to the major-league spring training camp as a non-roster player, if he wasn't taken in the December draft. He wasn't. Shepherd accepted the demotion, confident that he could make the major-league team. He has known no other baseball organization. "I've been here since I've been playing, seven years now, and it would be like leaving the family if I went to play with somebody else," he had said during the 1986 spring training when asked about the possibility of spending more time in Triple A. "I think it's a real good organization, the players are friendly. They've got a lot of young guys. It's not like there's a lot of older guys where you feel inferior. There's a lot of young guys you can come right in and mix with."

Shepherd, a six-foot-four 175-pound string bean, sometimes called "Manute" by his teammates (for the seven-foot seven-inch and painfully thin basketball player Manute Bol of the Washington Bullets), is a Blue Jay understudy who had given only brief glimpses of the promise that convinced the Blue Jays to persuade him away from football. "Before the Blue Jays came, I never thought about the major leagues," Shepherd said. "When they came in and explained how the system worked, the major leagues, the coaches and how it would help, I started looking at longevity in baseball."

In 1986, he spent most of his summer on the bench with the Blue Jays, hitting .203 with two home runs and four runs batted in. He is a whippet on the base paths and had been offered football scholarships as a receiver and defensive back and had intended to go to the University of Houston. (His brother, Larry, did play football at Houston, then was drafted and cut by the Los Angeles Raiders of the National Football League.) These weren't his first scholarship possibilities. Earlier in high school, he had received scholarship offers from several universities interested in him as an engineering student, but he ignored them to concentrate on athletics. Always good in mathematics, he had cried when he got his first B, in the eighth grade. Shepherd intends to pursue a college education and does not resent delaying it for baseball. "There was no guarantee and there still isn't, even with a college education, that you're going to get a good job. I've seen guys with engineering degrees who are working in 7-Elevens and little midnight grocery stores."

Thornton, two and a half years younger than Shepherd, was considered by the Blue Jays to be more vulnerable to the draft. He'd had less time to prove his potential. The Jays snatched Thornton from the New York Mets in the December, 1984, draft for $25,000 and he was kept on the major-league team for the 1985 season. The Mets had said they would make no deal to let the Jays demote him. Having spent the 1985 season with the Blue Jays, mainly on the bench with the other "turds," as the reserves called themselves, Thornton played in 1986 with the Syracuse Chiefs. Suffering from hamstring injuries, he hit .260 with two homers and 28 RBIs in 231 at-bats. He began his off-season with a semester at Auburn University – he receives tuition from his signing with the Mets through the major-league scholarship plan – before going to play in the Dominican Republic's winter league. He had to return early to his home in Montgomery, Alabama, when he fouled a pitch off his foot and suffered a bone chip.

It is a measure of how solid the Jays were in 1985 that they won their division despite having to carry Thornton and infielder Manny Lee, whom they took from the Houston Astros in the same draft. Neither had played above Class A and drafting one, let alone both, was a surprise. Al Rosen, then president of the Houston Astros, protested perhaps too loudly. Obviously Houston had gambled by not protecting Lee, who had been obtained from the Mets in a deal involving Ray Knight, the MVP in the 1986 World Series. Few thought the Jays could keep both Thornton and Lee on the roster through the whole season and finish first.

The Blue Jays, considered one of the finest scouting teams in baseball, have used the Rule 5 draft to advantage. (They've also made some mistakes, giving back pitcher Jose DeJesus, their December, 1985, pick, to the Kansas City Royals in 1986 for half the draft price.) Under this draft, the Jays have obtained cheaply such future major-league regulars as Willie Upshaw from the New York Yankees and outfielder George Bell from the Philadelphia Phillies. They also used it to get infielder Kelly Gruber from the Cleveland Indians, pitcher Jim Gott from the St. Louis Cardinals, and pitcher Jim Acker from the Atlanta Braves.

Although the Blue Jays thought they were obtaining a future third baseman in Gruber, members of the Indians' minor-league organization were delighted by the selection, too. No team had selected a player from them in several years and they felt that it showed a revival of their farm system. The Blue Jays were able to work out a deal with the Indians early in the 1984 season that allowed Gruber to be demoted to Triple A. The Jays gave up catcher/infielder Geno Petralli to the Indians, who wanted him for their Triple A team in Maine. It was difficult for Ash to deliver the news to Petralli, who had finally made the Blue Jays. Petralli's was the first contract that Ash had negotiated and now he had to tell him not only that he was traded but that he was returning to the minor leagues. By trading Gott to the San Francisco Giants, the Jays acquired left-handed reliever Gary Lavelle, who was useful in 1985 despite an elbow problem that finally required reconstructive surgery in April of 1986. He was attempting a comeback and the Blue Jays protected him on their 40-man roster even though he had not thrown a pitch in competition in more than a year. As a 10-year major-leaguer they would have had to seek his permission to demote him. By trading Acker, who had been a vital performer in the first half of the 1985 season but became disenchanted when his workload decreased, the Jays were able to obtain young starting pitcher Joe Johnson during the 1986 season.

The 40-man roster selected for the November 12 deadline included:
Pitchers: Luis Aquino, Bill Caudill, John Cerutti, Steve Davis, Mark Eichhorn, Don Gordon, Tom Henke, Joey Johnson, Gary Lavelle, Jose Mesa, Dave Stieb, Duane Ward, Jeff Musselman; *Catchers*: Jeff De-Willis, Jeff Hearron, Greg Myers, Matt Stark; *Infielders*: Tony Fernandez, Cecil Fielder, Damaso Garcia, Santiago Garcia, Kelly Gruber, Garth Iorg, Alexis Infante, Nelson Liriano, Rick Leach, Manny Lee, Fred McGriff, Rance Mulliniks, Mike Sharperson, Willie Upshaw; *Outfielders*: Jesse Barfield, George Bell, Silvestre Campusano, Rob Ducey, Otis Green, Glenallen Hill, Lloyd Moseby, Lou Thornton.

Campusano, from the baseball-rich Dominican Republic, was only 19 years old but a superb prospect, with all-around baseball skills that make scouts hyperventilate. He has been compared sometimes to a young Roberto Clemente, the Puerto Rican superstar who played 18 seasons for the Pittsburgh Pirates, with a lifetime batting average of .317.

The 40-man roster even included a Canadian, outfielder Rob Ducey of Cambridge, Ontario, who played for the Jays' Double A club in Knoxville, Tennessee, in 1986 and batted .308 with 11 homers after being promoted from Class A at Ventura. Ducey, the fourth Canadian to make the Jays' major-league roster, was one of several Jays playing winter baseball in Venezuela for the Lara Cardinales. The previous winter he had worked in a McDonald's at Sherway Gardens in Etobicoke ''flipping those burgers,'' as he called it, and telephoning the Blue Jay office from time to time to find out what was happening.

Pitcher Jim Clancy and catcher Ernie Whitt, two originals from the 1976 expansion draft, tested the free-agent market in the fall of 1986, which opened two spots on the 40-man roster. Both Clancy and Whitt wanted to stay in Toronto, however, and the Blue Jays were able to sign them in January of 1987, though not without some drama in Whitt's case. Amid players' cries of collusion, free agency was less lucrative than it had been only two years earlier. Even George Steinbrenner, the Yankee owner, had been quiet on the free-agent market.

On December 1, the Blue Jays demoted catcher Jeff DeWillis, 21, to Triple A to open up a spot on their roster so they could take another dip into the Rule 5 draft. They took a right-handed pitcher, Jose Nunez, from the Kansas City Royals organization. Nunez, 21, who had pitched in Class A and Double A in 1986, had a potentially good major-league breaking ball, according to the Blue Jay scouts. The Blue Jays lost two left-handed pitchers, Stan Clarke, 26, who had pitched at Syracuse and Toronto, and Clifford Young, 22, who had pitched at Knoxville in 1986, to the Seattle Mariners and the Oakland A's respectively. For Clarke, who had had several trials with the Blue Jays, it was a chance for the change of scenery he had wanted. He and pitching coach Al Widmar were not on the best of terms and Clarke, who wanted to be in the majors so badly that he had trouble controlling his emotions, had grown frustrated.

In the Triple A draft, the Blue Jays selected three players for $12,000 each–right-handed pitcher Ray Young from the Los Angeles Dodgers, infielder Mark Pottinger from the Philadelphia Phillies, and right-handed pitcher Darren Balsley from the Oakland A's. They lost left-handed pitcher Gibson Alba, who threw hard but not always with control, to the Cleveland Indians.

In the Double A draft, the Blue Jays took infielder Roberto Fuentes from the Boston Red Sox for $4,000, while losing right-handed pitcher Tom Wasilewski to the San Francisco Giants. These drafts are conducted by the team's minor-league affiliates.

After the December meetings, during which the Blue Jays made no trades, they would demote four more players from the major-league roster – it was a safe time to get them through waivers because the rosters of the other teams are usually full at that time – catcher Jeff Hearron, infielder Alexis Infante, left-handed pitcher Steve Davis, and right-handed pitcher Luis Aquino. This made room for the signings of Clancy and Whitt. All the demoted players would attend the major-league camp as non-roster players, the same as McLaughlin, Shepherd, and DeWillis.

Then on February 2, Damaso Garcia, the second baseman since 1980, and pitcher Luis Leal, who also began with the Blue Jays in 1980 but had languished in the minors since July, 1985, had been sent to the Atlanta Braves for pitcher Craig McMurtry, who was trying to regain his rookie form of 1983 when he was 15–9. Leal's deal was conditional; the Braves could return him. Garcia and Leal would be joining their former manager, Bob Cox, now the Braves' general manager. For Howie Starkman, the public relations man, the trade was not one day too soon for his media guide. It was at the printers, but not printed. If the trade had been made a day later, it would have taken a week to adjust the guide. This way, the delay was only a day or two and hardly a major inconvenience.

"FOR ALL PRACTICAL PURPOSES, we're in a fortress here," Paul Beeston said, leaning over his oversized blonde desk, blowing cigar smoke toward an office window overlooking the sidewalk outside the stadium and, beyond that, the frozen expanse of Lake Ontario. "We've really got nothing to walk to. Once you get in here, you're stuck.'"

Beeston is a chartered accountant, known throughout the stadium complex simply as "The Beest" or "Beest." Beneath a full head of hair, longish at the back, he has the impish look of a schoolboy. His grin is never far from exploding into a roof-rattling blast of laughter. He is often heard when he cannot be seen. Beeston and Gillick, his baseball counterpart, form a baseball Odd Couple. Matching wooden signs, Oscar and Felix, provided by Gillick's wife, Doris, sit amid Beeston's clutter and the neatness of Gillick's office.

They aren't quite a classic Oscar-Felix combination: the cigar-smoking Beeston wears a suit and tie to work – he works without the suit jacket and the shirt cuffs usually rolled up above the wrist – and Gillick prefers open-necked shirts, sweaters, and cowboy boots. Beeston is the beer drinker and only recently has gone along with the trend from Labatt's 50, the ale, to Blue, the lager. Gillick will have one glass of wine with dinner. Atlhough he's improving, Beeston's happiest moment on any flight is when the plane lands; thus, he likes to go first class on business trips because he feels it keeps him in a good mental state, ready to work. Gillick, a constant traveller, is a student of airline schedules and is delighted when he can obtain a discount rate. In land travel, Gillick believes new cars are a bad investment and owns two used cars, a 1972 Oldsmobile and a 1979 Honda. While Beeston is everybody's friend, Gillick is more difficult to know, although he has the loyalty of those who work for him. When meeting people, Beeston is a hearty backslapper; Gillick's manners are impeccable, almost old-fashioned. Gillick, the former professional left-handed pitcher, jogs in the morning even before the most crucial negotiations; Beeston looks as if his primary exercise is letting his fingers do the walking through the ledgers.

Yet, the differences between the two are not so clearcut. Bill Giles, the president and part-owner of the Philadelphia Phillies, talks fondly of Beeston and his image of the Blue Jay tandem is one of Beeston rolling the dice at a casino with Gillick standing beside him, arms folded. Perhaps yielding to the accountant in him, Beeston in fact wouldn't gamble at a casino or on a horse race. Gillick is the one who likes to have a small bet on a football game, or will enjoy taking in a few races at Woodbine with his daughter Kimberley. Both own stocks, with Gillick admitting that Beeston has the edge. Beneath the jocular nature, Beeston has a toughness that should not be underestimated. Gillick is a more curious mixture. He has the fibre to make the difficult decisions that can cost a player his job and sometimes a sizeable income, yet it can be emotional for him. He was in tears when he told designated hitter Willie Aikens that he was being released early in the 1985 season. Aikens, obtained in a trade with the Kansas City Royals, had come back from serving a prison term on a cocaine charge in 1984.

The Blue Jay management liked Aikens and his approach to his problem, and talked about him as a person they'd consider hiring for the organization.

"He makes his decision based on the best interests of the club," says Gord Kirke, a lawyer who draws up the Blue Jay contracts, "but when it's made and as it's made you see him time and again really labouring and suffering through something he knows is going to be hard on a player. I've been with him when he's told a player essentially his career is over and I'm sure the player hurts more than Gillick does – but not by a whole lot. He's a very sensitive man."

There is an informal air about the Blue Jay offices even during the busy times of winter. The mood is relaxed and the biggest gripe might be from the non-smokers, which includes almost everyone, about the smoke coming from Beeston's office. One morning, there was some alarm when Beeston lit a cigar and promptly set his wastepaper basket on fire. But usually, there are a lot of good-natured barbs and laughing. There is no clock-punching. Beeston calls his secretary, Sue Cannell (née Browne), "Downtown." She has worked with him almost since the Blue Jays began. Others in the baseball department have been there from the beginning: Judy Van Zutphen has been Howie Starkman's secretary since 1976; Sue Turjanica worked for Gillick from the beginning until leaving in the winter of 1986 to raise two children, with Fran Brown taking her place.

Beeston, the first executive hired by the fledgling team, rises at his Moore Park home at 6:00 a.m. and arrives at the stadium at about eight. In summer, when the Jays are in town, he stays for the evening game and rarely gets home before midnight. For lunch he often goes to Joe Allen, a trendy eatery near the downtown core, a ten-minute drive away. In summer he might walk over the pedestrian bridge near the stadium to one of the restaurants at Ontario Place, a tourist attraction on a man-made island in the lake.

Beeston is from Welland, Ontario, and is a devout fan of baseball – as a boy he and his father would drive to Tiger Stadium, where they could count on getting a seat behind a post whether the ticket was bought by mail, at the box office, or from a scalper – but he is also the chief number-cruncher (though he often gives the appearance of being more intent on crunching cigars). He sometimes refers to the team on the field as the "product" or the "commodity" or the "fixed asset." He apologizes for sometimes saying things like "Those twenty-four or twenty-five guys on the field are The Product. That's what we sell."

Beeston isn't big on accountant talk, however. He was not a conventional accountant when he worked for Coopers and Lybrand in London, Ontario, where he became known as an accountant who actually made audits fun. He likes the players, is frequently found chatting to one of them or to a coach in the dugout before games. Besides being the product, he says the players are the most important part of a baseball organization. "The minor-league system, the front office, the scouting, the development people, the ticket sellers, they're all working for those twenty-four, twenty-five guys on the field."

There is an important subtlety in Beeston's phrase "twenty-four, twenty-five guys." The success of the Blue Jays in 1985 proved to other major-league teams that the 162-game schedule could be played with twenty-four guys instead of twenty-five. Saving the team the salary of the twenty-fifth guy, with the major-league average approaching $450,000 a year and with the minimum at $60,000 ($62,500 in 1987), the saving can be significant. In 1986, all 26 major-league teams used the 24-man roster, except in September when 40 is the limit. The players claimed it was an owners' conspiracy and filed a grievance. The rules state that the maximum is 25 players, the minimum is 24, and in unusual circumstances a team might dress 23 but must have the number of players in uniform up to 24 within 48 hours. By using 24 players for the season, the major-league players association argued that the teams had violated the spirit of the basic agreement.

Beeston has become inured to the six-figure sums paid to the game's stars, and even to the *seven*-figure salaries paid to some superstars. Of course, Beeston's duties have expanded and he no longer signs salary cheques. Today, the cheque signing duties belong to Bob Nicholson, the vice-president of finance, but Beeston admits that in 1977 he probably winced at the $100,000 salary paid to starting pitcher Bill Singer. It was a lot of money then, and Singer, twice a 20-game winner in the majors, did not finish the 1977 season because of a shoulder injury.

Beeston's good rapport with the players includes those who might be perceived to be moody or critical of management. He got along well with Damaso Garcia, the second baseman who was the moodiest of all. "He's one of those few guys who would be very good at anything he puts his mind to," Beeston said. "If he wanted to be a doctor, he'd be a doctor. If he wanted to be a lawyer, he'd be a lawyer. He's got a lot of pride, but he's got ability, and he'll put in the time and the effort. He's very complex. There's a message to Damaso Garcia."

25

In Feburary of 1983, Garcia had taken his case to arbitration and, though he won, he was hurt by the weaknesses of his game – such as his lack of bases on balls – that the team mentioned in its case. Arbitration is an adversarial process in a court-like setting. Each side submits a salary figure and then argues the case before the arbitrator, who must choose one or the other. After hearing some of the Blue Jays' arguments, Garcia talked loudly about wanting to be traded. A Garcia trade demand, often followed by a change of heart, would be made so freqently over the ensuing years that no one paid attention. But in 1983, it was still somewhat new.

The next winter, as the Blue Jay brass tried to hammer out a contract with Garcia, Beeston and Garcia became teamed spiritually on one side with Gillick and Garcia's agent Tom Reich on the other. "I think what really disarmed Reich," Beeston said, "was Damo coming with four boxes of cigars for me from the Dominican Republic."

In the end, the Blue Jays signed Garcia to a contract covering five years. It was guaranteed for three years; that is the maximum under club policy. But Garcia could guarantee a fourth year by appearing in 135 games in 1984, or by playing in 270 games in 1984 and 1985. He could guarantee a fifth year if he appeared in 135 games in 1985, or by appearing in 270 games in 1985 and 1986. As it turned out, Garcia made enough appearances to guarantee his contract for five years. His base salary would be $600,000 in 1984, $650,000 in 1985, $700,000 in 1986, $800,000 in 1987 and 1988. Garcia also would receive an extra $20,000 when he reached 450, 525, and 575 plate appearances in a season. He received a signing bonus of $150,000. He would get another $25,000 if selected for the UPI All-Star team. There was a stipulation in Garcia's contract that would give him an extra $50,000 on each year left on it after he was traded. When he was traded to Atlanta his contract jumped to $850,000 for 1987 and for 1988.

This was typical of the contracts the Blue Jays at that time were giving to their top young players before they became eligible for free agency. The Blue Jays were sending out the message that they were not cheap and were willing to make the moves to build a winner. In the early years, when Toronto was happy just to have a major-league franchise, if only to see the Yankees and the Orioles and the Red Sox and the Tigers up close, the Blue Jays began to gain a reputation for stinginess. According to Beeston, "We were a losing organization, with the perception of being cheap, taking guys down to the wire. It was a bad place to play."

He edges his teeth up on the Monte Cristo, takes a puff, and another stream of cigar smoke sails across the desk.

"We weren't going to win that first year – you can just look at our opening day lineup. And we weren't going to win the second year or the third year. It was obvious as the dots on a playing card that there were two ways of going, one to draft and develop, the other to go on the free-agent market. We weren't going to the free-agent market because free agents weren't going to come here. We had to have patience, and not get rid of the young kids. That was the key, not trading the young kids."

The Blue Jays began to make their move in February, 1983, when they signed pitcher Dave Stieb to a six-year contract (with a potential value of between $5 and $6 million depending on incentives achieved). In the three previous seasons Stieb had had contract squabbles with the Blue Jays, and he had lost his arbitration case in 1982. The key was to get Stieb to agree to the three-year guarantee. If Stieb, the team's most valued player at the time, could agree to it, then it would be easier to convince the others to accept it. At this time, five-year guarantees were still in vogue. Soon after, pitcher Jim Clancy was signed to a four-year deal, the first three years guaranteed with an option for a fourth year. Before the 1984 season, they signed Garcia, first baseman Willie Upshaw (minutes before a scheduled arbitration hearing), outfielder Lloyd Moseby, and shortstop Alfredo Griffin to long-term contracts that could run as long as five years. Having forged a strong, contending nucleus, the Blue Jays then explored the free-agent market and considered serious trades for the missing pieces.

First they chased the big, intimidating Yankee reliever Rich (Goose) Gossage but lost out to the San Diego Padres. But the Blue Jays had kept their options open: they had told Dennis Lamp, a reliable middle reliever, occasional starter, and sometimes short man for the Chicago White Sox, that they would be interested in signing him if they did not obtain Gossage. They got Lamp for the 1984 season, though he did not prove to be the much-needed "bullpen stopper." For 1985, sensing the club needed only one or two additions for glory, the Blue Jays traded for Bill Caudill, a quirky reliever with the Oakland A's – he tended to pitch well only in even numbered years – and Gary Lavelle, a left-handed reliever who for 11 years had toiled with unheralded distinction for the woeful San Francisco Giants. Regardless of how they turned out, the deals were a signal to major-league baseball and a front-office pep talk for the Blue Jay players.

"There comes a time when you've got to do it for the players,"
Beeston explained. "They're not just hunks of meat out there, or a
circus we bring into town. When you go out and get a relief pitcher,
you don't get him for the ego gratification of the owners, or for the
financial reasons, or even for the fans – you do it for the *players*. They've
trusted us, and they've busted their asses day after day after day.
Getting Lamp for '84 and Caudill and Lavelle for '85 was a signal to the
players that we're trying our best. It's more fun if you win. Look at a
great player like Ernie Banks – he never had a chance to play in a World
Series."

In his frequent speaking engagements Beeston says, "Simply put,
baseball can now best be described as a medium-sized entertainment
business of individual partners, each partner comprising an economic
unit of say $40 million, or a combined total in excess of $1 billion."

He will point out that in 1950 the 16 major-league clubs drew 17.5
million fans, or an average of 1.1 million spectators per team. Thirty-
five years later, the 26 major-league teams were drawing a total of
46.8 million, an average of 1.8 million per team.

"This is good, because it is the one direct measure available to quan-
tify interest in the sport," he says. "When people stop coming to the
ballpark, then the industry will know what the definition of a major
problem really is . . . while the salary structure may need a little corrective surgery, I still am not aware of any club that is selling tickets
solely to see their mascot, I am not aware of any club that is selling
their licensed material strictly on the ambiance of their park and I am
not aware of any club that is selling their radio and television rights
based on the potential of a probing and interesting interview with members of the front office. It's the players who sell the tickets, create the
interest, and are the cause of the growth of the game. So why shouldn't
they get paid? As a native of Welland, I didn't rub shoulders with too
many millionaires. Now I just walk through the clubhouse."

He was talking in September, 1986, and even then Beeston could flip
through his appointment book and realize he would have to turn down
engagements for that winter, knowing what was ahead in the so-called
dormant months of baseball. There would be some tough negotiations
with free agents Jim Clancy and Ernie Whitt and then later on contracts for outfielders Jesse Barfield and George Bell, who each had
108 RBIs while Barfield led the majors with 40 home runs. Little did he
know that one engagement he had accepted back in March of 1986 for

January 8, 1987, when he spoke to the Lambton County Chartered Accountants Association in Sarnia, would complicate negotiations with Whitt.

During the late summer, Gillick had prepared a budget for player salaries with estimates for the 1987, 1988, and 1989 seasons, using the resources of the Player Relations Committee and of Tal Smith, a former baseball executive who had been one of Gillick's bosses with the Houston Astros and New York Yankees and who now negotiates salaries and handles arbitration cases on behalf of teams.

Since the inception of the free-agent era, predicting the direction of player salaries has become the trickiest aspect of the business of baseball. Beeston can predict from year to year what the team's expenses can be, with adjustments for inflation and unforeseen costs. Gate receipts used to bring in most of the revenue, but now the revenue from home and away gate receipts made up just less than half of the team's total revenue of $37 million in 1986 and slightly more than the team earns from Canadian and U.S. media rights.

Beeston could predict with confidence that for 1986 major-league equipment would cost in the area of $100,000, major-league team travel about $1 million, scouting about $2 million, and the minor-league system $4.5 million when costs are converted to Canadian funds. But the growth of major-league salaries has been less conducive to long-range planning. Major-league salaries cost the Blue Jays $13.3 million (U.S.) in 1986 and they were budgeting the same amount for 1987. Yet on a year-to-year basis, Gillick has been good at not exceeding his budget, and usually has hit within $50,000 to $200,000 of the allotted amount.

"You'd like to think that you have long-term five-year projections, short-term three-year projections, and then your one-year projection," says Beeston. "At best, your one-year projection has a chance of making it, if you put in your contingencies. The three-year and five-year have been so out of whack in the last seven or eight years. There's no possible way that one could have anticipated that you'd go from a $3 million salary level in 1982 to a $13 million salary level in 1986."

Beeston sets the mood of the office because he's more of a presence, and more present, while Gillick is often away, perhaps visiting the Dominican Republic where the Blue Jays have a complex for young players, or off talking about a trade or looking at a prospect. There is no view from Gillick's rectangular windowless office, but there is an abundance of pictures and figurines of real blue jays. There is a conference table. At one end of the office his desk faces the big organizational board on the wall. Beneath the board is a row of black binders – scouting reports. On one of the bookshelves behind his desk is a collection of blue binders containing his annual season-end reports and the projections for the future. He prepares them as the season winds down in September. The reports are the front-office game plans for the next season; studied in retrospect, they constitute an intriguing diary of the Blue Jay franchise.

Gillick's report or plan is one of several presented to the board of directors, usually in October, which is when the budgets for the next year are being submitted for approval. The board members are R. Howard Webster, Peter Hardy, Peter Widdrington, Larry Greenwood, and John Craig Eaton. The board usually meets once a month throughout the year. The chairman is Webster, but for health reasons he no longer attends meetings. William Ferguson, who is executive vice-president of Webster's Imperial Trust Limited, represents the Webster interests on the board. Eaton, of the department store family, also represents Webster. He married one of Webster's nieces. Greenwood represents CIBC interests. Hardy, vice-chairman of the board, is in the Blue Jay offices once a week, usually Thursdays. A man who likes to avoid publicity's glare, he is chairman of the board of John Labatt Limited and has represented the company on the board since the Jays' beginning. He became the Blue Jays' chief executive officer in May, 1982, about six months after Peter Bavasi, the club's first and only president, departed, and he is admittedly not the type who turns first to the major-league box scores in the morning. Widdrington is the president of John Labatt Limited, which has many business interests besides beer. Through its ownership of the Sealtest and Silverwood dairies, Labatt's actually earns more from dairy products than beer. Of all the members of the board, Widdrington takes the keenest interest in the games on the field and is the most knowledgeable.

"It's an interesting thing to me," Widdrington says. "You know in business, you can do some pretty good things over a period of time; real estate guys put in a development and after twenty years the development is worth a lot more and they go to the bank and cash their cheque and that's it. But in this situation, you're in a crazy game where every day you win one or you lose one, so you've got an instant evaluation. It was kind of a thrill for the ball club to get some recognition over the past three or four years."

Widdrington enjoys baseball people.

"The association, too, is a lot of fun," he says. "I enjoy the baseball side of it, the baseball people, they're interesting, they're fun and they're extremely knowledgeable."

In 1980, when former Ontario premier John Robarts was a Webster representative on the board and David Lewis was representing the Canadian Imperial Bank of Commerce (before moving to the Continental Bank), the report came late in a season in which the team, for the first time, lost fewer than a hundred games. The report listed five blue-chip prospects in the farm system: shortstop Garry Harris, catcher Brian Milner, outfielder Paul Hodgson, shortstop Tony Fernandez, and infielder-outfielder Danny Ainge. Harris never worked out; Milner and Hodgson retired prematurely because of injuries; Ainge eventually abandoned baseball to play basketball for the Boston Celtics. By 1986, Tony Fernandez turned out to be one of the finest shortstops in baseball – if not the best.

The 1980 report also noted three pitchers as solid prospects: Colin McLaughlin, Luis Leal, and Mark Eichhorn. Six years later, McLaughlin was still in the farm system, still a prospect. Leal had made it to the Blue Jays and stayed until July, 1985, when he was sent down to Syracuse. Entering the 1986 winter meetings, he was no longer on the 40-man roster or the Triple A roster. He was on the Double A roster, which made him, and his $490,000 guaranteed salary for 1987, available in the Triple A draft for $12,000. There were were no takers (although, subsequently, he was traded to Atlanta, along with Damaso Garcia). After a brief major-league stint with the Jays in 1982, Eichhorn wallowed in the minors for the next three seasons, which included rehabilitation from a shoulder injury. He blossomed as a reliever with the Blue Jays in 1986, thanks to a new and wicked sidearm delivery he had developed the year before in the minor leagues.

The report continued:

. . . the farm system is not anticipated to pay dividends through graduation of other players until 1982 and 1983, and therefore while 1981 should be an encouraging year, it will nevertheless produce frustrations and disappointments at the major-league level for the sports media and public looking for immediate improvement.

We must remember that in 1977, the club won fifty-four ball games. In 1978 and 1979, fifty-nine and fifty-three respectively. The 1980 club should win sixty games even with disastrous injuries [the Jays won sixty-seven]. But what the 1980 club has that the previous Blue Jay teams did not have are two solid front line pitchers, two infielders and two outfielders, who barring injury or trade, will be with the major-league club when it becomes competitive.

The player personnel group has a tremendous challenge facing it with no substitute available to it for giving the young quality players the necessary experience. Expectations should not be raised materially for the 1981 Blue Jay won/loss record, although improvement should be evident. But what can be expected is the continued development of quality players on the farm system of some quantity. This will manifest itself in a competitive team more surely and less expensively than any program available to it.

The 1981 report recommended hiring a full-time batting instructor (Bobby Doerr was part-time at the major-league level) and listed as objectives the acquisition of a catcher, a third baseman, a left-handed pitcher, a bullpen stopper, and an outfielder with some power. It continued: ''Young players like Lloyd Moseby and George Bell began to establish themselves as legitimate major-leaguers. They were joined in September by shortstop Fred Manrique and outfielder Jesse Barfield, who are expected to be important players in the Blue Jay future.''

For 1982, the first season under new manager Bob Cox, Gillick's report predicted, ''While the roots of the roster-development plan would remain in the farm system, the emphasis for 1982 will shift to a future-is-now concept of roster building. The farm system will not be disturbed, but a more aggressive approach will be taken in securing veteran playing talent. In adopting this approach – and if the right players are selected and perform up to expectations – it is presumed that the club will perform better artistically. It is also presumed that with this approach the Blue Jays will do no better than break even financially.''

Gillick's year-end reports, despite some clunkers from time to time (Danny Ainge!), have proved remarkably prescient, especially in terms of overall team success. He predicted 75 wins in 1982 and the Jays won 78 to finish tied for sixth in the American League East. The future-is-now concept became evident in 1983 when the Jays first won more games than they lost (89–73), finishing in fourth place. The Jays were 89–73 again in 1984, good enough for second place but 15 games behind the supercharged Detroit Tigers.

Gillick was happy to have the club where he wanted it, poised to win if things went right. For two consecutive seasons, the Blue Jays had exceeded eighty-five wins, an almost mystical number. "If you can always stay in that 85 to 90 win area, if you can stay injury free and somebody has a hot year offensively or a pitcher has a great year, you might get 95, 96, or 99 wins." At all costs Gillick wants to avoid the team slipping to 75 wins or worse. He watched it happen to the Milwaukee Brewers, who won the American League East in 1982, then collapsed and finished the 1984 season in the cellar.

After winning the AL East in 1985, the Blue Jays finished a disappointing fourth in 1986, but they still won eighty-six games, one more than Gillick's eighty-five. Even in the tough American League East, the team was still in the thick of it.

The Blue Jays, formerly ugly ducklings, have eased their way into baseball's mainstream as a team to be respected. In less than a decade, the Blue Jays have become one of major-league baseball's elite teams. The Blue Jays' first winning season was 1983, and since then a composite standing of all teams, in both leagues, through 1986 has the Blue Jays fourth in the major leagues – only four games behind the Detroit Tigers. This record could have been better if the Blue Jays had not lost seven of their final eight games of the 1986 season. It is noteworthy that three of the top four teams are from the American League East.

At the bottom of the list, in 26th place, were the Seattle Mariners, the other new kid on the block when the Blue Jays began in 1977. If

Top 10 Major-League Teams, 1983–86

	W	L	PCT	GBL
1. Detroit Tigers	367	280	.567	–
2. New York Yankees	365	282	.564	2
3. New York Mets	364	284	.562	3.5
4. Toronto Blue Jays	363	284	.561	4
5. Houston Astros	344	304	.531	23.5
6. St. Louis Cardinals	343	304	.530	24
7. Boston Red Sox	340	307	.526	27
8. Baltimore Orioles	339	308	.524	28
9. Los Angeles Dodgers	338	310	.522	29.5
10. California Angels	333	315	.514	34.5

1982 is to be included, when they won 78 games, the Blue Jays are third in the major leagues in wins over the five-year span, but the race is not so close. The Tigers remain first for that five-year period at 450 wins followed by the Yankees at 444 and the Blue Jays at 441.

In the game within the game, the Blue Jays were at least as distinguished. During the same four years, the top ten list in home attendance included Toronto in the fourth spot.

Major-League Home Attendance, 1983–86

1. Los Angeles Dodgers	12,932,938
2. California Angels	10,181,312
3. St. Louis Cardinals	9,464,742
4. Toronto Blue Jays	8,964,826
5. Detroit Tigers	8,720,476
6. New York Yankees	8,562,408
7. New York Mets	8,479,487
8. Kansas City Royals	8,257,404
9. Baltimore Orioles	8,193,418
10. Philadelphia Phillies	7,954,717

The Montreal Expos, the Blue Jays' major-league cousins, attracted 6,558,157 fans, the Seattle Mariners only 3,630,828. If it is obvious that Seattle has done something terribly wrong, as well as being in a smaller market, it is as obvious that Toronto has done something right. But the best stroke of fortune could have been what had been a crushing disappointment – not bringing the Giants to Toronto. The Giants, despite occasional signs of resurgence, had been mired in mediocrity until a surprisingly good season in 1986.

By that time, the Toronto fans, who bemoaned the loss of an established team in a league in which Montreal could have provided a natural rivalry, felt blessed. They had taken in a fresh, new team, one with the vibrancy and ingenuity that comes with youth, a team unencumbered by past failures. And as difficult as the American League East could be, it was the most competitive and interesting division in baseball. There was another advantage for the owners. Buying the Giants would have cost $13.5 million. If the National League had voted to expand in 1976 when the American League did, it would have charged each new team $10 million. An American League expansion franchise proved the best deal of all at $7 million.

Looking out over the snowswept stadium, with its concrete and aluminum that could seem cold even in summer and positively frigid in winter, one longed for a summer day, the earthy smell of a grass field and the vagaries of quaint Fenway Park, or even the volatility of Yankee Stadium. The new Yankee Stadium was one year older than the Toronto Blue Jays, who had become one of its most feared visitors. As the snow blew, travelling secretary and trainer Ken Carson was at home in Florida putting the final touches on charters and hotels for next season's trips. As the wind swirled in toward home plate, thoughts easily shifted to the future – a new stadium, with a retractable roof yet. Baseball under any dome, removable or not, was a chilling thought. Yes, it would make the Blue Jays better at the game within a game, but it would also take away some of the fun. It wouldn't matter anymore if it snowed on opening day. Come to think of it, it didn't matter on April 7, 1977, either.

S E C O N D

DOING IT
ON THE ROAD

EVERY YEAR, major-league baseball teams are scheduled to play eighty-one road games, and in 1986 that required the Toronto Blue Jays to make 39 separate flights. In every city, from Boston to Anaheim, the team needs hotel rooms, buses to and from the airport and stadium, and a truck to carry trunks and equipment bags – uniforms, hats, bats, shoes, socks, helmets, gloves, batting-circle "doughnuts," jock straps, warmup jackets, undershirts, and various balms and medications for aches and sprains and for toes and ankles hit with foul tips. As well, the truck transports civilian clothes and everyday personal paraphernalia – family photographs, golf clubs, guitars, Bibles – that make life on the road bearable if not comfortable.

Road-trip expenses for the major-league team, including hotels, airline fares or charters, and meal money, come in at about a million dollars for a season. In 1986, it was $950,000, including $550,000 (Cdn.) for flights with the rest in U.S. funds, bringing the total to about $1.1 million (Cdn.) when the exchange is figured in. In 1986 only the trips to and from the West Coast were on commercial flights, but in 1987 it was becoming more difficult to hire charters and eleven of the flights were to be commercial.

In the American League, visiting teams get 20 per cent of the gate after taxes, which brought the Blue Jays $2.3 million in 1986, a particularly welcome amount to the club as this provides a rare source of U.S. funds. Of course, the teams visiting Toronto are paid their percentage in Canadian money, but the strong attendance at Exhibition Stadium helps offset some of that disadvantage when compared to some of the weaker franchises.

Cliff Johnson, the grizzled designated hitter, once joked that by big-league standards the Blue Jays used to rough it ''like Boy Scouts'' on road trips when he first joined the team in 1983. No more. Nearly all the flights are chartered, with first-class accommodation, and the players' basic agreement states that on commercial flights the club must buy three seats for every two players – all the better for a hand of cards in the midnight skies between Minneapolis and Cleveland. Several seasons ago a travel agent forgot this requirement for a twenty-minute flight from Seattle to Vancouver and the players filed a grievance. They won, too. The Blue Jays offered to pay the difference to charity, but the players refused. It was a matter of principle, they said. The settlement worked out to $17 a player.

The buses vary from the clean and air-conditioned with washrooms at the back to the city buses with the hard seats that always seem to be waiting at the Milwaukee airport. If a bus doesn't have air-conditioning on a hot summer day, the director of team travel will hear about it from the players.

On the road are the shrines of baseball: Yankee Stadium in The Bronx, Fenway Park in Boston, Comiskey Park in Chicago. These are stadiums with memories and traditions, with fields of real grass and dugouts that are dug out. Blue Jay players enjoy trips to Texas and California most because it means going home for so many of them. The families of the players enjoy Texas most of all because the Sheraton Centre Park hotel in Arlington is close to an amusement park featuring the Wet n' Wild. Even closer is the clubhouse entrance to Arlington Stadium, just a short walk away. In the right room, you have a panoramic view of most of the playing field. The Blue Jays' wives and children are entitled to travel on a charter free once each season and at Wet n' Wild they romp and splash under the hot Texas sun while the men of the house prepare to play the Rangers. It is so hot in Texas that even Sunday games at Arlington Stadium are played at night. In Houston, the Astrodome was built not to protect against rainouts but so the games could be played in air-conditioning.

37

For pure baseball the high points of the season are the road trips to New York and Boston. There is something about these old, begrimed cities, something about the stadiums and the fans and the teams who play in them with their traditional uniforms – the pin-striped Yankees; the crisp white with red and blue trim of the Red Sox – that arouses baseball passions. Spiritually, financially, and aesthetically the trips to New York and Boston have never been ordinary, not even when the Blue Jays were a stumblebum expansion team. There has always been a bitter rivalry between New York and Boston, and the big guys disdainfully regarded the early Blue Jays as "nuisance opponents."

All that began to change in the early 1980s when the Blue Jays crept out of the cellar and began a slow but inexorable move to the top of the tough American League East. It changed forever in 1985 when the Blue Jays won the division, holding down first place nearly the entire schedule, from May until the last out in early October. They finished two games ahead of the Yankees, but the real knockout punch came in a crucial four-game series in New York late in September. The savants of baseball were saying the Blue Jays could not take the heat, but they were wrong. In noisy, rancorous Yankee Stadium, the Blue Jays won three of the four games – did it after losing the first game as well – and the Yankees never recovered.

The Blue Jays made it to the American League playoffs against the Kansas City Royals, jumped to a 3–1 lead in games, then, in a heart-breaking collapse, lost the series in seven games. Still, in only their ninth season, the Blue Jays had come within one win of making it to the World Series.

In spring training before the 1986 season, another wave of baseball magazines appeared with the usual truckload of statistics, analyses, player profiles, and predictions for a new season. The Blue Jays, as expected, rated highly in nearly every category – offence and defence, up the middle, starters and relievers, infield and outfield, designated hitters, management. The phrase that kept recurring was that the Blue Jays were a "textbook" franchise, meaning that they had done just about everything right, becoming a model of how to build a contending team. *Bill Mazeroski's Baseball Annual*, one of the better pre-season fan magazines, exclaimed: "Strictly from a talent standpoint, Toronto may be the strongest team in baseball."

By late June of the 1986 season, with more than half of the schedule still to be played, the Blue Jays prepared for a road trip that would take them to New York again, and to Boston. This time it was the Red Sox who made the trip a crucial one.

The Red Sox were dominating the American League East, surprising everyone, thanks mainly to young Roger Clemens, a big, powerful, right-handed pitcher on his way to winning not only the Cy Young Award as the American League's best pitcher but also the Most Valuable Player Award. The Red Sox were in first place, five games ahead of the Yankees – nine and a half games ahead of the fifth-place Blue Jays. Despite the Jays' poor start, they had too much talent to be dismissed this early. There was also bad blood between the Red Sox and the Blue Jays, the result of a 1985 dust-up in Toronto in which outfielder George Bell charged the mound, levelled a karate kick at Red Sox pitcher Bruce Kison, walloped catcher Rich Gedman, then ran backwards to the Blue Jay dugout. Bob Stanley, Boston's formidable six-four, 230-pound, reliever promised he would get even with Bell.

IT WAS A DIVERSE GROUP, numbering fifty-one, that gathered in front of the Air Canada counter at Pearson International Airport in Toronto, waiting to board the charter flight to New York. Days off are to be savoured even if used for travel and this was one of them – the sixth scheduled day off, the seventh including a rainout.

Many had left their cars at Exhibition Stadium and had come to the airport on a bus the team provides. All the equipment had been packed in a truck and driven to the airport, an operation supervised by Jeff Ross, the equipment manager, and Ian Duff, who looks after the visiting team's clubhouse. There were seven trunks – one for weights, one for medical goods, one for the leg-stretching device, two for extra uniforms, one for such extra equipment as long-sleeved undershirts and gloves, one for caps and valuables bags. The trunks for extra uniforms include game uniforms and blue warmup tops for each of the players on the 40-man roster in case of a call-up. There are extra uniforms and warmup tops for the regular players in case an equipment bag is lost and a few extra uniforms so one can be made up immediately for a player acquired in a trade. Each player's equipment bag contains his personal equipment, including gloves, shoes, and uniforms.

Ross and Duff have been with the Blue Jays from the beginning. Ross is a trim, quiet man, with brown hair and a moustache. On most road trips he takes along his golf clubs and tries to get in a round or two with broadcaster Tom Cheek. Sometimes pitcher Jimmy Key, a good golfer, or Ken Fidlin of the Toronto *Sun* also plays. Ross usually plays cards with the players on the plane, but he had work to do at Exhibition Stadium and couldn't make this trip. Duff, slender, bespectacled, mischievous, and the wearer of a close-cropped beard, took Ross's place. The previous evening had been the official opening of Studebaker's, a night spot in which Ross, Duff, and batting coach Cito Gaston were minority partners. It had gone well.

Several of the players were with their families, which made the usually routine departure almost festive. Shortstop Tony Fernandez, outfielder Ron Shepherd, and pitchers Dennis Lamp and Don Gordon were cuddling children or steering strollers through the terminal. Some club employees had come along, too: husky, red-haired Mike Maunder from the ticket office; Len Frejlich, the lean, dark-haired assistant director of operations; clubhouse assistant Greg Kimoff; assistant clubhouse manager Kevin Malloy, a marketing administration student at Seneca College; Stan Stancheson, a dark-haired man with weatherbeaten features who looks after the umpires' room at the stadium. Also along was Gord Ash, administrator of player personnel, who seldom travels with the club. (Nor do Pat Gillick and Paul Beeston, though they might fly in on their own to see some road games.)

Since 1985, it has been Blue Jay policy to pay for one trip each season for club employees. The office support staff also get a free trip to the All-Star game every summer. Other major-league teams allow family members on certain road trips, but allowing office workers on trips is a rarity. It contributes to a family feeling. All expenses are paid, including $47-a-day meal money, the same as the players receive.

KEN CARSON, another original Blue Jay employee, dispenses the meal money in brown envelopes as soon as the plane is in the air. Carson was the team's first trainer and added the duties as director of team travel in 1980. This would be his last season in these jobs. A Canadian who lives in Dunedin, Florida, he would become the team's director of Florida operations in 1987.

As Carson doles out the envelopes, each recipient signs the meal-money sheet, which is handed back through the plane. It is an amusing ritual, with players who can earn as much as $1 million a season signing for envelopes that contain $352.50 for the seven-day road trip plus a half day's meal money because the trip left after 6 p.m. If the flight had left before 6 p.m., a full day's meal money would have been paid.

40

The contingent included the sports writers assigned by their newspapers to cover the Blue Jays throughout the season. They do not receive meal money or anything else from the club, but their papers do take advantage of the favourable hotel rate offered the major-league teams. The writers are with the team from late February, when the pitchers and catchers report for spring training in Florida and, regardless of how the team they cover finishes, are on the road through the World Series in late October. But there is not much of an off-season for the writers, either; winter is rife with baseball meetings, trades, contract negotiations, arbitrations, drafts, and the incessant rumours and rumours of rumours that need to be checked out and followed up.

Each newspaper that has a reporter travelling regularly with the team – *The Globe and Mail, The Toronto Star*, the Toronto *Sun, The Hamilton Spectator* – pays $8,000 to the club for air travel at the start of the season. It would cost the newspapers $9,800 if they had to arrange commercial flights for the reporters. Tom Cheek and Jerry Howarth, the radio announcers for the TBS Network, and Bruce Brenner, their engineer, also travel with the team. The TBS Network radio contract with the Blue Jays includes free travel for Cheek, Howarth, and Brenner. Howarth carries a briefcase containing a lap-top computer (a Tandy 200 from Radio Shack similar to the one many newspaper reporters use) and a portable disk drive and printer. Howarth has a disk for each team on which he stores information gleaned from newspapers, magazines, and conversations with coaches, players, and managers both of the Blue Jays and of their opponents. Since the Yankees are the next Blue Jay opponent, he makes a print-out of the information contained on their disk for use on the broadcasts. Howarth works hard.

Cheek and Howarth have a good professional rapport but seldom socialize. ''We're two different people,'' says Cheek in a deep voice that can carry the length of a bus or an airplane or across a hotel lobby. Cheek has worked every Blue Jay game played, all but a few on radio. The others were done on pay television when that was in its infancy. When Early Wynn, the 300-game winner, was his partner on the broadcasts in the early years, the two frequently went to dinner, meeting the people Wynn had known from his years in baseball. As for Brenner, in his early twenties, he often roams with the reporters, some of whom weave their own interesting routes through the American League cities.

Howie Starkman, the man in charge of public relations for the Blue Jays, was making this trip. Starkman was one of the first people hired by the fledgling Jays in 1976 after he had left the Toronto Maple Leafs of the National Hockey League. He usually alternates road trips with his assistant, Gary Oswald, a thin, fair-haired man with a sardonic wit, who has been with the team since August, 1982. Starkman, his dark hair forming a sort of crown around his small bald spot, is responsible on the road for providing the statistical data and other information on the Blue Jays. He'll also call reporters to tell them of any player moves or any abrupt changes in pitching rotation. It's a help to those who must write a story from their hotel rooms for early editions, the earliest of which invariably belongs to *The Globe and Mail*. Starkman is an avid reader and clipper of newspapers on the road to supplement the Canadian Press clipping service the team uses. (However, he often doesn't read the baseball stories in the Toronto papers until he files them back at his office weeks or months later. He sometimes enjoys a laugh at a story that did not prove out.) He also keeps a raft of statistics updated, a day book, for instance, on each player's performance beyond what can be gleaned from the usual statistics. He is able to tell at a glance that a player has one hit in his past 25 at-bats, and is not afraid to put it in the game notes. Starkman, 41, can be gruff at times. But those who deal with him daily learn to realize it's an amiable gruffness. People who deal with all sports in Toronto appreciate the professionalism of baseball public relations.

Until July, 1983, club PR men did not travel regularly. One reason was financial. After using United Airlines charters for the first season (the airline had a deal with major-league baseball), the Jays flew mostly on commercial flights in the early seasons. In those days, Starkman would send the Blue Jay game notes on a telecopier to the home team's PR office. They would be photocopied and included with the package of game notes – a staple for each major-league game in which each club provides two or three pages of notes containing essential and non-essential information plus complete statistics. Because telecopiers transmit over phone lines, however, what comes out is often of dubious quality and legibility.

The Hamilton Spectator began sending a reporter on road trips in 1983, another indication of heightened interest. The Blue Jays' immediate market extends far beyond Metropolitan Toronto's population of nearly three million. Hamilton, with nearly 500,000, is less than an hour from Toronto. In fact, fans trek to home games in Toronto from all over southern Ontario and the Golden Horseshoe, a huge, affluent sprawl that hugs the shoreline of Lake Ontario to the east and west. It is an enormous base of fan support, easily in the top five of major-league cities in North America. In the delirium of 1985, when it looked as though they were about to become the first "foreign" team to reach the World Series, the Blue Jays were described with enthusiasm and even affection as "Canada's baseball team." One must have grown up in Canada to appreciate the true significance of this socio-cultural metamorphosis. Canadians generally do not regard Toronto with much enthusiasm and affection. It was as if a Consolidated Edison fan club sprang up across the United States.

DON GORDON, his wife Deborah, and their infant daughter Christine, who was being held now by Mark Eichhorn, mingled with the group awaiting the charter. Earlier, at an afternoon ceremony at St. Michael's Cathedral in downtown Toronto, the pitcher and his wife watched as their child was baptized. It was such a happy and relaxed event that Christine fell asleep. Eichhorn, fellow pitchers Tom Henke and John Cerutti, and Cerutti's wife Claudia attended the ceremony.

Henke, a towering, bespectacled figure from Missouri, had been the bullpen sensation in the second half of the 1985 season, compiling 13 saves in 40 innings during the final 10 weeks. Eichhorn had been invited to spring training as a non-roster player, but he had developed the sidearm delivery that would make him the bullpen sensation of 1986. Eichhorn had been injured early in June, spiked while covering first base, so the Blue Jays had promoted the right-handed Gordon, a friend of Eichhorn's, from Syracuse. It was his second stint of the season with the Jays. At Syracuse in 1985, Gordon had pitched 113 innings with 12 saves and a miserly earned run average of 2.07. Gordon had grown up in Queens in New York, where his family still lived; he was looking forward to pitching in Yankee Stadium.

Jimy Williams, the third-base coach who succeeded Bob Cox as field manager for 1986, would not make the flight to New York that evening. With executive vice-president for baseball Pat Gillick, he was attending a dinner honouring Montreal Expo owner Charles Bronfman as the Toronto Jewish community's sportsman of the year. At the dinner, Gillick and Williams talked about the Yankee series. Since the days of Babe Ruth, Yankee Stadium has favoured left-handed hitters. There is a majesty to the place to be sure, with a huge expanse in left, left-centre, and centre field and a rather shallow right-field line. The foul pole in right is 310 feet from home plate, close enough that even a singles hitter can pull one over the fence. Williams and Gillick agreed at the dinner that they needed a left-hander for Yankee Stadium; they decided to send Gordon back down and promote Steve Davis, who had made an impression in his most recent outings in Syracuse.

A few others did not make the evening flight to New York. First baseman Willie Upshaw had left earlier in the day with centre fielder Lloyd Moseby and their families. Moseby is Upshaw's best friend on the team. Upshaw lives in Fairfield, Connecticut, a small industrial town west of Bridgeport on Long Island Sound. During the Yankee series, Moseby would stay with the team at the Grand Hyatt Hotel, next to Grand Central Station; but Upshaw would commute from Fairfield, less than an hour's drive to Yankee Stadium.

Bullpen coach John Sullivan skipped the charter as well. He lives in Dansville, N.Y., and after the Blue Jays had defeated the Milwaukee Brewers in an afternoon game the day before the open date, Sullivan drove the better than three hours home and then on to his father's home in Peapack-Gladstone, a residential borough in New Jersey about an hour's drive to Yankee Stadium. Sullivan wanted to attend his son's high school graduation; he would miss Sunday's game against the Yankees.

"Hurry up and wait" applies as felicitously to baseball travel as to the army. Rush to catch the team bus, which leaves unforgivingly on time, even if it means waiting for hours at the airport. The itinerary, prepared months in advance by Ken Carson, had the flight departing at 7 p.m. with the team bus leaving Exhibition Stadium at 5:45. Carson was informed that the Air Canada plane would not reach Toronto on time, and he altered the bus time and telephoned those making the trip. The flight was delayed by forty-five minutes, then an hour. The plane took off at 8:20.

There are two parts to any such wait. First is the wait at the ticket counter, where the players and families gather in animated groups. When Carson gives out the boarding passes, the second part begins. The passengers, like any other charter group, carry their luggage through U.S. customs, one of the little nuisances of playing in Canada. The equipment truck is checked separately before loading. Each player has been provided with a blue suitcase with the Blue Jay logo and a small plaque with his name and uniform number on it. On commercial flights this makes it easier to recognize the bags belonging to the team so they can be loaded on the truck going to the hotel. On a commercial flight, all baggage that is not "GI issue," as Bob Bailor, an original Blue Jay, referred to it, has Blue Jay stickers slapped on it. Once in the United States, the player does not see the bags again between hotels.

Delays aside, the players are treated well – luxuriously compared to the rigours of the minors – but it does not take them long to complain, perhaps jealously defending something they feel they have earned after years of bus rides. There is a rough, macho humour among professional athletes; like school children, it is usually at its worst in a group. Carson, or assistant trainer Tommy Craig, usually takes the heat. Craig gets it because he normally is designated to tell the bus driver to leave when the players are being transported from hotel to ballpark and back. Carson usually sits, or stands, at the front of the bus, smoking his pipe. If a driver gets lost, or there is some other delay, he reddens as the pipe smoke becomes thicker. He knows he is going to hear about it from someone. Even simple things can draw a player's ire. A few years ago, pitcher Joey McLaughlin complained that although he was served a first-class meal, as stipulated in the agreement between the players and the major-league teams, he had to drink from a plastic cup. McLaughlin threatened to file a grievance until Carson and the player representative smoothed things out.

As this trip began Carson's patience was wearing thin, mainly because of petty aggravations caused by Air Canada, the government-owned airline. First came the delays, then an attendant wanted unnecessarily to assign seats as another asked, for the umpteenth time, the exact number of passengers in the party.

The previous week in Milwaukee the series ended with an afternoon game. Air Canada told Carson the team could not have a plane until 8 o'clock in the evening, rather than 5:30 as the contract stipulated. Carson shopped around for a substitute flight; Ozark Airlines found it no problem. "I told Ozark to send the bill to Air Canada," Carson said. "I'd like to break the contract with Air Canada. I give up trying to figure out their logic. They just seem to make everything so hard."

It wasn't a complaint against individual employees; most of the flight attendants were highly competent and friendly. It was the frustration of dealing with bureaucracy when flight times had been set out months ago in the contract. Why make the commitment, Carson wondered, if they couldn't provide the plane?

Flight attendants on Canadian airlines were required to make all announcements in French and English, preposterous when carrying a planeload of ballplayers. However, there would be a delightful twist to this on the Blue Jays' final road trip of the 1986 season. They were returning from New York on another Air Canada charter when the flight attendant made her announcements, not only in English and French, but in Spanish. Tony Fernandez laughed with delight. The attendant then also made the announcements in German and Italian.

On charter flights, the manager and the coaches sit at the front. Behind them are the reporters and the radio crew and players with wives and children. The rest of the players sit farther back. Beer and liquor are served. The card games start. They are sometimes noisy. Many of the players carry attaché cases, looking like businessmen with their suits and ties. The cases often contain the players' tapes for their cassette players. Several players at one time might be wearing head sets on a plane or bus, their heads wagging and bobbing in different directions to their own music.

After their first season, the cost of airline travel increased dramatically. The Jays began to use commercial flights during their second season. Sometimes this would mean staying over the night after a game, getting up early to catch a flight, and then playing in another city that night. As the team became more competitive, the use of charters again increased. At first there were the Air Ontario propeller planes, and the equipment and luggage had to be loaded correctly for balance. During the loading, players would joke about getting a real airplane. Carson says the complaints were few, really. The biggest problem now is that the players often don't realize that their planes are also being used for commercial flights and can't always be at an airport waiting as soon as the team is ready to leave.

The flight to New York was smooth and uneventful. At La Guardia Airport, the well-dressed group – club regulations require suits or sport coats on trips – made its procession through the airport. Barfield and his wife Marla are always among the most stylish dressers. The last to leave the plane was pitcher Dennis Lamp, accompanied by his wife, Janet, and daughters, Hillary and Caroline, and a stroller. Lamp is usually one of the chattier players on a flight – he does superb imitations – but had been uncharacteristically quiet. There were two buses for the trip into town, one for players, the other for everyone else (including players with wives and children). On game days, there is a bus between hotel and stadium for players and reporters. The bus leaves the hotel two and a half hours before game time and leaves the stadium forty-five minutes after it's over. On getaway days, after the final game of a series, the bus leaves for the airport one hour after the game.

The players often take out their frustrations on bus drivers, barking out commands as the vehicle waits for the word to go from Craig or winds its way through the night city streets. Pity the driver who takes a wrong turn.

"Hey, bussy."

"C'mon bussy, let's go."

"Hey, bussy! Need a map?"

BOBBY MATTICK, the Blue Jay vice-president in charge of the minor-league system, played shortstop for the Chicago Cubs and the Cincinnati Reds between 1938 and 1942. He played in only 206 major-league games, compiling a modest career batting average of .233, with 64 RBIs and no home runs. He might have been better had a foul ball not smashed into his face above his right eye during batting practice in 1936 when he played in the Pacific Coast League. The injury fractured his skull and left him with double vision.

In 1980, Mattick was 64, the oldest rookie manager ever to start a season. He managed the Blue Jays for two non-vintage years, the second interrupted by a players' strike, and compiled a record of 104 wins and 164 losses. Mattick made his real mark in baseball as a scout, recruiting, signing, and developing such stars as Curt Flood, Vada Pinson, Rusty Staub, Tommy Harper, Darrell Porter, Gorman Thomas, Bobby Grich, Don Baylor, Gary Carter, Ellis Valentine, and the Blue Jays' Dave Stieb and Jesse Barfield.

When he managed the Blue Jays in 1980 and 1981, Mattick sometimes reminisced about the old days, especially when he heard his players grumbling about slow buses and delayed planes. "We had to claim our own luggage off the trains, carry it to the taxis, and pay our own fare from the depot to the hotel. We had to get to the ballpark from the hotel the best way we could, whether it meant taking a streetcar or three or four of us getting in a cab. You'd hope you would stay at a hotel near the park so you could walk, like in Pittsburgh and old Forbes Field. In New York, you couldn't do it. You'd take the subway to the Polo Grounds. In Philadelphia, you'd have to take cabs."

EXCEPT WHEN GOING THROUGH CUSTOMS, players are not expected to carry their own bags, and they never carry their own equipment. In

New York, a truck carried the equipment to Yankee Stadium, where the attendant for the visitors' clubhouse unpacked the bags, sorted the equipment, and hung up the Blue Jays' blue road uniforms in each player's locker, where they would be waiting the next afternoon. The day off had allowed the uniforms to be laundered in Toronto; otherwise they would be washed in the machines at Yankee Stadium and the visiting team charged about $4 per uniform. In some cities, where there are no laundry facilities, the uniforms are sent out to be cleaned.

At the Grand Hyatt Hotel, about 10 p.m., named envelopes with room keys – actually small cards that fit into a slot in the room door – were stacked on a table in a side lobby on the hotel's second level, where the buses and taxis can avoid the traffic. Some hotels will have sandwiches and soft drinks or beer waiting for the teams if they are coming in particularly late. At the Boston Sheraton, box lunches await the travellers in their rooms. The bags came later in a separate truck (cost for the truck on a road trip is between $700 and $800, to and from the airport). They are deposited in the main lobby and most are delivered to the rooms by bellmen, on request.

The team members and employees pay only for incidentals. The team agrees to rent one room for two players. However, 16 Blue Jays' contracts stipulate a single room. Another four take the single room and pay the extra. The remaining four players pair up; double rooms cost the same as singles. Major-league teams get special rates at hotels, usually half the regular price. The New York rate is $84 a night (plus $15.13 of combined city and state taxes for a grand total of $99.13), the most expensive on the schedule. The lowest rate is at the Warwick Hotel in Seattle, perhaps the team's favourite; it is quiet, and the rooms are good and half the price of those at the Grand Hyatt.

Hotels compete for baseball business. If one hotel puts up all 13 visiting American League teams, 40 to 45 rooms are steadily booked for six months, not to mention the bar and restaurant business generated by the players, coaches, and reporters. Usually the deals are for one year, but sometimes a longer deal is made and the hotel might agree not to increase the tariff. (Carson often receives calls from competing hotels; he listens and makes notes for future reference.) Most hotels provide suites for both Carson and manager Jimy Williams. The manager's is complimentary, and except for a couple of hotels that charge a single rate, so is the travelling secretary's. Carson has grown accustomed to baseball's perks. ''I never thought it would be like this,'' he admitted, ''but when I fly on my own now I'll try to get upgraded to first class. You get spoiled.''

Costs for the road trip to Boston and New York, excluding salaries and meal money, were:

Charter flights: $37,000

Buses: $2,500 ($1,500 in New York, $1,000 in Boston)

Trucks: $1,500

Hotels: $33,000

Total: $74,000 for seven days

Friday night, June 27, Yankee Stadium
Attendance: 30,815
Visitors' share: $52,226.15

THE NAME YANKEE STADIUM has magic in baseball, but not for New York City cab drivers. The team bus leaves the Grand Hyatt for the stadium at 4:45 p.m. for a 7:30 game, which seems time enough; but some coaches and some players get there early. The problem is that many cab drivers don't like to go Yankee Stadium, which is in one of the toughest sections of The Bronx. The traffic is often snarled on the route and the prospects of getting a return fare are practically nil. The fare from the hotel is $9, but cabbies often shrug: ''I'm new, I don't know how to get there.'' Or, ''Sorry, my shift's over.'' A driver took Carson once, but only as far as Harlem when he decided his shift was done. Another pulled over for a beer one hot summer day and left Carson in the cab with the meter running. When Carson shared a cab with Harry Warner, an early Blue Jay coach, they were rear-ended. It turned out the driver was a Yankee Stadium security guard on his way to work. They did make it to the park, all right, and the security guard checked to make sure there were no injuries, which there weren't.

After signing some autographs for the ubiquitous collectors outside the hotel, batting coach Cito Gaston, pitching coach Al Widmar, third-base coach John McLaren, and reserve outfielder Ron Shepherd found a willing cab driver. But the trip was not without incident. They were nearly sideswiped on the way to Yankee Stadium, barely avoiding a serious accident.

The coaches like to arrive early anyway, but this time it was because the Blue Jays were allowed some early batting practice before the Yankees began their pre-game hitting. Usually the home team hits first, but the Blue Jays wanted the batting cage for pitching practice. Mark Eichhorn, his punctured ankle healed, was ready to come off the disabled list and manager Jimy Williams and Widmar wanted him to test it. He would face bench players Ron Shepherd, Rick Leach, and Kelly Gruber, who took extra hitting whenever they could. John Sullivan, the 46-year-old bullpen coach and former catcher, donned the gear and squatted behind the plate. Pitcher Jimmy Key, coaches Billy Smith and McLaren, and clubhouse attendant Ian Duff shagged flies in the outfield. There is something exuberant, joyful, about an impromptu summer session on a field once inhabited by DiMaggio and Gehrig and Mantle and Maris.

In the batting cage, Shepherd foul-tipped an Eichhorn pitch and it bit into the netting with a hard click, like a hockey puck hitting the back of the goal.

"With him pitching, we won't need anyone shagging flies," Shepherd said, readying himself for the next sidearm delivery.

Gaston leaned his tall frame against the back of the cage. His broad shoulders go straight out, as if there were a clothes hanger in his uniform. He talks softly, reassuringly, to the hitters. "You know what you want now," he said to Shepherd. "Now wait for it."

After another futile swing, Shepherd stepped out of the cage, muttering about Eichhorn. "He's got some kind of funk, man." Eichhorn's nickname is Dr. Funk because of his delivery.

Eichhorn would throw for about fifteen minutes. Part way through the exercise, he asked, "Am I a little deliberate?"

"No, you're all right," Widmar said.

Eichhorn admitted he was a little tentative. The nine stitches in his foot were not removed until after the workout and he was reluctant to do that little hop on his follow through until he knew it was going to be all right. It was. Yet, his first two weeks back in action would be his most difficult as he tried to regain confidence in the foot.

Steve Davis, the young left-hander called up from Syracuse, was a surprise early afternoon visitor to the clubhouse. Davis was the first person Don Gordon noticed when he walked in the clubhouse door. He was startled. The first thought he had was the flight time of his plane back to the minors. Then he wondered if there had been a trade he didn't know about. He delayed putting on his uniform, thinking at any moment Jimy Williams would ask him into his office for the dreaded news. But Williams wasn't there, so he went ahead and put on his uniform and had thoughts of at least striding out on the Yankee Stadium turf so he could say, "All right, I made it." Just as he was walking out of the clubhouse, Williams was coming in after watching Eichhorn's workout. Gordon was asked into Williams's office for the bad news. He would be rejoining the Syracuse Chiefs in Richmond, Virginia. He expected he might be sent down when Eichhorn came off the disabled list in a few days, but there was always the hope that he would perform well enough to make the team alter its plans. He had hoped to be with the team for the Yankee series, at least, and maybe pitch a few innings.

There is no good way to tell a player that he is being demoted or released, and the Blue Jays were embarrassed by the way Gordon found out. Gord Ash explained that the decision to bring up Davis was not made until the dinner on Thursday night, after the charter flight had left for New York. Ash didn't find out until Friday morning, when he had to make the arrangements for Davis to be on his way to New York. Williams prefers to talk to players personally in these cases, but he was flying to New York Friday morning. Davis went directly to Yankee Stadium, bypassing the hotel so that Gordon and the other players would not see him; but Gordon had arrived ahead of the team bus. Williams felt badly about it, but Gordon took it well, even though he had asked for six tickets to the Friday night game for family and friends. He also knew that kids in Queens had bought forty tickets for the game and were selling them around the neighbourhood. As he was leaving Yankee Stadium, he said, "You've got to understand, that's the way it works. I understand what they're thinking. There's a potent left-handed lineup out there."

Early that morning Gordon had put Deborah and Christine on the train at Penn Station. Deborah would visit her parents in Aberdeen, New Jersey, then go to the game with friends. Gordon called his wife from the clubhouse and told her to meet him at La Guardia for the trip to Toronto, catching her just before she was leaving. Her parents drove her the two and a half hours to La Guardia. Gordon took a cab back to the hotel and quickly checked out, but he could not find a taxi to take him to the airport. Being from New York, he knew his way around well enough to find the $6 airport bus. He met his wife and daughter barely in time for the flight back to Toronto, where they were staying at Tom Henke's apartment. They arrived in time to hear the last part of the game.

The next morning they packed their wagon and drove back to their old apartment in Syracuse. On the Sunday morning, Gordon caught a 7 o'clock flight to Richmond, arriving at the ballpark at 11 o'clock for the day game. It was very hot, 95 degrees as Gordon would later recall. He got into the game in the third inning, wearing long sleeves and not having pitched in a week. The third batter he faced was Gerald Perry. He hit him with a pitch. Perry charged Gordon, a devout Christian. There was a brawl with Gordon winding up on the bottom as both teams converged at the mound. It was over in 30 seconds, but it seemed like two hours to Gordon. He emerged with bruises and a healthy curiosity about what could happen next.

FRIDAY NIGHT, Doyle Alexander stepped to the mound against the Yankees, his former team. Alexander was 35 years old, but in uniform he looked older. He seems to have been around forever, starting in 1968 in the Los Angeles Dodgers organization. In the major leagues he had played for the Dodgers, the Baltimore Orioles, the Yankees, the Texas Rangers, the Atlanta Braves, the San Francisco Giants, and the Blue Jays, who took him in 1983 after the Yankees had cut him and no one else seemed willing to give him a chance. He was one of five pitchers to have at least one win over all 26 major-league teams. There is a world weariness to the man, the dusty, grizzled visage of an old Hollywood western gunslinger in muddy chaps, one elbow on the bar, asking for a shot glass and bottle of whisky.

Alexander's pitching opponent for the Yankees was Ron Guidry, also 35, a leftie known as "Louisiana Lightning" or, to his teammates, "Gator." Alexander had pitched against Guidry six days earlier in Toronto, giving up only one run in nine innings, though the Yankees won 4–3 in extra innings. Alexander thought that might have been his farewell appearance as a Blue Jay. The morning that the Blue Jays arrived in New York, a newspaper story claimed Alexander was about to be traded to Atlanta, where Bobby Cox, the ex-manager of the Blue Jays, was the general manager. Someone called Pat Gillick in Toronto to ask about the rumour. Gillick replied, "Bullshit."

The Yankee pinstripe is woven through the fabric of the Blue Jays' brief history. Gillick was co-ordinator of player development and scouting for the Yankees from 1974 until 1976 when he joined the Blue Jays. Scouts Epy Guerrero, Dave Yoakum, and Wayne Morgan and personnel administrator Elliott Wahle followed. Alexander had two stints with the Yankees, in 1976 and in 1982 and part of 1983. Other Blue Jays who had played for the Yankees or had been in their farm system were Garth Iorg, Damaso Garcia, Willie Upshaw, and Cliff Johnson.

On this hot, humid night threatening rain, Guidry left in the third inning after Iorg struck a two-run homer, his first ever against the Yankees. Iorg, who once thought Yankee Stadium would be his home park, savoured the moment after the ball was swallowed up by the crowd down the left-field line. "Everything's got to be just right for me to hit one out of here," Iorg said. "Because it's so deep to other parts of the park that I can't reach it. A few years ago, I just missed one off Guidry, just hit one foul, and I said, 'Wow, I'll never get that chance again.'

"When I first signed with the Yankees, of course, there wasn't a Blue Jay team. I never really thought about going to another organization. What's on your mind is that you're trying to get to Yankee Stadium. Get here some way, somehow. I think this ballpark has so much lore behind it."

Alexander left in the fourth after a two-run homer by Rickey Henderson. In the end, the Blue Jays won 14–7, in a game that ended near midnight after a rain delay.

Saturday afternoon, June 28
Attendance: 43,187
Visitors' share: $67,339.03
ACCORDING TO THE ITINERARY, the bus was to leave the hotel at 11 o'clock, but most of the players thought it was 10:45. Catcher Buck Martinez took the first step leading onto the bus, put his head in, and said several players were still in the hotel lobby. The bus waited. Tom Henke and Tony Fernandez, the artistic shortstop from the Dominican Republic, led the group that boarded as Martinez and Rance Mulliniks in unison said, "Don't worry, we wouldn't leave without *you*, Tony." Fernandez was hot, on his way to 47 hits for the month, which would tie a club record.

Billy Smith's watch, it was decided, would provide the official departure time. "Forty seconds, bussie, by Billy Smith's watch," Lloyd Moseby said. "Okay, five . . . four . . . ."

From the elegance of Park Avenue – passing near the stately Plaza Hotel on Central Park Avenue South where Iorg, Jim Clancy, and Ernie Whitt were chosen in the American League expansion draft ten years earlier – the bus drove through the poverty of Harlem and then finally wheezed to a stop at Yankee Stadium in The Bronx, where the laundry hung from the windows of the tenements.

A crowd waited outside the press and players' entrance, restrained by wooden police barricades as they jostled for position when the players stepped from the bus.

"They're here to see you, Tony," Moseby said to Fernandez. As it turned out they would see plenty of Moseby, who would hit two home runs.

The crowd was more subdued, almost polite, compared to the masses at the stadium in the heat of the pennant race the season before when the Blue Jays, and even the Toronto press, were loudly booed on their arrival for all four games of that crucial series in September. The crowd even booed Canada's national anthem. Outfielder Jesse Barfield was incensed at the lack of respect for "our" anthem. Barfield, a soft-spoken, friendly man with one of the strongest arms in baseball, who was born in Joliet, Illinois, and lives in Houston, explained, "I feel like I'm a Canadian, in a sense. I've been up here my whole career. I feel like I'm part of the country."

For the second day in a row the Blue Jays beat the Yankees, this time 7–4. In the clubhouse after the game, pitcher Jim Acker, who had picked up the win Friday night, was not sure he wanted to stay in Toronto unless he could pitch more. On the morning his salary arbitration hearing was to take place in Feburary, 1986, he had signed a one-year contract that would be worth $367,000, including incentives. He was 27, single, and enjoying his bachelor days. Acker began the 1986 season in the starting rotation; but when left-hander John Cerutti had been called up, Acker was moved back to the bullpen. And with Henke pitching well in late-inning relief and Eichhorn a revelation, Acker wasn't seeing much action. The same thing happened the summer before. Acker, perhaps a victim of his own versatility, had not established a single role in his three and a half Blue Jays seasons. His uncomplaining acceptance of whatever he was asked to do made Acker a favourite with Cox, Sullivan, and Widmar in his first three years in Toronto, and at least one player would refer to Acker as Sullivan and Widmar's "son." But this year Acker wasn't feeling particularly favoured.

"I heard in a roundabout way that my name was mentioned in a trade and I was kind of excited," Acker said. "If Henke's not rested then Eichhorn's going to be out there for the save, which is the way you've got to do it, the way he's throwing the ball. I can't *ask* to be traded. I've only got four years and I can't say *nothing*. I'm just saying that my name was mentioned and I said, 'Great.' I just want to pitch."

Alexander, returning from the shower, overheard his best friend on the team. "Keep talking like that and you're going to get a bad name," Alexander said, laughing. "They'll blame it on me."

That evening, Jimmy Key, Rick Leach, and Jesse Barfield took their wives to see *A Chorus Line* on Broadway. Or perhaps their wives took them. It was a first for the reluctant Barfield. "My wife talked me into it," he said. "I didn't know what to expect. I was surprised. I enjoyed it." He began naming shows he was going to try to see in Toronto.

Sunday afternoon, June 29
Attendance 35,437
Visitors' share $58,203.52

THE *Daily News* headlined Saturday's Yankee loss: "A DAY OF PINSTRIPE INFAMY." It was the Yankees' ninth consecutive loss at Yankee Stadium.

But the big news was that the Chicago White Sox had traded Tom Seaver to the Boston Red Sox. It was a sensation in New York, where Seaver had been "Tom Terrific" for the Mets.

While John Sullivan was at his son's high-school graduation, his uniform was being filled, with the aid of appropriate padding, by Greg Kimoff, 22, a Blue Jay clubhouse assistant. Stuffing Tootsie Rolls in his mouth instead of the wad of tobacco that always puffs out Sullivan's cheek, Kimoff waddled about the clubhouse and then went onto the field with exaggerated Sullivan mannerisms. Tom Henke snapped a couple of pictures in the clubhouse. Sullivan would find a picture of the performance on the wall of the dugout at Fenway Park the next night. It was a decent impersonation, but his Sullivan voice was only fair. It sounded more like Archie Bunker.

Mimicry is a popular entertainment among the Blue Jays and pitcher Dennis Lamp was the best, including the one of Tom Cheek and Jerry Howarth working a game. "It's *still* the ninth inning; c'mon, let's get somebody out," Lamp says in deep Cheeky tones. Barfield is good with Harry Caray, broadcaster for the Chicago Cubs. Eichhorn does an outstanding Popeye. Many can do a solid Howarth, but Barfield's and Kimoff's are best–after Lamp. Howarth's "Back, back . . . THERE! SHE! GOES!" can be heard some nights in a dozen variations up and down the rows of a charter. Howarth would smile to himself.

The Blue Jays won again, this time 6–3 with three ninth-inning runs, the winner delivered on a pinch-hit single by the former Yankee, Cliff Johnson. John Cerutti got the win in his second relief appearance of the series.

Cerutti is a boyishly handsome leftie who grew up in Albany, N.Y., where his family still lives. As a youngster, Cerutti made some visits to Yankee Stadium, but he also followed the Red Sox as sort of a second team. "I didn't live or die with the Yankees, although in 1978, the year Guidry won 25 games, he really was my idol. That's when I started to come into my own as a pitcher. I was eighteen and I had a big year, also."

Cerutti made his first major-league start against the Yankees in the final game of the 1985 season in Toronto. He lost, but the game meant nothing in the standings. It was the day after the Blue Jays had clinched the American League East, and the day Phil Niekro of the Yankees won his 300th major-league game.

Cerutti's parents had considered making the three and a half hour drive to Yankee Stadium, but not knowing if he would make an appearance they decided to stay home and watch the game on television. His older brother Danny was at the stadium, as were some friends.

Cerutti started as a rookie professional in Medicine Hat in 1981, made it to Syracuse by the end of 1982, was back at Double A in Knoxville before returning to Syracuse in 1984, and finally got to the Blue Jays at the end of the 1985 championship season. After spring training of 1986, when the Blue Jays were in Fort Lauderdale to play two exhibition games against the Yankees, Cerutti learned he was going back to Syracuse. He had not pitched badly but could have been better. What finally turned him around was a change in his windup suggested by pitching coach Al Widmar, with an early-season reminder when Bobby Mattick had visited Syracuse.

"It wasn't a big change," Cerutti said. "It's an abbreviated windup. I eliminated some extra motion that had nothing to do with my arm. It was more of a rhythm thing. It made me more consistent going to the plate and enabled my arm to get in a proper throwing position consistently. It was early May, in Syracuse, when I got it down right."

Cerutti is a serious young man. He graduated in economics from Amherst College, a top school in Massachusetts, the same college attended by Milwaukee Brewer general manager Harry Dalton. Cerutti's major paper was titled "Determination of player salaries in the major leagues." He played winter baseball in Colombia in 1982, returning with a mild case of hepatitis and deeply affected by what he had seen.

"My life changed," Cerutti had said. "It was the first time I had seen poverty. I'd seen it in magazines, but from the bus, when you'd go through a small town, you'd see little kids in rags half-dressed running around on a dirt floor. I was thinking what would make them happy – probably just to go to bed with a full stomach. There were the very rich and the very poor, and there's a lot of the very poor.''

THE SUNDAY WIN meant a three-game sweep by the Blue Jays, their first over the Yankees. The Blue Jays had won six in a row at Yankee Stadium; the Yankees had lost ten consecutive home games, the worst since 1913, the year the team changed its name from the Highlanders and played at the Polo Grounds.

The ride to La Guardia was long and exasperating, as the bus drivers avoided the jammed expressways. Looking out of the bus window, players saw an elderly man lying on the road after being hit by a car. The ambulance had just arrived. It was a reminder of another bus ride, in Florida. The team was travelling to Lakeland for a game with the Detroit Tigers when they saw a little girl struck by a car on the road by the beach, but not seriously hurt. The driver tried to get away, but they had the bus driver hem the vehicle in.

Once at La Guardia, the drivers had trouble finding the entrance for the New York Air charter. The lead bus circled the front part of the airport three times before finding the gate and the buses were able to drive out onto the tarmac beside the plane.

The Blue Jays arrived at the Boston Sheraton at about 9 o'clock; the buses from the airport had to manoeuvre around a tree that had fallen across a downtown street. The feeling was buoyant. They had won five in a row and had taken five of their first seven games from the Yankees. It had been a good weekend for the game on the field. They had also drawn well – 109,439, an average of 36,480 a game – which meant a visitors' share of $177,768.70, all U.S. dollars. It had been a good weekend for the game within the game.

Fenway Park
Monday night, June 30
Attendance: 30,770
Visitors' share: $47,859
AT THE SERVICE ENTRANCE to Fenway Park, where the players and press enter, a sign over the door warns, ''Beware of Attack Dogs.'' In most other ways, Fenway Park suggests a time warp, a deliberate and

stubborn embrace of the past against all good advice to the contrary. Baseball people love it, or hate it, but it speaks well of the charm and timelessness of the game.

More than any other sport, with the exception of golf and yachting, baseball is tolerant of individualism, eccentricity. There are the new, brassy domes in Houston, Seattle, and Minneapolis. There is the blue cathedral of Yankee Stadium. There are the modern architectural gems – Royals Stadium in Kansas City, Dodger Stadium in Los Angeles. And there are the clunkers, including Exhibition Stadium in Toronto. Fenway Park in Boston and Wrigley Field in Chicago, where all games are day games because the neighbours won't tolerate the lights, stand as lovable Model Ts in an age of digital odometers and all-weather radials.

To begin with, there is "the Green Monster" in left field, a large fence, thirty-seven feet high, 315 feet down the line. There is only a gradual increase toward centre field because of the city street immediately behind it. A screen at the top catches fly balls; when a fly ball lands in the screen, it becomes a home run. This makes Fenway Park a lethal place for most left-handed pitchers. That would appear to make it a wonderful place for right-handed hitters, but, curiously, so many of the best Red Sox – Ted Williams, Pete Runnels, Billy Goodman, Carl Yastrzemski, Fred Lynn, and, most recently, Wade Boggs – have been left-handed. From a business sense, Fenway's small seating capacity – its record is 36,388 – limits the gate potential in a good season.

As a player, Bob Mattick would have loved the accessibility of Fenway. No need for a taxi, or even a bus, though the team bus dutifully transports the players from the Boston Sheraton, a fifteen-minute walk away. Inside, the press box and the media dining lounge are on the roof of the stadium, behind and above home plate. It was in the media lounge – scouts, club officials, and others also eat there before games – where Tom Seaver, a winner of 306 games with the New York Mets, the Cincinnati Reds, and the Chicago White Sox, held his first press conference as a member of the Boston Red Sox. ("Seaver Changes Sox," a newspaper headline had announced.)

Red Sox general manager Lou Gorman said negotiations for Seaver had begun seven months earlier, in November. The deal that sent Steve Lyons to the Chicago White Sox had been completed on Saturday night. Seaver, 42, began his major-league career in 1967 with the Mets. He said he would have retired if the White Sox had not traded him to either Boston or New York, because he wished to be closer to his home in

Greenwich, Connecticut. His contract called for $900,000 for the 1986 season (with incentives starting at $25,000 for 150 innings pitched) and $1 million if the Red Sox were to pick up the option for 1987, which they did not. At the time of the trade, Seaver had two wins, six losses and an un-Seaverlike earned run average of 4.38.

Seaver became a member of the White Sox inadvertently because of the Blue Jays. Trying to shore up a bullpen after the 1983 season, the Blue Jays had signed Lamp to a five-year contract, guaranteed through the first three years at a base of $400,000 for 1984, $500,000 for 1985, and $550,000 for 1986. By making a specified number of appearances in previous years, Lamp could guarantee a $600,000 base for 1987 and a $650,000 base for 1988. The contract became embroiled in controversy when Lamp did not pitch in enough games to renew the contract for 1987. He claimed he was kept out of games because of the terms of the contract, while the Blue Jays said he was not pitching well enough to deserve the appearances.

At the time of his signing, Lamp was rated as a Type A player according to a statistical formula based on the two previous seasons. The White Sox were entitled to compensation in the form of a professional player under the basic agreement between the Major-League Players' Association and the owners. All teams, except those who had declared that they would not sign Type A free agents, had to protect twenty-four players in their organization. A team losing a free agent could choose a player from the pool of unprotected players. The New York Mets, concerned with protecting such future stars as Dwight Gooden, thought it would be safe not to protect an aging and expensive Seaver. The White Sox took him anyway, and he started 33 games in 1984, won sixteen, and had an ERA of 3.17. It was the same draft in which the Jays took Tom Henke from the Texas Rangers in 1985 after losing Cliff Johnson as a free agent. (As it turned out, the Blue Jays later got Johnson back in a trade.) The rules have since changed; today, compensation for losing a free agent is a pick in the annual amateur draft.

At his press conference, Seaver said, ''They've got something real good going here. They don't care if I've won five hundred games or three hundred games. They don't want a memory coming in and pitching for them.''

Seaver liked Fenway. ''Aesthetically, from a historical point of view, from the feeling you get when you walk into it, I loved it. I think it's the essence of baseball here.''

THERE WERE NO RHAPSODIES to Fenway from Blue Jay pitcher Jim Clancy on Monday night. While he did not lose, in five innings he gave up eight hits and six runs. Clancy seldom does well at Fenway. In eleven starts over the years, his earned run average there stood at 6.67.

The game proved a microcosm of the Blue Jays' 1986 season. Down 3–0, they recovered to take a 9–5 lead in the top of the sixth but could not hold it. The Blue Jay pitchers, best in the American League in 1985, allowed the leadoff hitter to reach base seven times in 10 innings. Reliever Jim Acker did it in all four innings he pitched. Twice he hit Don Baylor, Boston's mountainous designated hitter who crowds the plate and never backs away. The second time was in the bottom of the tenth; it loaded the bases. Acker then walked Dwight Evans on a full count, forcing in the winning run.

In the clubhouse after the game, Acker said, ''I knew it was a ball as soon as it left my hand. It was way inside. If it had been Baylor, it would have been *behind* him.

Tuesday night, July 1
Attendance: 32,729
Visitors' share: $51,660.60
WHAT A DELICIOUS TWIST! Tom Seaver, the pitcher who didn't want to be just a memory, versus Doyle Alexander, the pitcher who did, at least for the Blue Jays.

The crowd started to applaud Seaver half an hour before the game started, when he strolled to the bullpen in right field to warm up. More applause came twenty minutes later when he walked to the dugout, where he doffed his cap. The applause continued, and he waved his cap. More applause poured forth when Seaver walked to the mound, where he doffed his cap two more times. ''That makes Seaver 4–0 over Ted Williams in cap tipping,'' one Boston writer said.

The Red Sox jumped out to a 7–1 lead; after seven innings, with the Red Sox ahead 9–4, Boston manager John McNamara sent in reliever Steve Crawford to start the eighth. The chant erupted, ''Seav-ah! Seav-ah!'' By this time, Seaver was icing his arm in the clubhouse. He said his attire was not appropriate for a curtain call.

Alexander, who was pitching on three days' rest (Cerutti had pitched twice in relief and had his start moved back two days), gave up seven runs in two and two-thirds innings and took the loss. For the past two seasons, Alexander had been the Blue Jays' steadiest starting pitcher, with seventeen wins each season. He had been the winning pitcher the previous October when the Blue Jays clinched first place in the American League East with a victory over the Yankees in the second-last game of the season in Toronto. It was doubly cruel for the Yankees because they were still paying most of Alexander's $850,000 salary because of a four-year contract he had signed with them in 1982. In 1984, he signed an extension with the Jays covering 1986, which paid him $700,000 in salary. In addition, the Jays paid him $670,000 ($420,000 deferred) for this option year. Alexander, who could have demanded a trade after the 1984 season under baseball rules, did not like the offer the Blue Jays made him for a contract beyond the 1986 season. He was unhappy and made it clear he wanted out.

The differences reached a crescendo late in June when Alexander had pitched a complete game against Roger Clemens of the Red Sox and lost 3-2. The game had been delayed two hours and 47 minutes by rain. Alexander criticized Blue Jay management for the long delay. The Blue Jays had had one home game rained out, in April, and it had been made up with a doubleheader. (Rainouts are expensive. When a good crowd is expected, a postponed game represents a $200,000 loss.) Besides, the weather reports had predicted a long enough break in the rain to get a good start on the game, but just as the game was to begin the rain returned. One of the perplexing problems of outdoor baseball.

No matter, Alexander seemed to be forcing the Blue Jays to trade him. He said the Blue Jays were "going nowhere." Publicly, Gillick said Alexander was entitled to his opinion; privately, Gillick worried that the remarks, especially about being lucky to win in 1985, might offend some of the players. Alexander's teammates didn't say much, for they could see what he was trying to do; but it was beginning to get on people's nerves by June.

For some players and coaches, differences with management are about more than money. Not far from Fenway, just beyond the Green Monster, former Red Sox coach Tommy Harper had been working for two months shuttling cars and picking up parts for a friend at Geneva Auto Parts. He had been fired by the Red Sox after 14 years, just before Christmas; the day Seaver made his triumphant debut, Harper found out that the United States Equal Employment Opportunity Commission had found in his favour, ruling that he had been fired because he had complained about club policies he considered racist. Harper, who is black, had a distinguished career in the major leagues, playing in Cincinnati, Cleveland, Seattle, Milwaukee, and Boston. He had complained about a long-standing policy of allowing passes to the Elks Lodge, an openly segregated lodge in Winter Haven, Florida, where the Red Sox have their spring training, to be distributed only to white players, coaches, and media. It was a delicate issue because the Red Sox have been criticized for deliberately remaining a predominantly white team.

At the park Tuesday, the Red Sox distributed a denial on the EEOC's conclusions. Harper was fired, the Red Sox said, because he was incompetent. It was a sad note on what should have been a triumphant night.

Wednesday night, July 2
Attendance: 27,493
Visitors' share: $44,550.20
THE MOOD AT FENWAY WAS FESTIVE. Roger Clemens was pitching. In the stands, beachballs bounced from arm to arm and head to head, usually ending up on the outfield grass. Fans in the right-field bleachers, near the clock, were ready to mount a poster stamped with a large red K on the wall behind the seats for each Clemens strikeout. The K-brigade started at Fenway on April 29 when Clemens struck out twenty Seattle Mariners to set a major-league record. It was a shameless imitation of Shea Stadium fans' celebration of Dwight Gooden's strikeout feats, but who cares? It's more distressing to watch spectators at Fenway Park do the Wave.

Clemens entered the game with fourteen wins, no losses. One more win would equal an American League record for consecutive wins opening a season. It had rained that afternoon, and a new $10,000 tarpaulin covered the infield, but there was a playoff frenzy in the air. Tony Kubek, the former Yankee shortstop who does television commentary for Blue Jay games and NBC, amused himself that morning in the lobby of the Boston Sheraton by planning the starting rotations for a World Series between the Red Sox and the New York Mets.

In his office in the visitors' clubhouse, Jimy Williams said he was eager to play against Clemens. "I think we can beat him," Williams said. He thought the Blue Jays had hit the ball hard against Clemens in the 3–2 loss in Toronto. The losses in Boston on Monday and Tuesday had been tough. After the five-game winning streak, the team's spirits had seldom been higher than when they came to Boston. Williams was angry at himself about a move he had made in Monday night's game.

And there had been a missed sign in a crucial late-inning situation. In the clubhouse after Monday night's loss – walking in the winning run is the worst way to lose – Williams was quiet and controlled, perhaps a little edgy. He does not erupt like Bob Cox, who used to scream obscenities, hurl uniforms on the floor, and smash bottles of shaving lotion.

As he waited for the Wednesday night game, Williams talked about Seaver. Seeing him pitch rekindled memories. Williams attended Fresno State College, where he studied animal science and, in his final years, twice made the All-California Collegiate All-Star team as a shortstop. When Williams was a college freshman, Seaver was a senior in high school. The freshmen often played local high school teams, and Williams remembered facing Seaver but didn't recall anything special about him. However, Seaver emerged from a stint in the Marines bigger and stronger, and he and Williams became teammates. Williams was playing for a team in Sturgis, South Dakota, when he was picked up by Seaver's team, the Alaska Goldpanners, for a National Baseball Congress tournament in 1964. They fell one win short of the championship. A year later, in the same tournament, Seaver pitched against the Wichita Dreamliners and lasted only a few innings. The Dreamliners had a wily left-handed pitcher, a former pro. He would be named the leading pitcher of the tournament in 1965 as his team won the title for the second time in three years. His name was Pat Gillick.

Jimmy Key beat Boston and Roger Clemens, 4–2, justifying Williams's pre-game optimism. Key lasted until two out in the eighth inning when, with a full count on Baylor, he felt something pop in his shoulder and Williams took him out. Henke got Baylor to foul out and struck out the side in the ninth.

This time the hero was the aggressive left-fielder George Bell, who is the most unpopular Blue Jay ever to play in Fenway Park. The fans remembered Bell's antics in the brouhaha at Exhibition Stadium the summer before and each time he came to bat they booed and shook their K signs at him. Red Sox pitcher Steve Crawford's dislike of Bell goes back to 1980 when they were both in the Double A Eastern League. As Crawford recalls it, Bell took a swing at him when he was being held during a brawl. Bell missed the pitcher but hit Crawford's manager, Tony Torchia. Crawford, who stands six-five and weighs 236 pounds, lumbered after Bell all over the outfield but couldn't catch him, even with Bell running backwards. The Blue Jays had their own grudges against Boston first baseman Bill Buckner. In the same 1985 brawl he used his feet to rub John Sullivan's face into the artificial turf at Exhibition Stadium, leaving unsightly turf burns.

In the fourth with two out, Clemens was working on a no-hitter, when Bell cranked a home run that silenced the crowd and stunned Clemens. Barfield compared it to a boxer being rocked by a blow. "Suddenly, he knew he could be hit," Barfield said. In the bottom of the fifth, Marty Barrett's two-run homer gave Boston a 2–1 lead. But a radar gun that had measured Clemens's fastball at 95 miles an hour in the sixth was catching him at 88 in the seventh. The Blue Jays tied the game on a double by Rance Mulliniks in the eighth, and in to relieve came Bob Stanley, who had vowed to settle matters with Bell. This was not the time for it, however, and John McNamara had warned his team to cool it. Bell hit the game-winning single.

Thursday night, July 3
Attendance: 21,123
Visitors' share: $36,033
IT WAS JOHN CERUTTI'S TURN to face the Red Sox, but his mind was on other things. His wife, Claudia, was expecting their first child, and his 15-year-old sister Lisa, the youngest of six children, had been injured in a bicycle accident. On her way home from cheerleading practice she had collided with a truck, shattering her cheek bone and breaking her jaw, which required surgery and wiring. At the hotel, standing by a pay phone with his younger brother Paul, Cerutti had just spoken to his mother in Albany. "Mom told me there was nothing I could do there and to go out and pitch a great game."

In the clubhouse before the game, many of the Blue Jays didn't know about the accident. When Garth Iorg found out, he sat down with Cerutti, put his arm around him, and talked. At 1985 spring training, Iorg's two-year-old son, Eli, fell three storeys out an apartment window. Luckily, he suffered only a broken leg.

Cerutti did not pitch a great game, but he won, for the third time in nine days. That meant two wins in a row at Fenway for the Blue Jays, and seventeen wins in twenty-seven consecutive games against the American League East. The Blue Jays had also drawn well in the seven road games. Their share of 221,554 paid attendance brought in $358,870 (U.S.).

Still, they were nine and a half games behind the Red Sox, the same

64

gap that existed when they left Toronto for New York a week earlier. It was a gap that would bedevil the Blue Jays all summer long.

On getaway days, the bus leaves for the airport one hour after the game ends. It is important to get to the airport early because jets are not allowed to land in Toronto after midnight. There have been some races to meet the deadline, but this time there was no chance. The game took more than three hours to play, which meant a flight to Hamilton and a bus to Exhibition Stadium. The plane landed in Hamilton at 2:30 in the morning. Two buses were waiting and in the back of one of them during the trip, Williams, Widmar, Sullivan, Smith, Gaston, Tommy Craig, and a couple of reporters played liars' poker, using U.S. dollars. Squinting under an erratic light, Smith can shatter any silence with his raspy high-pitched voice, "Ten eights? Who *said* that?" When the buses pulled up to Exhibition Stadium, the field lights were on and the workers were preparing for that night's game against the California Angels. The right-field fence wasn't up yet.

The equipment truck did not arrive at the stadium until a few minutes before four. Driver Dean Pulfer, with Duff sitting beside him in the front, wheeled the equipment truck under the stands and parked beside the door to the Blue Jay clubhouse, where some of the players waited for their bags to be unloaded by Malloy and Kimoff. Jeff Ross was also there. (During the wait for the truck, some card games from the plane and bus ride had continued.)

Duff went immediately to the visitors' clubhouse to prepare it for the Angels, who had already arrived from the West Coast on their off day. He did any laundry that needed to be done, prepared the shoes for cleaning although laundry and the shoes likely did not need doing because of the Angels' day off, and hung the uniforms in the players' lockers. Mike Maunder slipped home for a couple hours' sleep, reported for work at the ticket department at nine o'clock, and worked until ten at night with a couple hours off for a nap. It's all part of the life.

T H I R D

BACK TO
THE DRAWING BOARD

THE BLUE JAYS returned from their New York and Boston road trip in the early hours of July 4, and by the evening of July 5 Doyle Alexander learned he had been traded. Early the following day, Jim Acker had been traded. Both were going to the Atlanta Braves of the National League.

Bob Cox, the tough, inspirational manager who had guided the Blue Jays to the 1985 American League East championship came to town as general manager of the Braves to negotiate deals for the two recalcitrant pitchers and to take part as an honoured alumnus in the Blue Jays' first oldtimers' game. The festivities were part of the Blue Jays' tenth anniversary celebrations, ten years that had barely provided the Blue Jays with enough oldtimers to field a team. Most Blue Jay oldtimers were wizened geezers in their early and mid-thirties.

For a few hours that Sunday, Cox wore his old Blue Jay uniform and the spectators at Exhibition Stadium greeted him warmly, with only a few good-natured boos and catcalls. Most boos and catcalls at Exhibition Stadium are good natured because Toronto fans, quintessential Canadians, are unfailingly courteous, at least in the early innings before beer loosens the fetters of civility. Once when Baltimore's Earl Weaver was walking back from the mound from having talked to a pitcher, he encountered a hostile reaction from fans above the dugout. Weaver glared them down and yelled, "Shut up!" They did.

The deals for Alexander and Acker were done away from the anniversary partying, mainly by Pat Gillick. The Alexander trade was settled first, on the Saturday night before the oldtimers' game. In exchange for Alexander, the Blue Jays received 22-year-old Duane Ward, a right-hander supposedly blessed with a Rich Gossage-type fastball and the Braves' number one draft choice in 1982. The Blue Jays sent him to Syracuse for seasoning. On Sunday morning, Cox and Gillick completed the deal for Acker, which brought the Blue Jays Joe Johnson, a usable starter aged 24.

The transactions revealed much about the way the Braves and Blue Jays run a baseball team. The Braves, contending in the wretched National League West, wanted Alexander for the present. The Blue Jays obtained Ward for the future. They were happy to get Johnson because he is eleven years younger than Alexander and good enough to make the starting rotation. As well, the fans and some players were growing weary of Alexander's bitching and manipulating, although when the game was on he remained the consummate professional, concentrating on the game and never missing a pitch even between starting assignments.

Pat Gillick is not an impetuous trader. Even though Alexander made it clear at the end of spring training that he wanted to be traded, Gillick had waited until July. Actually, in November, long before Alexander made his discontent known, Gillick had been talking about trading the pitcher to Atlanta for what he would consider the right reasons, among them the fact that Alexander would be 36 in September. Gillick doesn't believe in trading only for reasons of personality, but by the time he made his move in this case the situation had reached the limits. "A lot of trades are made because of personality," Gillick said. "Sometimes it's a personality conflict between the manager and the player. If you analyse it, it's not unusual when you're together a minimum of 200 days a year, playing 162 games a season, with 30 exhibition games. That's more than you see your wife and family. There's going to be dislikes develop, and personality conflicts. What happens is that the manager says, *I want the son of a bitch off the club!*"

In most cases the players who are playing regularly are not a problem;

it's the players who aren't playing who create the problems. "What happens on some clubs, they choose the easy way and trade them," Gillick says. "That isn't solving anything. The next guy comes along and *he's* a problem, so you get rid of him too. On some clubs a personality clash develops between coaches and players or managers and players and now they go ahead and make a deal. It doesn't make a lot of sense to trade just to get rid of a personality problem – a management problem – not a playing problem."

Other trades are made to give the impression that something is being done, really nothing more than cosmetics. Then, there are the owners who meddle for all the wrong reasons. It has not been a problem in Toronto, but it has been with such teams as the Chicago White Sox, and the New York Yankees under George Steinbrenner. "They go to a cocktail party and somebody says, 'You've got a shit club. They're *terrible*!' " Gillick says. "They hear the same thing at another party and so they start making calls, saying, 'Goddammit, let's do something! I'm sick and tired of being embarrassed.' With George I know that would happen. He would get pissed off at some player because somebody would dig him about it and he'd want to get rid of him."

Gillick thinks he was probably too frank with Alexander at spring training in their discussions to extend his contract beyond 1986 and that's how the pitcher developed his "philosophical difference" with the team. Gillick told Alexander that they could not pay the $1.8 million per season that he was asking. But Gillick said that over the year and between the 1986 and 1987 seasons, changes could be made where older players would be replaced by lower-salaried younger players – Cliff Johnson and Buck Martinez were two examples – which would make more money available to increase the offer. Alexander took it the wrong way, Gillick believes, and decided that the club was interested in getting rid of some older players, and their higher salaries, and not necessarily interested in winning. "I don't mind keeping the older guys around," Gillick said, "but there comes a time when they're done."

There was a business aspect to the deal. Besides acquiring two younger pitchers, the Blue Jays unloaded Alexander's $700,000 salary with no incentives and Acker's salary of $325,000, plus incentives. Ward was earning $60,000; Johnson's contract paid him $75,000, and he would pick up another $30,000 from incentive bonuses. Financially, at least, the Blue Jays gained. Had they kept Alexander and he had become a free agent, the Blue Jays would have received only a draft choice.

Alexander was doing business, too, as he outlined in a meticulous, hand-printed statement he passed to Ken Fidlin of the *Sun*. Under the heading of "Reasons for Leaving Toronto," Alexander made his points:

1. The ballclub made no changes to improve the team over the winter of 1985–86. Other Eastern Division clubs made changes to improve. In my mind, it is doubtful the Toronto Blue Jays can repeat as Eastern Division champions.
2. Money!
On July 1, 1986, a new Canadian federal tax came into effect, creating an effective tax rate of 59 per cent. Tax shelters not advisable in Canada because of their high risk nature. Foreign tax credit offsets only about 70 per cent paid in Canadian taxes. A pending United States tax law will institute a flat 27 per cent maximum tax.
3. Minor problems:
Small hitters park.
Major traffic problems after games.
Airport closes at midnight. The team must occasionally take off and land in Hamilton.
Customs – no hassles, just inconvenience.
Ballclub decisions – has there ever been a game called because of wet or cold weather? Does a player's safety or level of performance ever mean more than one daily attendance?

The last heading in Alexander's statement was "The Bottom Line":

In my mind, Toronto wanted my services for 1986 only. After that, thanks and goodbye. I have fond memories of my first two and a half years in Toronto. I still think Toronto is a nice city. I still think the people of Toronto are some of the best I have known in my career. But baseball is a business for me, as it is for the Blue Jays. I cannot, and will not, let my emotions make business decisions for me.

It has become that kind of game.

A CROWD OF 36,197 showed up for the oldtimers' game, which preceded the regularly scheduled contest against the California Angels. It was a gorgeous July day – warm, clear skies, a pleasant breeze off the lake, the sort of summer Sunday afternoon for which baseball was created.

It was a day for the *real* fans, those intrepid loyalists who had attended the snowswept opener back in April, 1977, and suffered stoically through the dismal campaigns of '78 to '81, when the best the Blue Jays could hope for was to be loved, and the best they could aspire to was not losing more than a hundred games again.

There was oldtimer Roy Howell, the rawboned third baseman who endeared himself to Canadians by never wearing long sleeves. And there was Ron Fairly, one of the Blue Jays' first genuine big leaguers even if he had played for the Montreal Expos. And, hey, there was Rick Bosetti, the hot-dogging centre fielder whose ambition, it used to be said, was to urinate during a game on every natural turf field in the league. And Bob Bailor, the Blue Jays' first-ever draft choice, plucked number one in the expansion draft of 1976, the smooth rookie who batted .310 in the Blue Jays' first season. And there was Roy Hartsfield, the Blue Jays' first-ever field manager, and pitcher Tom Buskey, who once told the press that Roy Hartsfield was about the worst-ever field manager he had encountered. And there was Doug Ault, who belted those homers on that first-ever opening day to become the Blue Jays' first-ever hero. And John Mayberry, the gentle giant who is everyone's favourite father figure. And Baylor Moore and Tom (Tough Luck Tommy) Underwood, and Sam Ewing, and J.J. Cannon, and Dave Lemanczyk, and Mike Willis, and Hector Torres, and Jesse Jefferson—names tumbling out of the past like old letters found in the attic. And there was Rico ("Hone run! Hone run!") Carty, the first of what would become a distinguished exodus to Toronto from the Dominican Republic and the remarkable city of San Pedro de Macoris.

It mattered not a fig to the fans that many of these erstwhile Blue Jays, even in their primes, could not have made the bench of the 1986 squad. What mattered was that they were here, and they were family.

Arrayed against the homeside oldtimers were some of the canonized baseball players of our time. There was Ernie Banks, 55 years old, the Hall of Famer best known for his joyous enthusiasm for baseball ("Let's play *two*") and for never having played in a World Series in his 19 years with the Chicago Cubs. And Eddie Mathews, another Hall of Famer, the third baseman who four times hit more than 40 home runs in a season. And Bill Skowron, and Joe Torre, and Paul Blair, and Mudcat Grant, and Jim Lonborg, and Luis Tiant, and the brothers Gaylord and Jim Perry. And Ron Taylor, the local boy who pitched for the St. Louis Cardinals and the New York Mets in their World Series victories in 1964 and 1969. Taylor went to medical school after baseball and now is the Blue Jays' team doctor.

There were memorable moments. Mayberry belted a two-run home run off Tiant and the crowd roared as he boomed around the bases. Howell, red and rawboned as ever, got stung by a liner and had to be helped off the field. Cannon, whose lifetime average in the majors was .177, socked a homer off Lonborg to prove that in baseball, as in life, anything is possible.

The 1986 Blue Jays, preparing for their game against the California Angels, watched with much amusement and not a little awe, for three 1986 Blue Jays – Clancy, Whitt, and Iorg – were Jays way back then. The memories rekindled were bittersweet. The old Blue Jays won 6–3. The game lasted three innings. Enough was enough.

For the fans it was not so much baseball as an hour in a time warp.

On November 4, 1976, two days after Jimmy Carter was elected President of the United States, the movers and shakers of baseball gathered in the Terrace Room of the Plaza Hotel in Manhattan. Two weeks earlier the Cincinnati Reds had won their second successive World Series, sweeping the New York Yankees in four games. The movers and shakers were at the Plaza for baseball's first re-entry draft of free agents. The next day, the Toronto Blue Jays and the Seattle Mariners would participate in the American League expansion draft; Toronto and Seattle were both entitled to select thirty players from the twelve established teams.

Less than a year earlier, on December 23, 1975, arbitrator Peter L. Seitz had quashed the nefarious "reserve clause" that baseball owners had used since 1897 to bind players to teams for as long as the teams wanted them. Pitchers Andy Messersmith and Dave McNally had challenged the reserve clause, and Seitz had sided with the players, ruling that a contract could be renewed only for one year. The owners fired Seitz. The reserve clause was originally intended to prevent the wealthy teams from buying up all the best players. It was also intended to bind only a team's top five players, but in time it expanded to include the entire roster.

The real pioneer, and martyr, in the fight against the reserve clause was Curt Flood, a small and courageous outfielder who played fifteen major-league seasons with the Cincinnati Reds, the St. Louis Cardinals, and the Washington Senators. In 1969, while with the Cardinals, Flood

71

challenged the reserve clause all the way to the United States Supreme Court. The Court conceded that professional baseball normally would be subject to federal business laws because it was "a business and engaged in interstate commerce," but it held that baseball was established as "an exception and an anomaly" and the "aberration is an established one."

And so, in a five-to-three decision, with one judge abstaining, Curt Flood lost. Two years later he was out of baseball.

But the reserve clause was cracking. In 1974, Seitz granted Catfish Hunter of the Oakland A's his freedom, but not because of the reserve clause. Hunter had successfully argued that his contract with the A's was void because owner Charles Finley had failed to make payments on an insurance policy in accordance with the contract. The fact that Hunter was pursued so avidly, signing with the Yankees for $3.25 million over five years, showed what players could bring on the open market. Hunter, who had won more than twenty games four years in a row, went on to win more than twenty games for a fifth consecutive year.

After Seitz's ruling on Messersmith and McNally, the free-agent floodgates opened and baseball was forever changed. Seitz encouraged players and owners to disregard his ruling and negotiate a settlement – in fact, he had been urging both sides to settle from the outset – but the owners decided to challenge it in court. They lost.

There was little sympathy for the owners. For generations they had exerted enormous power, controlling players' lives and paying them as little as possible. They were perceived as the greedy and selfish authors of their own misfortunes. Established franchises, rich in tradition and loved by fans, were being moved around the country like Monopoly pieces. First the Boston Braves were shipped to Milwaukee in 1953, then the St. Louis Browns went to Baltimore and the Philadelphia Athletics moved to Kansas City. Those moves could be justified on the grounds of dwindling attendance in the two-team cities. But then Walter O'Malley hauled the venerable Brooklyn Dodgers out to Los Angeles with Horace Stoneham and the New York Giants riding on their coattails to San Francisco.

Al Widmar, pitching coach for the Blue Jays, was one of the last players of the old St. Louis Browns, pitching for them in 1948, 1950, and 1951. He reminisced, "We felt like ragamuffins. We felt like minor-leaguers and, in a sense, I guess we were because we lost so much." The Browns had so deteriorated that in the final game of the 1953 season the team ran out of baseballs. Plate umpire Art Passeralla had to scrounge up some scuffed, discarded balls and put them back into play for extra innings.

In the day of the reserve clause, the only way the player could protest was to withhold his services. In those days some players could make as much, sometimes more, in Triple A as in the majors. After a so-so season with the Browns in 1948, Widmar was 22-15 with a 3.03 earned run average for Baltimore's team in the Triple A International League. The Browns offered Widmar a major-league contract worth $6,000 for the 1950 season, $2,000 less than he had earned pitching in Triple A. "So I just told them I didn't want to play for the St. Louis Browns. I wanted to stay in Baltimore because I could make the same money the next year, or more."

The Browns told Widmar to report or he wouldn't work anywhere. "I probably would have gone to court over the fact that they couldn't force me to play or work for somebody I didn't want to work for. Right at the last day before the season started, the commissioner got involved in it. I guess he talked to Bill DeWitt, the president of the club, to give me the money. I got a raise of $1,500."

In time, two would move again. The Braves would be pulled out of Milwaukee for Atlanta; the A's would move to Oakland, putting two teams in the Bay area, which attendance figures indicated might have been one too many.

Bud Selig, president of the Milwaukee Brewers, still mourns the day that the Braves left town. He is a restless man who runs a car dealership in Milwaukee. He loves to walk into the press box and trade barbs with the writers. In his office at Milwaukee County Stadium, he pointed to a bookcase behind his desk where there is a large volume that details the legal hassles between the Braves and the state of Wisconsin. Selig calls it "Gone with the Wind."

The Braves had drawn more than two million fans a season from 1954 to 1957, just less than two million in 1958. Twice they made it to the World Series, winning in 1957, losing in 1958. "A lot of cities get complacent," Selig said.

John McHale was president of the Braves when they moved to Atlanta; he later became president of the Montreal Expos. "The leaders in Milwaukee were very blasé, very overconfident that baseball was there forever, whether they supported it or not," McHale said.

The crowds in Milwaukee dropped below a million in 1964, then plummeted to 555,584 in 1965 when it became apparent the Braves were going to leave. The new owners lived in Chicago and McHale feels absentee ownership is a mistake in most cities. While the decisions were being made in Chicago, the executives with the club in Milwaukee were the victims of personal and visceral fan reaction. "We were being terribly insulted by our fans, our houses were attacked, and our kids were fighting in school every day," McHale said.

"It was a disgraceful tragedy," Selig said of the move, years later. "The Braves' move disillusioned a lot of people. I think baseball did itself irreparable damage."

Selig has known what a major-league baseball team can do for the morale of a city since the 1960s, when he led a group that tried to keep the Braves in Milwaukee. There is a framed newspaper page on the wall of his office; its 1982 headline says, "YES, YES. A PENNANT AT LAST." That was when the Brewers won the American League pennant in the fifth game of the playoff with the California Angels. "I saw something here in 1982 that I'll never forget," Selig said. "We had lost Schlitz Brewery and industry was flying out of here. Milwaukee was in the throes of a horrible recession. We didn't realize it at the time, but for a three-month period this whole city, county, state rallied around this little baseball team. It became a symbol of hope. You have no idea what that means to people."

Selig walked to a window to check the crowd coming into the stadium.

"I remember the last game the Braves played here. It was against the Dodgers. We lost 7–6, and people were crying. I was sitting up in the stands, heartsick. I remember thinking a city isn't a major-league city without a major-league baseball team. It has lovely sociological ramifications. It means so much to people. You get letters from people in hospitals. We forget – we get so immersed in our business – it's all they have."

THE RE-ENTRY AND EXPANSION DRAFTS of 1976 were two historic days for baseball, and the Plaza was an appropriate site. It is a famous old hotel, a reminder of a slower, more gracious time that has always been an attraction of baseball. The morning of the re-entry draft was clear and brisk. There was the usual hubbub of New York outside, but across the street, parked at the curb, carriages and horses waited to clip-clop through Central Park. The metaphor was almost too obvious.

Howie Starkman, director of public relations for the Blue Jays, remembers the re-entry draft as an occasion of considerable excitement.

74

The Blue Jays and the Mariners, the two new expansion teams in the American League, were not allowed to participate in the re-entry draft, but Starkman watched, fascinated, from the mezzanine above the Terrace Room. Under bright chandeliers, representatives of the 24 established major-league teams sat at large, round tables around the thickly carpeted room. At the front, above a dais, was a large screen on which the names of selected free agents were flashed. There was something of the mood of an elegant art auction, but when the sleeves were rolled up and the cigars lit, it began to feel more like a cattle sale.

Toronto and Seattle unsuccessfully had tried to persuade the leagues that they be allowed to compete for free agents, so they had to start from scratch. Each team could select thirty players left unprotected by the established teams; the price of each player was $175,000, totalling $5.25 million. That price was included in the $7 million each franchise had to pay for the privilege of joining the league.

The Montreal Expos made the first free-agent selection. Charles Bronfman, chairman of the Expos – he had been married at the Plaza Hotel 14 years earlier – announced: "With a great deal of anticipation, we pick Reggie Jackson." Reginald Martinez Jackson (Mr. October) was thirty years old and an established superstar. His career had begun in Kansas City; he had played eight years for the Oakland A's, collecting World Series rings in three seasons, then moved to the Baltimore Orioles for 1976.

Alas, the selections at the re-entry draft were only for negotiating rights to players and Jackson never went to the Expos, despite efforts that included a lavish dinner at the Bronfman home during a two-day visit to Montreal. Jackson went to New York instead and helped the Yankees to victory in the 1977 World Series, during which he hit five home runs.

The re-entry draft took an hour and 45 minutes. The 24 free agents eventually signed contracts worth $25 million. Besides Reggie Jackson, there were Joe Rudi, Don Baylor, Gene Tenace, Rollie Fingers, Sal Bando, Steve Stone, and, yup, Doyle Alexander. The expansion draft the next day took seven hours, but when it was over both the Blue Jays and Mariners had selected thirty flesh-and-blood (albeit marginal) major-leaguers from the established teams.

It was the third expansion draft in American League history. The first had been in 1960 when the league expanded to ten from eight teams for the 1961 season, adding franchises in Washington and Los

Angeles. The original Senators had moved to Minneapolis, where they became the Twins. The new Senators would eventually move from Washington to Arlington, Texas, and the Angels would move down the turnpike to Anaheim and Disneyland. The National League added two teams for the 1962 season, the Mets in New York and the Colt-45s in Houston (later renamed the Astros). The second expansion came in 1968 when both leagues added two teams for the 1969 season: the Royals in Kansas City, the Pilots in Seattle, the Padres in San Diego, and the Expos in Montreal. The Pilots stayed only one season in Seattle. Forced into receivership by poor attendance, they were moved to fill Milwaukee's void. In 1976, the National League considered and voted against expansion; the American League felt obliged to expand to Seattle because of the loss of the Pilots and a resultant suit.

The Toronto Blue Jays and the Seattle Mariners were born into a new age in baseball, an age of great freedom but also turmoil and controversy. As often happens in a revolution of rising expectations, the force that finally broke the shackles swung wildly in the opposite direction. It accomplished nothing less than the emancipation of professional baseball players and, for a time, gave the players considerable advantage over the owners. It became an age of negotiation, arbitration, player agents, and, all at once, an age when baseball reached new heights of popularity.

During the next ten years, the average salary of a major-league baseball player would rise to $412,500 from $51,500. After one spectacular season, an otherwise unspectacular player could become a millionaire. Bud Selig, who is chairman of baseball's player relations committee, estimated that probably 20 or 21 of the 26 major-league teams had lost money in 1985. ''It's staggering,'' Selig said.

The game within the game would become crucial. The next ten years would provide a textbook study of how, and how not, to operate a modern-day major-league baseball franchise.

THE EXPANSION DRAFT was set up so that each of the twelve established American League teams would lose five players; at $175,000 a player each team received $875,000. Each of the established teams could protect fifteen players. There would be five rounds of drafting. Toronto and Seattle would select six players a round. The established teams could not lose more than one player in each round and could protect three additional players after each of the first three rounds and two more after the fourth round. Seattle picked first in the first and third rounds Toronto in the second and fourth. Toronto won a coin toss to pick first in the fifth round.

Pat Gillick, Al LaMacchia, Bob Mattick, and some Blue Jays scouts did not attend the free-agent re-entry draft the day before. Instead, they sequestered themselves in a suite at another hotel to study the choices in the expansion draft. For three months, Blue Jay scouts had logged 14-hour days to prepare for the expansion draft.

The way to go had been discussed at a long dinner in Kansas City earlier in the autumn. "We got together and discussed how we'd go about building an expansion club," LaMacchia said. Once a pitcher with the St. Louis Browns (1943–46), he had joined the Blue Jays after sixteen years with the Braves. "We decided to go out and get as many young prospects as we could rather than older guys in the twilight of their careers."

The Blue Jays knew they would have time to become a contender. Seattle had been exposed to major-league baseball and might demand success more quickly. The honeymoon would be longer in Toronto; the fans would be happy just to have a major-league baseball team. One of the early role models for the Blue Jays was the Los Angeles Dodgers. This was not surprising because Peter Bavasi, the young executive vice-president and general manager of the early Blue Jays, had grown up with the Dodgers. Peter's father, Buzzie, had been a Dodger executive in Brooklyn and Los Angeles. Gillick had also grown up in southern California and he was at the University of Southern California when the Dodgers arrived in Los Angeles.

At the start, at least, a more realistic model for the Blue Jays would be an expansion team that had excelled rapidly, the Kansas City Royals. They played their first American League season in 1969 and won the American League West eight seasons later, in 1976. The Royals always seemed to have a steady flow of talent and emerged quickly because of some shrewd early trades by general manager Cedric Tallis. The Royals traded for young players with potential. For example, in the 1968 expansion draft, the new Seattle Pilots drafted Lou Piniella, then traded him to Kansas City. Piniella became the American League rookie of the year in 1969.

Exempt from the 1976 expansion draft were players who had played their first professional season in 1975 or 1976 and players with a minimum of ten years in the majors, the last five at least with the same team. These players in collective bargaining had been given the right to refuse a trade. Toronto and Seattle could talk to these "ten-and-five players," and if they were not on the protected list they could even draft them, but at considerable risk. If an expansion club did not sign a ten-and-fiver before December 1, the player's rights would revert to his previous club, with no compensation to the expansion team.

The Blue Jays were interested in ten-and-fiver Carl Yastrzemski. He had played sixteen years for the Red Sox and would have made an outstanding pick for the Blue Jays; but he refused to consent to be drafted. Knowing this, Boston did not protect Yastrzemski, using his spot to protect another player.

The Blue Jays argued to no avail that the ten-and-fivers should not have been given special consideration – more and better players would have been in the expansion draft. Yet, despite the restrictions, there were some excellent prospects available and Toronto and Seattle missed some plums. Outfielder Dwayne Murphy and pitcher Matt Keough, both 21 years old, somehow slipped through all five rounds and stayed with the Oakland A's.

"Those were just two," Gillick said.

Lou Gorman, then vice-president in charge of baseball operations for Seattle – he later moved to the Mets and is now general manager of the Red Sox – stressed the importance of drafting young players. He explained, "You start with the premise that of your 25-man squad, probably half won't be there in three or four years. Develop your own talent, build an aggressive scouting staff, build a solid farm system, keep developing and be patient. You've got to put a reasonably competitive team on the field in the beginning to get some fans in the ballpark, but the emphasis is to build your farm system as quickly as you can. Take the nucleus of what you've got and as you improve keep weeding out."

Gorman had the right idea, but he did not get needed support in Seattle. In Kansas City, Ewing Kauffman provided stable and understanding ownership – much like the management of the Blue Jays in Toronto – and Gorman helped fashion the Royals into the most successful new franchise in the history of baseball. The situation in Seattle was different.

One of the original owners of the Mariners was Danny Kaye, the entertainer. Kaye had grown to love baseball as a Dodger fan at old Ebbets Field, and, as a Dodger fan in Los Angeles, he loved the mood and symmetry of Dodger Stadium. He did not like the Kingdome. As one of six partners in the Mariners, Kaye took an active role at the 1976 expansion draft and fairly gushed with enthusiasm: "I am one lucky man. I have seen my fantasies become realities."

Comparing baseball to theatre, he said, "I've got to admit I had that certain tingle, the butterflies in my stomach, just as I've had with the curtain going up."

He posed for pictures with commissioner Bowie Kuhn minutes before the draft began. "It's like picking the cast for a show," he erupted. "You know, who will fit best here? Who will fit best there?"

Kaye loved the attention, the limelight, and between rounds he raced excitedly from the floor of the Terrace Room to the Mariners' suite upstairs. The only representative of the Blue Jays' ownership was R. Howard Webster, a shy Montreal businessman. He attended to accept the charter for the new franchise, then sat for a time next to Starkman charting on a piece of paper some of Toronto's early choices. Webster left the Terrace Room before the draft was over. From the beginning, the Blue Jay owners have stayed in the background and pushed their baseball people to the forefront.

When the show began, Seattle first chose outfielder Ruppert Jones from Kansas City. It was an excellent pick. In the Mariners' inaugural season, Jones hit .263 with 24 home runs, missing only two games all season. Gillick later admitted that if the Blue Jays had picked first, they would have taken Jones.

The Blue Jays' first choice was a surprise, a 25-year-old shortstop with the Baltimore Orioles, Robert Michael Bailor of Connellsville, Pennsylvania.

WHEN THE EXPANSION DRAFT BEGAN began at the Plaza Hotel, Bob Bailor – "Buzz" to his teammates – was out in the Pennsylvania woods with his brother and two friends. They were hunting turkeys. The men stayed at Bailor's log cabin, which had no electricity. They used Coleman lanterns at night and there was no radio. "I knew the draft was going on," Bailor said, "but I was kind of involved in the hunting." When he arrived home with two turkeys later in the day, his father was standing on the porch hollering that he had been selected by the Toronto Blue Jays.

Earlier in the day, back at the Plaza, Howie Starkman prepared publicity sheets after each round. Starkman's first-round publicity sheet quoted Gillick as saying, "Bob Bailor will be a key player. He is young, aggressive, a real team player as well. He has outstanding speed and range. He's an ideal choice and we're very delighted to have him at this key position."

Bailor was surprised that the Blue Jays picked him first. So were the Orioles. He'd had problems with his shoulder the previous season, the result of playing in Venezuela during the winter. He had appeared in only nine Orioles games in 1976, managing a triple and a single in six at-bats. That the Blue Jays were interested in Bailor could not have been a total surprise. When the 1976 season ended, he noticed Gillick hanging around the Instructional League in Florida asking questions. With Gillick was LaMacchia, who studied Bailor in the batting cage, watched him going for grounders, throwing to first. "I watched his eyes," LaMacchia said. "That's how you know if someone's hurting—the eyes. If a ballplayer has to make a tough throw, he'll wince if it hurts."

Bailor started the 1977 season for the Blue Jays and wore uniform number "1." He proved a versatile player, performing at shortstop, in the outfield, and as a designated hitter. (In subsequent seasons, Bailor also played second and third and, using a sly knuckler he fiddled with in pre-game warmups, pitched in three games in 1980.) Bailor's .310 average was the highest for any rookie in 1977 and the best of any rookie on a first-year expansion team. Picking Bailor first made the Blue Jays look like prophets.

The Blue Jays expansion-draft picks were, in order:

FIRST ROUND
Shortstop Bob Bailor, from Baltimore.
Pitcher Jerry Garvin, from Minnesota.
Pitcher Jim Clancy, from Texas.
Outfielder Gary Woods, from Oakland.
DH Rico Carty, from Cleveland.
Pitcher Claude (Butch) Edge, from Milwaukee.

SECOND ROUND
Pitcher Al Fitzmorris, from Kansas City.
Outfielder Alvis Woods, from Minnesota.
Pitcher Mike Darr, from Baltimore.
Pitcher Pete Vuckovich, from Chicago.

Pitcher Jeff Byrd, from Texas.
Outfielder Steve Bowling, from Milwaukee.

THIRD ROUND
Pitcher Dennis DeBarr, from Detroit.
Pitcher Bill Singer, from Minnesota.
Shortstop Jim Mason, from New York.
First baseman Doug Ault, from Texas.
Catcher Ernie Whitt, from Boston.
Second baseman Steve Weathers, from Oakland.

FOURTH ROUND
Second baseman Steve Staggs, from Kansas City.
Pitcher Steve Hargan, from Texas.
Second baseman Garth Iorg, from New York.
Pitcher Dave Lemanczyk, from Detroit.
Pitcher Larry Anderson, from Milwaukee.
Pitcher Jesse Jefferson, from Chicago.

FIFTH ROUND
Infielder Dave McKay, from Minnesota.
Pitcher Tom Bruno, from Kansas City.
Outfielder Otto Velez, from New York.
Pitcher Mike Willis, from Baltimore.
DH Sam Ewing, from Chicago.
Pitcher Mike Hooten, from Oakland.

The Mariner choices, by position, were outfielders Ruppert Jones (Kansas City), Dave Collins and Carlos Lopez (California), Tommy Smith (Cleveland), and Luis Delgado (Boston); designated hitters Steve Braun (Minnesota) and Lee Stanton (California); third basemen Bill Stein (Chicago) and Juan Bernhardt (New York); shortstop Tom McMillan (Cleveland); second baseman Julio Cruz (California); first basemen Dan Meyer (Detroit) and Joe Lis (Cleveland); catcher Bob Stinson (Kansas City); and pitchers Gary Wheelock (California), Dick Pole (Boston), Grant Jackson (New York), Frank MacCormack (Detroit), Stan Thomas (Cleveland), Rick Jones (Boston), Glenn Abbott (Oakland), Dave Pagan (Baltimore), Roy Thomas (Chicago), Pete Broberg (Milwaukee), Bob Galasso (Baltimore), Steve Burke (Boston), Alan Griffin (Oakland), Bill Laxton (Detroit), Steve Barr (Texas), and Joe Earardi (Milwaukee).

Toronto and Seattle had bought some players before the expansion draft. From the White Sox, Toronto acquired catcher Phil Roof, who once played for the Toronto Maple Leafs of the International League. From Hawaii, where Roy Hartsfield had managed, Toronto acquired catcher Dave Roberts, third baseman John Hilton, and outfielder John Scott, the opening-day leadoff batter. Seattle had purchased pitcher Dave Johnson from the Orioles, infielder Jose Baez from the Dodgers, and pitcher Jim Mishall from the Pittsburgh Pirates.

Two Seattle picks eventually played for the Blue Jays – Braun in 1981 and Collins in 1983 and 1984. Three Toronto picks – Clancy, Whitt, and Iorg – were still with the Blue Jays after ten seasons. The only original Mariner in Seattle in 1986 was pitcher Roy Thomas, though he had been traded to Houston in 1977, played three years in St. Louis, and made it back to the Mariners in 1983. Each team selected a Canadian in the expansion draft. Seattle took Dave Pagan, a pitcher from Nipawin, Saskatchewan; Toronto took Dave McKay, an infielder from Vancouver, who said that in his three years with the Blue Jays he always felt like "the token Canadian."

Toronto surprised Seattle by taking so many young pitchers: Garvin was 21, Clancy, Byrd, Darr, and Edge were 20. Al Widmar, then working for the Brewers, was surprised the Blue Jays took Edge when the medical report given the Blue Jays showed that he had emotional problems.

In all, seven of Toronto's first twelve picks were pitchers. "We decided to bite the bullet," Peter Bavasi said. "We thought they were the best young arms available, so we took them." For Elliott Wahle, the administrator of player personnel, it was a matter of matching what was needed to what was available. "We knew we had artificial turf and we knew the two things we had to do was go for speed and pitching," he said. "Speed was not available in the draft in abundance, I can tell you. But young pitching, guys you could take a chance on, were there – Clancy, Byrd, Edge. We felt they would be our future. Some of the other guys we drafted were marginal, and some of them were real *reaches.*"

The Blue Jays wanted Fitzmorris, even though he was 30 years old, because they had worked out a deal to trade him to Cleveland for catcher Alan Ashby and first baseman Doug Howard. Fitzmorris had been a steady, reliable starter for Kansas City for eight years, and he was one of the few "name" players selected in the expansion draft. Two years later, he would be out of baseball. Ashby remains a dependable catcher with the Astros. The Blue Jays took Rico Carty from the Indians basically because their other unprotected players were so unappealing. Carty had some outstanding seasons but was 35. At least that was his listed age.

Another "name" player drafted by Toronto was Bill Singer, the starting pitcher in the opening-day snow at Exhibition Stadium. Singer had been a 20-game winner with the Dodgers in 1969 and the Angels in 1973. He was the one player the Blue Jays had who was known and had been connected with a winner. After two starts, however, Singer developed shoulder problems. He pitched only 60 innings for the Blue Jays, winning two, losing eight, and compiling an earned run average of 6.75. He was gone from baseball before the 1977 season ended.

Lou Gorman of the Mariners liked two of the Blue Jays' picks, Clancy and Vuckovich. Gorman is a heavy, grey-haired man with Master's degrees in English and Education and can compress a great number of words into a short period of time. "I'd always liked Vuckovich's makeup in college, and our reports on Clancy were very good," he said. "We had thought of taking Clancy in the third round, but the Blue Jays took him in the first. Those were the only two players that I really wanted and didn't get. The rest of our players, I was as pleased as I could be. I thought our nucleus was as good as Toronto's, and we had some good young players coming."

Gorman's assessment of Vuckovich and Clancy proved prescient. Vuckovich played only one season with the Blue Jays, winning seven and losing seven, then moved to St. Louis where he performed solidly as a Cardinal for three years. His next stop was Milwaukee, where in 1982 he won the Cy Young Award as the best pitcher in the American League. Clancy was still in the Blue Jays' starting rotation ten years later.

The Seattle *Post-Intelligencer* rated the Mariners stronger than the Blue Jays in pitching, at first, second, and third, and in the outfield; the Blue Jays were superior at catcher (after acquiring Ashby), shortstop, and designated hitter. It was an accurate appraisal as far as it went; the newspaper did not rate team management, and there was no way it could have rated the subtleties of team ownership. Eventually, Gorman left the Mariners and joined the Mets, where he helped to develop such stars as Dwight Gooden, then he moved on to the Red Sox, where he put some important touches on the team that won the 1986 American League pennant and came within one out of winning the World Series.

Gorman likes the way the Toronto owners provided stable leadership and let the baseball people do the baseball things. In Florida in 1986, when the Blue Jays came to Winter Haven to play a spring training game with the Red Sox, Gorman elaborated on his thesis: "You've got to have ownership that has total confidence in what you are doing and lets you go and do it. They've got to be patient. They've got to have confidence in what you're doing and give you the means to do it. The people in Toronto did just that. They stayed with the plan. In Seattle, the ownership was in turmoil almost the whole time."

There was some minor grumbling in the executive offices of the early Blue Jays when Bavasi infuriated Gillick and Wahle by signing Bailor for $38,000, twice the major-league minimum, in his rookie season.

"Pat and I were just miffed beyond belief how Bavasi could be that extravagant," Wahle said. "In retrospect, it's kind of comical, isn't it?"

THE THREE ORIGINALS still with the Blue Jays in 1986 – Jim Clancy, Ernie Whitt, Garth Iorg – were not at Exhibition Stadium on opening day of 1977, but over the years they became a symbol of the continuity and stability Toronto set out to establish. No other new team in the majors had kept this many players from an expansion draft for this long.

Clancy was at his parents' home in Twin Lakes, Wisconsin, when he heard he had been selected in the first round of the expansion draft. Someone with the Blue Jays called him from the Plaza Hotel, but he doesn't remember who. He does remember being surprised that he was picked – he thought the Texas Rangers had plans for him. Ten years later, he said, "I didn't know nothing about Toronto. And I was kind of scared, going to a new place. I had to get a map to find out where it was."

On Starkman's release manager Roy Hartsfield appraised the pitcher. "We rated him the best young right-hander available from the standpoint of having an excellent arm. We'll be able to build around him."

Clancy had completed his third year as a pitcher in the Texas Rangers organization in 1976 with six wins, eight losses, and an unhealthy ERA of 6.41 for San Antonio in the Double A Texas League where Bob Miller, who would be the Blue Jay pitching coach, had watched him

84

while managing Amarillo. His most distressing statistic, however, was the number of walks. In 125 innings, Clancy walked 98, threw 10 wild pitches, and struck out 77. He could fire it, though, and he was big and strong.

Clancy is six-feet four-inches and weighs 220 pounds. He has a thick neck and sloping shoulders. He has always been quiet and unassuming. He smiles generously, but almost shyly with a tilt of his head. In his early years as a Blue Jay, he was awkward with the press. Ten years later he is still quiet and unpretentious, but after a game he will sit at his locker with a beer and a cigarette and discuss the finer points of his game with the baseball writers – win or lose.

When he was growing up in the Chicago suburb of Mount Greenwood, Clancy was a Cubs fan. The Cubs played only day games at home and Clancy could follow them on the television. Even as a Blue Jay, Clancy will revisit his old neighbourhood, then go directly to Comiskey Park on the south side. "I didn't think there was really anything for me to go downtown for," he said. "Everything was in our community that you needed. Even in the past four or five years, I have only been downtown once when I took a bus just to see what it was like."

Clancy began playing baseball when he was five, with cousins and friends from the neighbourhood. He played outfield, first base, and catcher, until his strong right arm became too obvious to ignore. He was wild even then, and opposing sandlot players sometimes were afraid to face him. It was not until his junior year at high school that he considered himself a major-league prospect. He had attended St. Rita High School on a football scholarship. Clancy was a roll-out quarterback despite his size and strong arm. During a practice he broke his left collarbone on a roll-out. The coaches didn't think he had broken anything; they told Clancy to go home and treat it with ice. After supper that evening his parents decided to take him to the hospital, and the next day Clancy appeared at high school in a body cast. When he was over that, he injured the shoulder again on a roll-out and decided to concentrate on baseball. That ended his football scholarship and Clancy paid his own tuition for his final year at high school.

In 1974, Clancy was drafted by Texas and signed by Joe Marchese and two years later, when he was twenty, he had moved up to Double A. The next year, at the first Blue Jays spring training camp, Clancy was disappointed when it seemed that he was overlooked in favour of veterans.

"I was kind of mad when they sent me down. They didn't really

85

have a place to send me, so they optioned me to Cleveland. First you get adjusted to the guys here, then all of a sudden you have to go to another spring training camp. I had to fly all the way out to Arizona. We were there for two weeks, then I was sent to Jersey City, which is not the best place.''

But Clancy understood the situation.

''Being an expansion club, they had to put players on the field that people would come out and see.''

For Clancy, the best thing about Jersey City (then in the Double A Eastern League) and its dimly lit stadium was the road out. He was promoted to Toronto on July 26 and his salary zoomed from the $1,000 a month ($6,000 for the season) he was receiving with Jersey City to a princely $19,000, the major-league minimum. With Singer ailing, the Blue Jays desperately needed pitching. Clancy knew he would not have been called up if he had been with Texas.

In his first three seasons with the Blue Jays, Clancy won 16 and lost 29, all for a team that lost more than a hundred games each season. In 1979, he twice required surgery for a dislocated tendon in his right foot. After the 1979 season he attended the Florida Instructional League, and there he met Al Widmar, the Jays' new pitching coach. ''I had to start all over again as far as my motion was concerned because everything was pushing off the right leg,'' he said. ''Widmar started working with me on the changeup. That was the pitch I needed. That's when I started to become a pitcher.''

In 1980, Clancy's first season under Widmar, he won 13 and lost 16, with an ERA of 3.30 – more than respectable on a last-place team that considered it an achievement to avoid 100 losses for the first time. He won 16 games in 1982, 15 in 1983. His control improved. All the while, Clancy's salary had been gradually increasing: from $30,000 in 1978 to $55,000 in 1979, $67,500 in 1980, $167,500 in 1981, and $210,000 in 1982, all with incentive clauses added. They reflect not only the development of a career, but the escalation in the game's salary structure.

Prior to the 1983 season, Clancy signed a four-year contract, guaranteed for the first three years with the club holding the option for the fourth, 1986, with a $100,000 buyout if the option was not exercised. Clancy took much of his salary in deferred payments. In 1983, his contract paid him a total of $475,000 but $250,000 of that was deferred with interest. It was more of the same for the next three seasons: he received $230,000 each year and in addition would get deferred payments of $250,000 for 1984, $350,000 for 1985, and $450,000 for 1986. He had incentives for each season that included $10,000 for 200 innings pitched; $15,000 for 220 innings pitched; $35,000 for 240 innings; $25,000 for being an All-Star; and another $25,000 if he finished in the top three of the Cy Young Award voting.

His teammates began to call him "Diamond" (as in "Diamond Jim"). He showed flashes of brilliance, as in September, 1982, against the Minnesota Twins – a perfect game through eight innings. Then Randy Bush led off the ninth with a broken-bat, bloop single.

Clancy struggled in 1984 but seldom looked stronger than he did for spring training in 1985. Then, late in March, he had to have his appendix removed. He did not start for the Blue Jays until April 30. When he settled into a groove he developed tendinitis in his shoulder in July. Despite the setbacks, he finished 1985 with nine wins, six losses, and a 3.78 ERA. A healthy Clancy, as far as Widmar was concerned, would have had an outstanding season.

Someone once showed Widmar a picture of himself in action as a young pitcher and there was a startling similarity to Clancy. Widmar has a soft spot for Clancy. He affectionately calls him "a horse" for the way he works without complaining. He could count on Clancy for a league-leading 40 starts in 1982, 34 starts in 1983, and 36 in 1984. There was talk of Clancy being traded after the 1984 season, but he was adding a curveball and developing his changeup. By 1986, he used his breaking ball and changeup more. He'd still admit to relying a little too much on his fastball with men on base, but hitters were learning that they could no longer wait for it.

Clancy's contract expired after the 1986 season and he became a free agent, which suddenly had diminished in status with the talk in baseball of "fiscal responsibility." Many top-ranked free agents in the off-season of 1986-87 received little more than nibbles from other teams. And the contracts being offered by teams to keep their free agents were of shorter duration. One of the most endearing things about Clancy is that he seems to be a man without guile. He had become a marketable pitcher but kept saying that he enjoys playing in Toronto and wanted to stay. He once even wondered quietly how much money anyone really needed. It's not quite the litany of the modern-day baseball player.

ERNIE WHITT, one of Clancy's best friends on the Blue Jays, began to catch when he was seven years old, in Roseville, Michigan. Actually,

Whitt was a year too young for the league, but the team needed a player and the only opening was at catcher. Ernie's older brother Mike pitched for that same gang of peewees.

Whitt was a Detroit Tigers fan. He arrived early in the left-field bleachers at Tiger Stadium to chase balls hit into the seats during batting practice. His were the Tigers of Charlie (Smokey) Maxwell, who seemed to hit an inordinate number of homers on Sunday afternoons. And there were Jim Northrup, Willie Horton, Norm Cash, Al Kaline, and – Whitt's boyhood hero – Detroit-born catcher Bill Freehan, who spent his entire fifteen-year career in the majors with the Tigers. Whitt was 16 years old when the Tigers won the World Series in 1968. The next time the Tigers won, in 1984, Whitt was behind the plate for the Blue Jays, who finished second in the American League East.

As a boy, Whitt expected to play for the Tigers some day. He had been scouted by them and there had been discussions, but the Tigers didn't rate Whitt as more than a Double A player. Then, boom, in July, 1972, he got a phone call from Morri deLouf, a Boston scout: "Do you want to play professional with the Red Sox?"

"It just shocked me," Whitt remembers. "All I knew about Boston was that they had Yastrzemski and that year Carlton Fisk was the rookie of the year."

In 1976, Whitt began at Bristol, a Red Sox Double A team, worked himself up to Triple A, then the Red Sox brought him up in September and he appeared in eight games. His first major-league hit was a home run off Milwaukee's Jim Colborn. He caught the eye of the Blue Jays' Al LaMacchia. "I happened to catch Boston against Baltimore and he got two base hits that day," LaMacchia remembered. "Got out in front and hit that ball sharp. I told Gillick that Whitt had stung the ball pretty good, that he's got to improve as a catcher but he's worth a chance because he's a left-handed bat. There aren't that many left-handed hitting catchers."

Whitt heard that he had been drafted by the Blue Jays when he got home from visiting the hospital where his wife, Chris, had given birth to their daughter Ashley two days before.

Boston's scouts had liked Whitt's attitude but rated him as a marginal defensive catcher. Roy Hartsfield, the Blue Jays' first manager, agreed. Whitt played 25 games for the Blue Jays under Hartsfield – 23 of them in the 1977 season after he had been called up in June from Charleston of the International League where he was making $2,100 a month. (His major-league contract was worth $23,000 plus incentives.) In August, he was gone after dislocating a tendon in his left foot while making a tag.

Whitt played the entire 1979 season at Syracuse for $3,200 a month and hit .249 with seven home runs, made only three errors, and was voted to *The Sporting News* minor-league Silver Glove team. The Blue Jays had had two good young catchers: Ashby, a switch-hitter traded to Houston after the 1978 season, and Rick Cerone, who was traded to the Yankees after the 1979 season.

In the spring of 1979, Whitt had a confrontation with Hartsfield. "That was a situation where either Hartsfield was going to leave or I was going to leave, one or the other," Whitt said. "We had just played a game over in St. Petersburg and I threw out four straight guys – Lou Brock *twice.*"

Later, Hartsfield told Whitt, "You're never going to play in the big leagues. You're never going to throw anybody out."

"You obviously don't know how to manage," Whitt replied.

When Gillick joined the meeting, Whitt told him, "He doesn't like me. The best thing is to move me someplace else."

After Hartsfield left, Gillick and Whitt continued talking. Whitt returned to Triple A, assured that Hartsfield would not always manage the Blue Jays. When Cerone was traded to the Yankees and Bob Mattick became manager for 1980, Whitt came up to share the catching with Bob Davis. Whitt started slowly, one-hopping throws to second, but Mattick stayed with him and before one early-season day game at Cleveland Stadium he and the coaches worked on Whitt's throw. Whitt said he wasn't preparing his arm properly and began to do more long throwing to strengthen the muscles.

LaMacchia gives much of the credit for Whitt's success to Mattick. "Sometimes a manager wants immediate success and it's tough when you've got young kids," LaMacchia said. "You've got to realize when you've got a young club like that you're going to have people who are going to struggle and you think they're never going to put it together. Ernie didn't give up, just kept working harder and harder. When Bobby took over the job, I remember him saying, 'Hell, I'm just going to get Ernie and catch him.'"

In 1980, Whitt hit .237, with six home runs. When Buck Martinez joined the Blue Jays in May, 1981, he and Whitt became an effective catching platoon. Hitting mainly against right-handed pitching, Whitt found his home-run swing, with 11 in 1982, 17 in 1983, 15 in 1984, 19 in 1985, and 16 in 1986. Whitt was selected to the American League All-Star team in 1985.

Whitt hit .268 with 56 RBIs in 1986, the last season of his three-year contract, which brought him $325,000, including incentives. Whitt's major-league salary had not climbed as rapidly as Clancy's. From a base of $30,000 in 1980, he went to $55,000 in 1981, $100,000 in 1982, and $145,000 in 1983. There also were incentive clauses, which in 1983 totalled $20,000. When Whitt's three-year deal was drawn up, he received a $25,000 signing bonus. He also received a deferred package of $410,000 and the club paid his disability insurance. He received $175,000 for each of the first two years and a $275,000 option for 1986, with a $50,000 buyout clause. As incentives, Whitt received $16,666.66 for appearing in 90 games, another $16,666.66 for 110 games, and the same amount for 125 games. By the day's standards, he was falling behind.

As Whitt prepared to become a free agent, and representing himself, he admitted he might accept less money to stay in Toronto. "I am very impressed by the Blue Jay organization," Whitt said as he sat at his locker in the cramped visitors' clubhouse at Fenway Park, talking above the clamour of the card game nearby.

He said he feels particularly fortunate when he hears some other players talk about their teams. But he remembers the early Blue Jay years. "In the beginning, they were more concerned with marketing the team than actually putting the players out on the field. They made statements to the effect that we were a team with a future, they were going to build through the farm and that's what they're doing. Look at some of the guys right now who came up through the farm system."

With the maturity of the franchise, Whitt has seen the change in the way the players are treated – little things like better seats for the wives, so they don't have to climb so many stairs toting young children and in a more protected area behind the homeplate screen. "They didn't treat the players worth beans in the beginning," Whitt said. "I mean we were just, as Peter Bavasi said, the sizzle with the steak to come, and that's basically the way it was."

In recent years, Peter Hardy, the team's chief executive officer, introduced a financial planning company, The Etherington Group, to the players. The group doesn't invest the money but develops a plan for them. There was no obligation and Hardy does not think it's his business to know who has used the service. Whitt was the first Blue Jay to try it. "I was like the guinea pig," Whitt said. "Now they're picking up half the tab and I'm paying the other half. They sit down and talk to you and find out what you want to do, how much you want to live on when you've done playing baseball, and put some realistic goals together and what you probably need to earn to keep that going. It's rare, I think, for a club to do that. I think we've got six or seven guys using it now."

The off-season would be a big test for Whitt as he had decided to represent himself in the increasingly murky waters of free agency. He had thought of becoming a player representative one day. During the off-season of 1986–87, a good test of his bargaining acumen would be to see what Ernie Whitt could do for Ernie Whitt.

THE THIRD ORIGINAL, Garth Iorg, knows what it is like to act as his own agent. He did it for two years. He knows that Beeston and Gillick are tough negotiators. "But I don't see anything wrong with that," Iorg said. "I don't mind that a bit. If they're tough across the board that's okay. They're not being tricky. It's basically all up front. If I had a team, I'd like them to run it."

Twice when he did his own negotiations, he signed a contract when he felt that he might have done better.

Like Whitt, Iorg persevered to make the majors. He became a reliable utility player in 1980, filling in at first, second, shortstop, third, in the outfield, and as a pinch-hitter, pinch-runner, and designated hitter. Players like Iorg are handy to have around.

He didn't expect to be picked in the expansion draft. He had broken his leg in 1976. When he was with the Yankees' Instructional League team in Sarasota, his coach, Mike Ferraro, tried to tell him he had been picked third in the fourth round.

"Ferraro was trying to call me all night to tell me I had been drafted," Iorg said. "I never heard about it until the next morning when he called me real early and asked me where I'd been."

Iorg, a Mormon and a non-drinker, had gone to the beach at Sarasota with friends and stayed there past the midnight curfew.

"We were just messing around, having a good time. I wasn't really aware of the draft. At first, Ferraro got me a little scared. He told me I had been drafted by the Blue Jays and I didn't know if that was good or bad.

"What's the deal?" Iorg wanted to know.

"They picked thirty guys and you're one of them," Ferraro said.

Iorg is the younger brother of Dane Iorg, a key role player with the St. Louis Cardinals when they won the 1982 World Series and with the Kansas City Royals when they won the 1985 World Series. In the 1979–80 off-season, Garth Iorg had been dropped from the Blue Jays' 40-man roster, but he worked hard and started well at Syracuse in 1980 and by May was with the Blue Jays.

It was not until 1982, under manager Bob Cox, that Iorg developed as a solid – if not full-time – third baseman. Cox adroitly platooned certain players, but his most unusual platooning was at third, a position usually associated with power and regularity. Against left-handed pitching Cox used Iorg; against right-handers he used Rance Mulliniks. Iorg occasionally played at second when Damaso Garcia was hurt or wasn't up to playing.

Iorg is a sparkling personality, bright and chipper, and goes about his work with joy. It wasn't always that way. His attitude was bad when he was demoted to the minors in 1978 after starting the season in the majors. In 1977, Iorg played for $1,400 a month in Triple A at Charleston. His major-league contract would have paid him $25,000 for the 1978 season; his demotion to Syracuse meant playing for $2,300 a month. His wife, Patty, was caring for a year-old baby, the first of their four children.

"The hardest thing is to start a major-league season and be sent down," he said. "It's different if you get sent down at spring training and can come back in the middle of the season. I was young and very ignorant – very immature. I see a lot of guys doing it now, same as I did. Instead of going down and really doing well, they go down and just kind of die and prove the team was right. But when they took me off the roster in 1980, it woke me up. I went to spring training that year as a utility man in Triple A. I didn't even have a position, so it was make or break time for me."

His Triple A salary had gone from $2,600 a month in 1979 to $3,100 a month in 1980 and by this time he had two children. His graduation to the majors that year meant a $30,000 salary.

Elliott Wahle remembers how hard Iorg worked to get there. "He went through some hard times when we dropped him off the roster," he said. "He got a little bit negative. I remember him sitting there in the evenings at spring training with his brother really trying to help him out. It turned Garth around. He has a tremendous approach to the game, and to life. We thought of him as a utility player, but all the son of a gun did was get better.''

Iorg has an odd batting stance he developed in the minors. He stands square to the plate, deep in the batter's box, with his weight entirely on his right foot and the bat held so far back it seems to pull his left foot off the ground. He'd never seen what it looked like until he saw it on a television replay in Toronto. He was surprised at how drastic it was; he's modified it somewhat since. He does not often hit for power but sprays the ball to all fields. With young Kelly Gruber showing promise as a power-hitting third baseman in the minors, there was talk after a poor 1984 season that Iorg would be traded. But he had his best season in 1985, hitting .313 with seven home runs.

As Iorg's family grew to four children, his contracts went from $45,000 in 1981 to $75,000 in 1982, $135,000 in 1983, and $165,000 in 1984, all with incentive clauses. In 1984, Iorg's new representative was Chuck Berry, who works with Tom Reich. Berry was negotiating a three-year deal for Iorg that would start in 1985. Despite his agent's recommendation to turn down an offer tendered by the Blue Jays, Iorg signed. ''I felt comfortable with it,'' he said. It brought him a $50,000 signing bonus. The base salary was $225,000 in 1985, $275,000 in 1986, and the option year in 1987 was for $350,000, with a $50,000 buyout. The contract for 1987 was guaranteed if he had either 300 plate appearances in 1985 (he exceeded it) or 600 combined in 1985 and 1986. If traded, he'd receive $25,000. The incentives included $15,000 for 300 plate appearances and another $15,000 for each plateau reached of 350, 400, 450, and 500 plate appearances, which include walks and sacrifices that don't count as at-bats. If, somehow, he reached 600 plate appearances he would receive another $50,000. All-Star status would bring him $25,000.

Like Whitt, Iorg has taken advantage of the financial planning offered and wishes it had been available earlier in his career. Iorg always worked in the off-season, usually at the lumber mill in Arcata, California, a town of about 9,000 where he lives. ''I feel likes it's a waste if I don't do something,'' he says.

As he approached a 1987 season that held some uncertainty for him, he had been helping to run a steel dealership with two partners and seven employees, obtaining steel and selling it to businesses in the area. They had invested in an existing business that had been faltering.

"It's a tough and unique business," he said. "It's been real rewarding but I can't say it's been lucrative so far. There's a lot more pressure trying to make a payroll with no money in the account than it is hitting with runners on base."

But Iorg knows all about businesses that struggle for a while before achieving success. He remembers how the Blue Jays began to gel in 1982. After a sluggish April, the Blue Jays finished 1982 with 78 wins and 84 losses, creeping up on .500. That year Pat Gillick and Paul Beeston began running the team and Cox became manager.

At spring training in 1986, Iorg sat on a bench in the clubhouse at Grant Field in Dunedin and reflected on all that had happened since the early-morning call in 1976. "When Gillick and Beeston took over, that's when the team did an about-face," Iorg said. "Toronto had been living on the novelty of having major-league baseball. The product had been bad on the field. Attendance was down. Guys just didn't want to go to Toronto. Nobody wants to go to a team that's bad."

Iorg felt sorry for Bob Mattick when he took over as Blue Jay manager in 1980. "He inherited a team with a lot of problems. We had guys who were just going to be here a short time. They were trying to get another year in the big leagues and pick up a paycheque. We had no chance of getting guys to come to Toronto. Guys wanted out of Toronto. When Gillick and Beeston took over, when Cox was named manager – gee, what a difference! Being a player, you could feel electricity in the air during the warmup. You could *feel* the change."

F O U R T H

CHASING THE DREAM

THERE WAS EXCITEMENT in the early years, too, but it was not the excitement of watching a contender, nothing as dramatic as a pennant race.

In the early years – and no one knew this better than the brains behind the Blue Jays – there was excitement in just having a major-league baseball team in the city. It was as if one morning Toronto woke up, raised the shades, and saw the Empire State Building pushing through the smoke of Manhattan across the street.

Having a major-league baseball team meant *being* major league. No other sport makes such a thing of major-leagueness as professional baseball. Even such an undistinguished municipality as Cincinnati struts a little knowing it is the home of the Reds.

FOR YEARS Toronto had a reputation as a terrific minor-league baseball city, but no matter how this is stated it sounds patronizing. The truth is, Toronto had a great baseball tradition well before the Blue Jays came to town. If Toronto (and Montreal before the Expos) had been situated in the United States it might have had a major-league team at the turn of the century, certainly before the likes of Kansas City or Minneapolis or Oakland or San Diego.

Hall of Famers who played in the minors in Toronto include Wee Willie (''Hit 'em where they ain't'') Keeler, Nap Lajoie, Charlie Gehringer, and Ralph Kiner. Some of the other notables who did their undergraduate work in Toronto were Urban Shocker, Burleigh Grimes, Dick Fowler, Joe Altobelli, Elston Howard, Frank O'Rourke, Carl Hubbell, Rocky Nelson, Reggie Smith, Sparky Anderson, Chuck Tanner, Ozzie Virgil, Rico Carty. Babe Ruth briefly played for the Providence Grays, but he became part of Toronto baseball history one afternoon in 1914 at Maple Leaf Park, a pleasant 18,000-seat stadium with covered grandstand at Hanlan's Point, on an island across the harbour from downtown Toronto. Ruth, nineteen, pitched a one-hit, 9–0 shutout and stroked his first professional home run, the only homer he hit in the minors.

By the mid-1920s, attendance at the island stadium was dwindling; the burghers of Toronto decided to build a new baseball stadium at the foot of Bathurst Street, not far from where Exhibition Stadium stands today and even closer to where the new stadium is being built. It took five months and $750,000 to build the 20,000-seat stadium, considered the jewel of the minor leagues.

As early as 1899, when franchises were being sought for the new American League, Toronto was considered a strong candidate for major-league baseball. Toronto was mentioned again in 1926, when Maple Leaf Stadium was built.

In the 1950s, the Maple Leafs, who played in the Triple A International League, flourished under flamboyant owner Jack Kent Cooke, a Torontonian who later would own the Los Angeles Lakers of the National Basketball Association, the Los Angeles Kings of the National Hockey League, and the Washington Redskins of the National Football League. With Cooke's constant promotions, more than three million fans attended Maple Leaf games in the fifties at the stadium that became known as the ''Fleet Street Flats.'' *The Sporting News* named Cooke minor-league executive of the year in 1952 when the Maple Leafs drew 446,040, the highest total that year in the minor leagues. Cooke steadfastly worked to obtain a major-league franchise for Toronto. He tried to persuade local politicians to build a major-league park, which would not have been difficult or unduly expensive with Maple Leaf Stadium as the base. Whenever he detected an ailing franchise, he offered to buy it. He tried for the Braves, but they moved instead from Boston to Milwaukee where a new stadium had been built. He tried for the Browns, but they moved instead from St. Louis to Baltimore where they became the Orioles. When the Briggs family was forced to liquidate its estate, Cooke offered $5.2 million to buy the Detroit Tigers, but he struck out again.

In 1959, Cooke had the Toronto franchise in the Continental League, formed by New York lawyer William Shea after he had failed to find a National League replacement for the Dodgers and Giants. But major-league expansion that resulted in the Mets killed the Continental League and with it went Cooke's last attempt to bring the majors to Toronto.

Cooke had always believed passionately that Toronto was a major-league city and in time he managed to convince the fans. By the 1960s, Toronto was becoming a sophisticated megalopolis that would soon surpass Montreal as the largest urban centre in Canada. Televised baseball created an appetite for major-league games and major-league stars. In 1960, the Maple Leafs won the International League pennant by seventeen games, but drew only 203,700; the year before, when they finished eighth, they drew 207,505. Despite championship seasons under manager Dick Williams in 1965 and 1966, the crowds kept dwindling. It didn't help when Montreal, Toronto's big-city rival in Canada, set about to acquire a major-league team. Only 67,216 showed up to watch the 1967 Maple Leafs and so, after 79 years, the team folded. The owners sold the bankrupt club to Louisville and wreckers tore down Maple Leaf Stadium, the coolest place in town on the hot summer days and the last true professional baseball stadium the city has known.

IT BECAME EVIDENT in the 1970s that if Toronto was serious about acquiring major-league baseball, it needed a place where the game could be played. Paul Godfrey, a young alderman in the Toronto borough of North York, was an enthusiastic baseball fan. He travelled – always at his own expense – across North America to meet with baseball executives. He tried serendipitous encounters with the wheelers and dealers, hanging out in hotel bars. Like Woodward and Bernstein, he arranged midnight liaisons in underground parking garages – anything to discuss ways of getting Toronto big-league baseball.

Once he flew to Florida to attend an important baseball meeting in Bal Harbor. He began to prowl the lobbies and bars and eventually ended up at the Sheraton. "I sidled up beside Frank Lane, one of the biggest wheeler-dealers of players at the time, took a deep breath, and bought the guy a drink. We talked. I bought. We talked. I bought. Ted Williams came over. I bought him a drink, too."

Around midnight, Godfrey felt he was making progress. He got down to specifics of how a city goes about obtaining a major-league baseball team. Lane pointed to a towering man standing at the other end of the bar.

"He's the fellah you've got to talk to," Lane said. "That's the new commissioner, Bowie Kuhn."

Godfrey slipped off his stool, walked over to Kuhn, introduced himself, and made his pitch.

Kuhn looked down at the young man, put a fatherly hand on Godfrey's shoulder, and said, "Son, I'll tell you how it works. First you've got to build us a stadium, then baseball will decide whether or not you get a team."

In 1973, Godfrey became chairman of Metro Toronto Council, a non-elected but powerful civic position, a sort of super mayor. In the fall of 1973, he attended in his official capacity the annual Grey Cup game at Exhibition Stadium in Toronto. Godfrey talked to Ontario Premier William Davis as they waited for Governor General Roland Michener, who was to make the ceremonial kickoff and was late. Godfrey told the Premier that for $15 million Exhibition Stadium could be renovated to accommodate major-league baseball. If the province paid half, Godfrey said, Metro Council would put up the rest. Premier Davis agreed. He told Godfrey the province could provide an interest-free loan for half the cost of the renovation, to be paid from the profits generated by baseball.

By the mid-1970s, for $17.8 million, Exhibition Stadium had been renovated to hold more than 40,000 baseball spectators. It has turned out to be a good deal for Metropolitan Toronto. The stadium has always shown an operating profit. Even in 1981 when a players' strike interrupted the season for 50 days, the stadium showed a $6,000 profit despite losing 30 Blue Jay home games.

The rental percentage paid by the Blue Jays for use of the stadium probably ranks among the top one-third in North America – favouring the stadium. The Blue Jays pay 7.5 per cent of admissions as rent on the first 1.5 million spectators each season and 10 per cent on any attendance above that. In addition there is a 25-cent user fee on each admission over $2. This is on all stadium events and has raised $6 million since 1976, which is designated toward capital improvements. Versa Foods, which handles the concessions, gives 16.2 per cent to the Blue Jays and 10 per cent to the stadium from its take from the concessions. The Blue Jays do not share in the parking. In 1986, the stadium took in $3,235,000 from baseball operations with costs of $1,482,000, a net surplus of $1,753,000 – including the 25-cent per ticket user fee, which for an attendance of 2.4 million raises $600,000 for the capital improvements. (The Blue Jays also must pay 10 per cent to the province, 20 per cent of the gate after taxes to the visiting team, and between 2 and 4 per cent to the American League depending on its needs for the season – in 1986, the league charged 3.5 per cent on gate receipts but most years it is 4 per cent. Add it all up and the Blue Jays have more than 40 per cent of their gate receipts skimmed from the top.)

There are 14 private boxes behind home plate, of which seven are rented at $75,000 each per year, not including tickets to the event. Of the remainder, two are for the use of the board of governors of Exhibition Place. Another goes to the Blue Jays for free. The Blue Jays have three other boxes and are charged by the square foot, which works out to about the same as the rental cost. Carling O'Keefe, owners of the Toronto Argonauts of the Canadian Football League, another stadium tenant, are charged for one on the same arrangement. There are 14 more private boxes in the area of the football press box above the north grandstand, hanging over the left-field bleachers. Twelve are rented for $40,000 per season and two others for $35,000 each – and 12 tickets for each game are included.

Overall, the stadium revenues for 1986 were $5,726,000 with expenses of $4,295,000. The operating surplus was $1,431,000 for the stadium and Metro Council received $1,383,900. Metro pays back the province using a formula involving the basic operating profit of $115,000 in 1975. Half of any profit above that amount is used to pay off the province's interest-free loan.

"It gets a lot of knocks, but it did what it was supposed to do," said stadium general manager Gord Walker. "Toronto would never have had the team without it. With the number of dollars spent, the public has been well served."

Under its agreement with the stadium, the Blue Jays could request additional seating if they drew at least 1.2 million fans in any three consecutive seasons. They exceeded that in each of their first three seasons. A study was done and it was found that improvements that would add 10,000 chairs would cost $16 to $17 million. Another plan that would have added 17,000 seats, which provided a cover and a parking garage, would have cost $31 million. But Metro Council had its eyes on something bigger, something with a dome, and the improvements did not get past the study stage.

In this quirkiest of stadiums, there is another small oddity involving the right-field foul line. Listed at 330 feet, it has been reported to be as short as 315 feet. A mistake was made in the construction and the foul pole was placed on the wrong side of the fence. So, according to Walker's calculations, the distance from home plate to the foul pole in right field is about 327 feet.

As flawed as it might be, the transformation of Exhibition Stadium into a baseball park started some stirring among several potential owners.

ONE OF THE PRIME CONTENDERS was Labatt Breweries of Canada, a brewing giant that wanted a promotional vehicle to sell beer. There was also a group known as the Toronto Baseball Company, headed by Syd C. Cooper and Montreal financier R. Howard Webster, chairman of *The Globe and Mail*. A third group was headed by Lorne Duguid, a former professional hockey player who was vice-president of Hiram Walker and Sons, and supposedly included Harold Ballard and Maple Leaf Gardens. A fourth group emerged later, headed by brothers Phil and Irving Granovsky, who were believed to be fronting for Carling O'Keefe, another brewery giant with a substantial share of the Toronto beer market. Also in this group were Jimmy Kay, David Dennis, and Fred McCutcheon. Their lawyer was Trevor Eyton, who, ironically, has since become chief executive officer of Brascan Limited, which includes John Labatt Limited among its holdings.

Cooper's group commissioned a study of the Toronto market for major-league baseball; the results showed that Toronto and southern Ontario indeed were ready for it. The study anticipated a minimum attendance of 1,300,000 in the first year with 1,500,000 a reasonable goal. It showed that Metropolitan Toronto's population (2,400,000 and rising) ranked eighth among cities with major-league franchises. Toronto's "sales activity index" was 132, 45 per cent higher than Montreal's 92. Toronto's "quality buying power index" was 113, 10 per cent higher than Montreal's 104. Toronto ranked second in

"Median household income" of North American cities with major-league teams.

Peter Widdrington, president and chief executive officer of John Labatt Limited and a member of the Blue Jay board of directors, said Labatt's wanted a tie-in with an important sports franchise to enhance corporate visibility in Ontario, especially in Toronto. He explained: "In the beer business, there has always been a strong association with sports. We had been tied up with the Canadian Football League, and on a minor basis there was a long association with sports, but we didn't have a strong affiliation with a major franchise."

Molson's sponsored the popular *Hockey Night in Canada* and also had a long association with the Montreal Canadiens through sponsorship and, eventually, ownership. Carling O'Keefe sponsored the Montreal Expos' televised games on the CBC and would become involved with the Quebec Nordiques of the World Hockey Association, which merged with the National Hockey League.

Widdrington thought that merely trying to obtain a major-league team for Toronto would enhance the brewery's image in that region. In the 1960s, when he was the general manager of the British Columbia division, Labatt's had tried to move the Oakland Seals of the National Hockey League to Vancouver. The attempt failed, but Widdrington found strong community support for the effort.

The people at Labatt's felt that if they brought major-league baseball to Toronto, it would help offset the increased market share that Molson's had gained over Labatt's in Ontario, and particularly in Toronto, which was rapidly becoming Canada's dominant financial and head-office centre. Labatt's had had five years without a significant improvement in market share, except through acquisition. It was then the largest brewery in Canada, with 36 per cent of the market share; but Molson's was coming on strong. In Ontario, Molson's held 39 per cent of the market share, three percentage points more than Labatt's. Early in 1974, 36-year-old Don McDougall took over as president of Labatt's Brewery; he would become a key figure in the move to bring major-league baseball to Toronto.

"Baseball came along as one of those opportunities that would move us to the centre stage in Toronto and that was what we wanted," McDougall said in a 1977 Labatt's Corporate Newsletter. "Owing to the fact that a Toronto baseball franchise was a sound business proposition in its own right, when you add the synergistic effect to the beer business it becomes a major breakthrough."

According to McDougall, an increase in Labatt's market share would earn back the initial capital investment in a major-league baseball team in three to five years. "We were completely confident that we more than recouped our investment in the team through increased sales," McDougall said during the Jay's tenth season, when he was no longer with Labatt's.

Pinpointing when the brewery had earned its way out through increased share of the market is difficult, however, says Widdrington. "The only time you look at something that way is when you decide to sell. And we're not in that position."

It is also difficult to determine exactly how much the team has contributed to Labatt's increased market share because other factors were involved. "At the time the Blue Jays opened we got a very good reaction and our market share in Toronto probably went up a couple of points, which was pretty good," Widdrington said. "Since that time we've introduced about five new brands. They've all increased our market share. We've introduced the twist top, that increased our market share. We've had heavy advertising with some good ad programs, that increased our market share. You keep adding things on like that and it's very difficult to measure at this point what part of it the Blue Jays would play. The Blue Jays did provide us with a good advertising program during the summer months – which we paid a lot of money for – but that's been a positive. It's been a good vehicle."

In late 1986, Labatt's had an estimated 42 per cent of the national market followed by Molson at 32 per cent and Carling O'Keefe at 22 per cent.

"Since that time 10 years ago, there have been 15 major promotional or product events that the brewery has become involved in," Widdrington said. "All of them have left their mark somewhere in terms of our total market share. To go back and figure out what is what is very difficult. . . .It should also be noted that after that for various reasons, the market share went below where it should have been."

Widdrington mentions another problem: figuring out exactly why people drink a certain brand. "If you walk into a bar and asked 10 people who are drinking Labatt's why they are drinking it, I doubt if you would get one of them saying it's because of the Blue Jays. One way or another, the Blue Jays might have had an effect on a couple of them; but they wouldn't tell you that. They'd tell you they drink Labatt's because it's smooth. . . . Here's the thing about beer, because it's a

personal choice thing he doesn't want to be caught without a reason –
it's smoother, and maybe he hadn't even thought what smooth was."

There is another side to the high visibility of a sports franchise.
"There is also the potential of some negative impact, if the club . . .
is perceived as being not managed well. It's a two-edged sword,"
Widdrington said. "We have the highest visibility of the partners."

LABATT'S PURSUIT of a major-league baseball team began in 1974, when
it tried to buy the Cleveland Indians. John Alevizos, who was vice-
president of administration for the Boston Red Sox, wanted his own
major-league team and he was very keen on Toronto. Alevizos knew
the ropes. He went to the Ontario government, then to Metropolitan
Toronto Council, then to Labatt's. "He knew what it would take to
buy the Cleveland Indians," said Neil MacCarl, the veteran baseball
writer of *The Toronto Star*. "He convinced the provincial government
that Toronto had the potential to be a major-league city, that it had the
best potential of any city that wasn't in the major leagues."

Labatt's was interested and McDougall listened to Alevizos's proposition.

"We would basically put up some money and he would provide leadership and own a piece of it," McDougall said. "Alevizos wanted to
pursue the Cleveland Indians, or, after that – whoever. It almost got
away from us because he put on a pretty good show. He knew all the
names in baseball."

The Labatt's people, inexperienced in the ways of major-league
baseball, nearly reached a deal with Alevizos. McDougall arranged a
breakfast meeting with R. Alan Eagleson, a Toronto lawyer big in hockey
and the Progressive Conservative Party. Eagleson knew a lot of names,
too. He was friends with McDougall and John F. Bassett, who had
been involved with several sports franchises, and Herb Solway, the
lawyer for the Toronto Argonauts.

"I didn't feel too comfortable with the deal we were putting through
with Alevizos," McDougall said. "I wanted to go through it because
we were supposed to begin drafting and signing documents. Anyway,
at the breakfast meeting, Johnny Bassett – God bless him! – said in the
world of professional sports getting people to run these things is not a
problem. He said there are dozens of people quite capable and you
don't have to give them 20 per cent for nothing. That's when Johnny

Bassett stood up and said, 'I don't care how great Alevizos is, I wouldn't do it.' "

McDougall and Eagleson decided to fly to Boston for a meeting with Alevizos and his lawyers.

"They were there with the papers all ready to sign," McDougall said. "Eagleson and I were there to say it's no deal. It was as close as we ever came to making a fatal mistake."

LABATT'S CONTINUED in hot pursuit of a major-league franchise. Joining McDougall, Solway, and Godfrey were Ed Bradley, then marketing director of Labatt's, and Dave Cashen, Labatt's Ontario sales manager. When they were younger, McDougall and Godfrey had worked for the Young Progressive Conservatives in the period between 1964 and 1968.

In making their pitch for a major-league team, they would emphasize that Toronto was the largest market in North America without a major-league baseball team. Moreover, the Toronto market was far enough away so as not to infringe on franchises in Detroit, Montreal, and Cleveland. They even had charts that showed Toronto's weather was no worse than Boston's, Detroit's, and Chicago's (and a heck of a lot better than Montreal's). In Godfrey's travels in pursuit of a team, his assistant Ray Biggart usually accompanied him. Biggart would carry a huge model of the new stadium, almost five feet by five feet and weighing nearly a hundred pounds. Between trips it would be kept at Biggart's house. "Even if we never got a team," Biggart said, "at least my kids got to play with the most expensive set of building blocks in town."

After eschewing the Alevizos-led try for the Cleveland Indians, the Labatt's group flirted with acquiring the Baltimore Orioles – after recent ownership change it looked as if the Orioles might be available – then concentrated on getting a major-league franchise in the National League. The Montreal Expos wanted Toronto in the National League because of the long-standing rivalry between the two Canadian cities.

The Labatt's group trained its sights on the ailing San Francisco Giants of the National League. After leaving the deteriorating Polo Grounds in New York following the 1957 season, the Giants thrived for a while in San Francisco, drawing more than a million fans a season from 1958 to 1967. In 1960, the Giants drew 1,795,356, continuing their rivalry with the Dodgers.

Bad times fell on the Giants when the A's moved to Oakland, the sprawling seaport city across San Francisco Bay. In 1968, attendance at Candlestick Park dropped to 833,594 – lower than a million for the first time since they left New York. There were justifiable complaints about Candlestick Park, which is too cold and windy for comfortable baseball playing and watching. The A's did not do much better at the gate, attracting 837,466 their first season in the Oakland Alameda County Coliseum, but – alas for the Giants – they played much better baseball. The colourful, feuding A's of Reggie Jackson, Gene Tenace, Rollie Fingers, and Catfish Hunter (and irascible owner Charlie Finley) won the World Series in 1972, 1973, and 1974. By the mid-1970s, it seemed apparent that the Bay area was not big enough to support two major-league teams, though the Giants and A's have somehow survived.

Given a choice, baseball people probably would have preferred to keep the Giants in San Francisco; it had more prestige than dreary Oakland. The A's were something of a gypsy team, having resided in Philadelphia and Kansas City before moving west. But Horace Stoneham of the Giants was $2 million in debt. The Giants had fired their manager, Wes Westrum, and the coaches, and cut office salaries by a third. The team owed $1 million to the Bank of America. It had mortgaged property in Arizona and borrowed $500,000 from the National League to finish the 1975 season. The Giants could not even pay the $125,000 rent on Candlestick Park. Thus, in September, 1975, an inter-league committee recommended Toronto as a site for the Giants.

Labatt's had approached Stoneham about buying the Giants when Webster, the Montreal financier, joined the Labatt's group. Webster had been peripherally involved with the Montreal Expos – his nephew Lorne had invested in the team – and in the early 1970s had tried to buy the San Diego Padres and move them to Toronto. The partnership was expanded to include the Canadian Imperial Bank of Commerce, which did business with both Labatt's and Webster. Labatt's and Webster were in for 45 per cent each, the bank for 10 per cent. It added up to considerable financial clout: the country's biggest brewery (annual sales upwards of $500 million), a wealthy individual sportsman, and Canada's second largest bank (assets of more than $33 billion). Larry Greenwood, the bank's representative on the Blue Jay board, says the addition of the bank as a minor partner also helped to show the "substantial financial responsibility" necessary to obtain the franchise. The bank limited its investment to 10 per cent because of the Bank Act. At the time the partnership was formed, the limit under the act was 49 per cent on an investment of under $5 million. But there had been speculation that would change with the Bank Act's revision, which comes every 10 years, and, sure enough, with the revision the Act stated a bank could not own more than 10 per cent, no matter what the investment.

The alliance between the two major owners seemed almost offhand. McDougall said that the contact was made through the bank. Jake Moore, then chairman of John Labatt Limited, sat on the board of the CIBC. Page Wadsworth, then chairman of the bank, mentioned to Moore that he had been reading about Labatt's interest in obtaining a major-league baseball team. He said he had a client who also was interested in acquiring a team. A meeting was set up with McDougall, Bob Luba, then vice-president of finance of John Labatt Limited, Webster, and Wadsworth. There had been discussion within Labatt's about whether a big-league team should be pursued alone or a partnership should be formed. It was agreed that if Webster was interested, a partnership would make sense. Too many groups acting independently might dilute the effort.

"Our interests seemed to dovetail," Widdrington said. "And . . . the bank does a lot of business with both of us so it made pretty good sense that they might come along and they expressed an interest. These were pretty casual phone calls and conversations."

The important thing is that there was no conflict between the goals of the two major partners: the brewery could gain some promotional value; for Webster, it was more of a sporting and business enterprise. "If it had been somebody else, who was looking at the same things we were," said Widdrington, "we couldn't have gotten together."

When the franchise was finally secured, the ownership agreement was drafted by lawyer Gord Kirke. He had practically severed the middle finger on his right hand moving a ping pong table at his home. A plastic surgeon had put the finger back together and Kirke worked on the agreement at home. He had no dictaphone there, so he wrote it out by hand. When it came time for the bandage to be removed, the plastic surgeon, who had been proud of his handiwork, invited some colleagues to observe. He was startled by the irregular shape of the finger – it looks today as if it had stopped one too many foul tips. He asked Kirke what he had done. It was then that Kirke realized the pen pressing against the injured finger as he wrote had left him with a permanent memento of Toronto's baseball dream.

IF LABATT'S could count on spinoff beer sales to make up for any operating losses, there was no such advantage for Webster; he would thus become less tolerant of continued significant losses. William Ferguson, the executive vice-president of Webster's Imperial Trust – a holding company for some of the family's business interests – and his representative on the Blue Jays' board, says that Webster does not look at the baseball team as a money-maker. "It was strictly another asset that Howard was putting into Toronto. That's really what he was looking at," said Ferguson, who is from Saint John, New Brunswick, and attended Clarkson College in Potsdam, New York, on a hockey scholarship in 1957 and 1958.

"He owned a number of things in Toronto," Ferguson said. "He owned *The Globe and Mail*, he was involved in the Lord Simcoe Hotel, he had other investments in Toronto, including the Eaton Centre. He's always been involved in business in Toronto."

By early 1987, Webster's only Toronto business interest was the baseball team, although he had considerable land in nearby Uxbridge, Ontario.

Because of his health, Webster doesn't attend games but watches them on television. Ferguson talks to Webster every day and baseball often comes up in the conversation. Ferguson says Webster derives great enjoyment from the team, watching the young players progress. "But he doesn't enjoy losing the money," Ferguson said. "We're looking forward to the day when we move into the new stadium."

In the present situation, Webster's only hope of a solid profit in his baseball investment would be from selling his share in the team, but Ferguson didn't see that happening. "Howard would be happy to keep it close to the line, he has no view of selling it at a profit, really, because of his feelings toward sports.

"Besides," Ferguson added with a smile, "we get good seats."

THE CANADIAN IMPERIAL BANK OF COMMERCE kept a low profile at first as far as using the team as a promotional vehicle. The bank deferred to Labatt's because of its greater investment. "They could use it to their advantage," said David Lewis, the bank's first representative on the ball club's board, "and the bank didn't want to seem to be intruding." Lewis was on the Blue Jays' board of directors for the first five years, then he left CIBC for the Continental Bank.

The team was not looked on as a money-maker by the bank, says

Larry Greenwood, the CIBC representative on the board. But there is positive fallout from involvement with the team if it is, and is perceived to be, a well-run organization.

"Money's not everything, you know," Greenwood said. "The team is an excellent thing for Toronto. It's given Toronto an added something, like the symphony orchestra. Economically, it keeps money in Toronto. I'm not saying we're totally altruistic; it's good for the bank."

During the first years, the bank's main baseball promotion was to put out a schedule. The bank is less reticent now; it proudly advertises itself as the Bank of the Blue Jays.

It took some prodding. Mike Gouinlock of Chris Lang and Associates, a company involved in sports and promotional events, remembers walking past a downtown Royal Bank in 1982. It was having a Blue Jay day with decorations pertaining to the baseball team. The team was beginning to shake off its expansion label. Gouinlock was puzzled. Wasn't it the CIBC that owned part of the Blue Jays? He developed and presented a program through which the CIBC could take advantage of its investment, help its image with the public, and boost internal morale. The first year of the program was to be strictly internal, to let the employees know that the bank did own 10 per cent of the Blue Jays.

The CIBC used tickets to games, trips to spring training, and other Blue Jay-oriented prizes as incentives for branches. Prizes might be offered, for example, to the branch that came closest to meeting its quota for issuing VISA cards in a specified month.

The bank also puts out a poster – in 1986 it featured Damaso Garcia – and arranged autographing sessions with a player at twenty-five branches during the season. In 1986, twenty different players made the visits. There also was a Saves for Charity promotion, in which money was donated for each save recorded by the Toronto relief pitchers.

Autographing sessions attract fans; pitcher Dave Stieb, for example, drew 2,200 to the Commerce Court in 1985. Crowds would be smaller at most branches, but still significant – 500 to 1,500. "Three-quarters of the people there are customers, anyway," said Barbara Sheedy, assistant to the CIBC manager of consumer promotions and special events. "It's a community thing, not tied in to sales. The bank manager meeting customers he otherwise wouldn't meet. It's a special event for the staff."

THE COMMERCE might been the bank of the Giants. On January 9, 1976, it was announced that Labatt's, Webster, and the bank had bought the Giants for $13.5 million – $8 million for the franchise, the rest to buy out of the nineteen years left on the stadium lease. Then, as quickly as the deal had been pushed through, it fell apart. George Moscone, the new mayor of San Francisco, obtained a temporary injunction that blocked the move to Toronto and prevented the National League from voting on the transfer. Supreme Court Judge John Benson gave the city a temporary restraining order so that a local buyer could be sought to keep the team in San Francisco.

Bob Lurie, a San Francisco financier who had been interested in buying the Giants for some time, put up half of the $8 million needed to keep the team at home. He had been working on a partnership with Bob Short, who had owned the expansion Washington Senators and moved them to Texas (where they became known as the Rangers) before selling them. After much discussion, the National League owners accepted Lurie's proposal, but the deal collapsed. As the March 1 deadline loomed, it looked as if the Giants were headed for Toronto. But the Giants do their spring training in Phoenix, Arizona, and mayor Moscone got a phone call from Bud Herseth, a Phoenix meatpacker: another partnership in the works, this time between Herseth and Lurie. Two and a half hours before the deadline, Herseth and Lurie put together a deal that kept the Giants in San Francisco.

Herb Solway still has a Toronto Giants sign from the January 9 press conference.

The Labatt's group renewed efforts to get a National League team for Toronto, convinced the rivalry with Montreal was the best way to go. It was a myopic obsession that nearly killed its chances of getting major-league baseball.

"For marketing and other reasons we thought a National League team would be best," McDougall said. "We almost blew it completely."

There had been a new development during Toronto's frenzied courting of the Giants, one that would change the thinking of the Toronto group. Early in February, 1976, the twelve-team American League awarded Seattle an expansion franchise. This meant that it would have to add another expansion team for balance – seven teams in each division – or the National League would add a team and the two leagues for the first time would play interleague games.

There had been a $14-million suit filed against the American League by Seattle, King County, and the state of Washington over the loss of the Seattle Pilots to Milwaukee in 1970. The Pilots had come to Seattle in the same expansion that brought the Royals to Kansas City. The Royals and Pilots began playing in the 1969 season, the same season the Expos started in Montreal and the Padres in San Diego.

The Pilots, underfinanced and undersupplied in an inadequate, appropriately named Sick Stadium, soon went broke and were sold to Bud Selig's Milwaukee group for $10.8 million. The handshake agreement was reached at Baltimore's Memorial Stadium during the eighth inning of the first game of the World Series, October 11, 1969. It was to be the only Orioles win in that five-game series taken by the amazing eight-year-old New York Mets. The deal was made under a portrait of former Baltimore Oriole catcher Gus Triandos in the Bird Feed room, an area for season ticketholders.

Seattle fought hard to keep the team, but the move to Milwaukee was legally approved on April 1, 1970, a week before the season was to open, after several days of testimony in bankruptcy court.

The American League thought it had a good case for the suit that resulted from the move. But the trial would be by jury and it would be held in the state of Washington. Rather than take the risk, the American League settled by awarding the new franchise to Seattle, which now had the Kingdome, a huge and hideous domed stadium that seats nearly 60,000. ("Damned domes!" Bob Cox once exclaimed unprovoked as he sat in the visitors' dugout of the Kingdome before one Blue Jay game there. Cox felt that having to play his home games in a dome could drive him from managing.) At the Kingdome, baseballs that hit the loudspeakers above the field are fair. If they are caught by an outfielder the batter is out; if they drop to the field the batter can get as many bases as he can. It is like playing in a pinball machine. Short porches in left and right field make it a home-run paradise. Pitcher Shane Rawley once remarked, "If you can pitch in the Kingdome and not allow home runs, you can pitch in a phone booth and not allow home runs."

There was little time to become disappointed at losing the Giants. McDougall and friends, mainly Herb Solway, renewed their quest for major-league baseball. They would travel wherever the owners were gathered, which meant long vigils in hotel lobbies and bars waiting for the chance encounter that might prove fruitful. "We'd go to the bar the night before to meet owners," Solway said. "We'd chat with them and we'd think we were going to be on the next day, so we'd wait around the lobby all day and late in the afternoon a door would open and the owners would pour out carrying their bags and say, 'We've got to catch a plane. See you at the next meeting.' We'd have flown God knows where to get in and make some kind of presentation and then we'd just sit there feeling completely let down."

In March, 1976, McDougall and Solway spent a couple of days watching spring training in Fort Lauderdale, trying with little luck to rub shoulders with some owners. On the day they were scheduled to return to Toronto the two men headed to the beach for some morning sun. As McDougall dozed off, Solway riffled through the newspapers and found a story that said both leagues were holding meetings at the Plaza Hotel in New York the next day. He leaned over and nudged McDougall awake.

"We better go to this meeting," he said to him. "We haven't missed one yet."

"I wanted to stay sleeping on the beach," McDougall remembered. "I always call Herb my designated fretter. He was always fretting we were going to miss something."

Solway's concern proved correct. They arrived in New York that evening, checked into the Plaza Hotel, and scouted the bar downstairs, then tried the Club 21 bar, where they figured some baseball people could be found. Solway left early, but McDougall stayed on. He walked back to the hotel with Chub Feeney, president of the National League, and they had a long, amiable discussion. Feeney suggested that McDougall and Solway make a presentation the next morning, a Saturday.

At breakfast, McDougall told Solway, "Listen, they're talking expansion in *both* leagues. There's going to be a motion at the National League meeting to expand to Washington and Toronto."

American League owners were getting anxious. They wanted a new team for a balanced 14-team league. They knew Commissioner Bowie Kuhn desperately wanted Washington back in the majors, and worried they might lose Toronto to the National League. Lee MacPhail, the American League president who once was business manager for the Toronto Maple Leafs, felt that the foul-up of the Giants' transfer to Toronto had opened the door for the American League to try to get

111

Toronto. "We had agreed that we would stay out if the National League intended to go in," MacPhail said, "but we finally warned that there was a time limit to our waiting. We had given them one year."

After McDougall and Solway spoke, the National League owners voted 8–4 to expand. It was not good enough because unanimous consent was required for the National League to expand, while the American League required three-quarters of the owners to vote in favour.

There was a motion to adjourn the meeting, but Bill Bartholomay, chairman of the board of the Atlanta Braves, spoke against it. The adjournment motion failed, seven votes to five. There was some chaos, and it was decided to break for a few minutes. "I think we can get to some of these guys," Solway recalls Bartholomay telling him.

August A. Busch, whose Anheuser-Busch brewery owns the St. Louis Cardinals, told McDougall that he was not in favour of expansion but that for the sake of Labatt's, a fellow brewer, he would support it. The final vote reached 10–2 in favour of expansion and it stayed there with Cincinnati and Philadelphia standing firmly against. They were not opposed to Toronto but were against more expansion on principle.

Bill Giles of the Phillies thought the league made a mistake by not moving the Giants to Toronto – he says Chub Feeney and Los Angeles Dodger president Walter O'Malley changed the owners' minds about moving the franchise out of San Francisco. But Giles, and the Carpenter family who then owned the team, were against expansion because they didn't feel it was necessary. "If it hadn't been for Ruly Carpenter and myself and Bob Howsam of the Reds, there would have been expansion," Giles said. "I just thought the league was healthy the way it was, why change it. We had enough teams coming in that were weak drawing cards so why put in two more teams that couldn't draw. People tried to twist Mr. Carpenter's arm and he wouldn't do it."

It was decided to reconvene the National League meeting in two weeks. McDougall and Solway were told to "hang tough" while the owners worked on the two holdouts.

Elsewhere in the hotel, the American League owners were meeting. In a corridor, McDougall and Solway bumped into Ewing Kauffman, owner of the Kansas City Royals.

"Listen fellahs," Kauffman warned McDougall and Solway, "you guys are going to be shut out."

Kauffman had a place in his heart for Toronto. His wife Muriel had attended Queen Victoria Public School and Parkdale Collegiate in

Toronto. Kauffman had become a strong ally of the Toronto effort, and with her husband's blessing, Muriel Kauffman passed on information to the Toronto group through her daughter who lived in Toronto and knew Dave Cashen of Labatt's.

Kauffman "was a very strong advocate within the American League," McDougall said. "He particularly succeeded, I think, in erasing negatives that might have arisen in some American League owners' minds because we had the National League as our first choice. It had nothing to do with the league, it was Montreal."

McDougall and Solway learned that Lee MacPhail, president of the American League, would be going to Toronto in a few days – but didn't know when – to meet a group headed by Phil and Irving Granovsky. The Granovsky brothers owned Atlantic Packaging and it was generally believed that they were backed by Carling O'Keefe. Phil Granovsky, however, denies that Carling was any part of his ownership group, but that they had helped them with graphics for their bid. However, he did say there was a possibility that the brewery would have had a chance at sponsoring the games on television and radio if his group had been successful, but no details had been discussed.

Phil Granovsky, who says he is a lifelong fan of baseball, was a friend of Jerry Hoffberger, chairman of the Baltimore Orioles, who informed him that the American League wanted to add another team to go with Seattle. Granovsky was told that his group might have some advantages in that it was individual ownership rather than corporate ownership, for individual owners had proved more successful. Another advantage he thought he might have was that the Labatt's group had been wooing the National League. With little time to work, Granovsky talked to Oriole manager Earl Weaver to get an idea of what went into a major-league baseball team: the costs of setting up a minor-league system and all the other necessities. They were a late entry, to be sure, but they were about to try an end run.

"It was very much public knowledge, the American League had already voted to expand to Toronto if the National League didn't," McDougall said. "There was no secret about that."

On the plane back to Toronto, McDougall and Solway discussed strategy.

"You know," McDougall said, "we're going to blow this thing if we stick with the National League. The American League has got to expand. Everybody keeps giving us all these assurances that we'll have the stadium and we'll be in the National League, but if we stick here we're dead.''

Solway agreed.

The next morning, a Sunday, McDougall tried an end run of his own. He met with top executives of Labatt's at his office in London, Ontario. McDougall explained the dangers of continuing to pursue a National League franchise. ''It would be a crying shame to be shuffled off the main stage by sticking with something that may never happen,'' he said. ''We can't control whether Philadelphia or Cincinnati will change their minds, but we can do something about an American League franchise.''

So, McDougall called MacPhail at his home at noon, told him the Labatt's group had decided to pursue an American League team, and said he would like to visit MacPhail to talk about it. The Labatt's group was on good terms with MacPhail.

''You don't have to come very far because I'm going to be in Toronto tomorrow,'' MacPhail said, explaining that he was to meet and attend a press conference with the Granovskys on Monday. McDougall arranged to have MacPhail picked up at the airport and driven to the Granovsky press conference.

Meanwhile, McDougall called a press conference at the Harbour Castle Hilton on Sunday evening to announce that MacPhail was coming to Toronto to meet the Labatt's group. It worked. When the Granovskys held a press conference on Monday to announce they were pursuing an American League team, it appeared as if they were merely jumping on the Labatt beerwagon.

On Monday night, McDougall and his men had dinner with MacPhail and learned that the American League was going to accept Toronto at a meeting the following Saturday in Tampa. The only question was who would get the franchise, the Granovskys or Labatt's? The Granovskys had one staunch ally in Hoffberger, who owned National Brewing. Carling O'Keefe had purchased National and Hoffberger had been named chairman of the board of Carling's U.S. division.

Labatt's strategy was to lobby all the other American League owners. McDougall took about two-thirds of the owners, Solway took the rest, including Cleveland Indians owner Nick Mileti, whom he had known through their involvement in the World Football League. When Solway called Mileti, he said, ''Nick, I need your vote.''

''I've given Ted Bonda the right to run the team,'' Mileti answered. ''I'm the general partner but I don't interfere anymore.''

"Nick, I need your vote," Solway persisted.

"I can't get involved, Herb."

"Nick, I wouldn't call you unless I needed you. I need your vote."

Mileti paused for about a minute, then said, "Okay, you've got it."

Labatt's felt sure they had nine of twelve votes. McDougall and Solway had trouble reaching Calvin Griffith of the Minnesota Twins and George Steinbrenner of the New York Yankees; they didn't bother to approach Hoffberger. The owners would vote in a secret ballot, but, unlike the unanimity needed in the National League, a 75 per cent majority would be enough. Solway worried that things were too easy; he suspected something fishy.

What worried him was Hoffberger, whom he suspected controlled three votes apart from his own, even though some of the three others had unofficially indicated that they would support Labatt's. He figured Hoffberger would keep the four votes in his pocket and when the ballots showed an 8–4 split, he'd say, "Look, you need a fourteenth team and you need Toronto. You don't have Toronto unless you take my group, the Granovskys."

As the meeting approached, McDougall spoke to the Twins and got a mild assurance that Griffith was with Labatt's. The last call they received was from Steinbrenner, who said he'd support them as well. John Fetzer of the Detroit Tigers, a man in his seventies, flew all night from San Francisco on the redeye in order to cast his vote for the Labatt's group.

Phil Granovsky said he had talked to some American League owners "but I guess not enough." He admitted that the Labatt's group had the advantage because it had done the groundwork in trying to obtain the Giants.

The Labatt's group made its presentation, but before the vote was taken Solway encountered Milton Richman of United Press International. Richman told him that the vote would be 11–1. When Solway expressed surprise, Richman said, "I was talking to Charlie Finley last night, he sent his cousin Carl to the meeting, and when I asked him how it was going to be, he said, 'You know that room we're having the meeting in? There'll be a cop outside the door. You know what the cop's for? He's to make sure that those Labatt guys don't get out of the room until they pay their money.' He said, 'You, guys have so much money, do you think they're going to let you out of the room without taking the franchise?' "

Richman broke a number of stories in baseball and he was right on the money this time as well. The Labatt's group won 11–1. And it subsequently was discovered that Solway's theory was right, except that Hoffberger was left with only his own vote. But there was one more skirmish ahead.

The National League still wanted Toronto and asked Bowie Kuhn to intervene, arguing that the National League should expand to Washington and Toronto and the American League should find another city. Kuhn told the American League to consider its commitment to Washington and told the National League to decide on expansion. Two weeks later the National League met but could not reach a unanimous decision to expand, and no backers could be found for a team in Washington. Early in April, 1976, Toronto was officially in the American League East, with the Yankees, Orioles, Red Sox, Tigers, Brewers, and Indians.

Altogether, baseball's toughest division.

THE FLEDGLING TORONTO TEAM had a five-man board of directors, but no name. R. Howard Webster was chairman and Peter Hardy, then vice-chairman of the Labatt board, was vice-chairman. The board was completed by John Robarts, the former Ontario Premier, David Lewis, then senior vice-president of the Canadian Imperial Bank of Commerce, and McDougall.

From the start, the board decided to let the baseball people run the baseball team. It's a basic business principle: hire people who know what they are doing, let them do it, and make them accountable. Although it doesn't always happen that way in the grand old game, it did for this new team. The directors stayed in the background, but Hardy would quietly develop into a powerful force as the conscience of the team.

In 1976, Hardy would have been better known by the horseracing fraternity. His father used to race thoroughbreds, none of top class, on the old Ontario circuit. Hardy became a member of the Ontario Racing Commission in 1973 and its chairman in 1980, the same year he became chairman of John Labatt Limited. In 1982, he would become the chief executive officer of the Blue Jays; he left the racing commission in 1984.

Hardy is a man of small but authoritative stature. He has fluffy, thinning grey hair and a neatly trimmed full beard; he smokes expensive cigars. He has been associated with Labatt's since 1949. He is admittedly not a baseball fan, but says he likely would attend some games even if he were not connected with the team. Hardy may not be found poring over box scores every day, but he does understand the vagaries of sport. "I may have a better appreciation for this because of my horseracing experience, where people go out and buy yearlings for a million dollars and the son of a gun never gets to the racetrack, or he gets to the racetrack and can't run a lick."

In an age when George Steinbrenner's rampages make headlines, Hardy has patience and stays silent. If the team does poorly, he doesn't necessarily blame the manager. "All the field manager can do is do the best with the tools that he's been given by the general manager," Hardy says. "And all the general manager can do is the best he can with the allocation of funds by the board. So no one person is responsible."

Hardy believes in delegating responsibility. Once the board approves the operating plan, management has the authority to carry out the defined areas of responsibility with freedom.

"It's been my business experience, and certainly of the Labatt's company since I've been part of it, to have a philosophy of what we term participatory type management. That's really what we have here. Participation. You try to put the decision-making down as low as possible. Define the job functions and job responsibilities and authorities so people know what they can do and what is expected of them."

Hardy has dinners for the players at spring training and at the end of the season where he tells them the team's financial status. He and Beeston also will bring in players to answer any questions they have about the organization.

"It's the same as any company," Hardy said. "It's not you and us, it's we. And we're all part of the same thing with this organization, with the same objectives. If the organization enjoys success, then we're in a position to share our financial success. We share it with the people in the organization. Without the players, we haven't got a ball team. Without us, they've got no place to play. We're all one part of an organization. I guess what we try to strive for around here, and I think we've had some success, is when I became involved on a day-to-day basis, I started to realize that there's no security in the minds of people. Everybody was always looking over their shoulders, waiting for someone to take their jobs. I think around here, we've endeavoured within the organization to indicate to people that you have security here. You've

117

got a job to do, do it well, in a satisfactory way and you've got long-term security. That's true in any organization. We try to encourage people to look at it as if they have a career with the Blue Jays.

"Communications is another thing we've tried to improve and that's part of the reason of meeting with the players to let them know that as a partner, they're entitled to know, as any member of a company is, what's happening in the organization. We've never hesitated to call them in at the end of the year to tell them they've done a good job, we lost $800,000 or we made $300,000 this year. We've imparted that knowledge to them."

It is an unusual approach for baseball management. At first, when Hardy began telling them the team's financial status, some of the players were dubious.

"Some of them don't know because they haven't been with other organizations," said catcher Ernie Whitt. "But I think more and more are starting to feel that the concerns of Mr. Hardy are genuine and that he is really concerned about the players. But you are always going to have doubt among players; I don't care who you are. There are going to be certain players who do not believe management and that they are just out to stick you."

One thing the players don't have to worry about with Hardy is that he will become a media star like some owners. Just the opposite. Hardy does not enjoy having a high profile. He has turned down all requests to be interviewed on the Blue Jay telecasts for which Labatt's owns the rights. "I don't like the limelight," he said. "That's one part of baseball I don't like."

ONCE THE FRANCHISE HAD BEEN GRANTED on March 26, 1976, with opening day little more than a year away, the work of building the team could begin. First, it was necessary to assemble a staff to run it.

The first employee was Millie Figliano, who had worked at Labatt's. She had been secretary to the president of Labatt's Ontario and then had become the first female logistics manager in the plant. She handled the early secretarial duties for the new franchise. She was joined by the vice-president of administration, Paul Beeston, the unorthodox, 30-year-old accountant – long-haired, irreverent, cigar-smoking – who had actually made auditing fun and was bringing in new clients for his firm. (Beeston had thought he would be the financial man earlier, when the partnership apparently had purchased the San Francisco Giants.)

A friend of Beeston's, Peter Fowler, an orthopedic surgeon, lived beside McDougall in London, Ontario, and they'd sit around the pool talking sports. But it was Beeston's ''technical qualifications'' that prompted McDougall to offer him the job with the new franchise. ''Baseball's not exactly a big business as far as accounting is concerned,'' McDougall said. ''We had to have someone with some personality and some sense of getting things done. You didn't want someone who was spending all their time accounting.''

Beeston had been expected to become a partner in the accounting firm of Coopers and Lybrand, but that changed when Toronto got an American League team. On May 10, 1976, he took the new post, sharing a small office with Figliano at the Goodman & Goodman law offices, then at the Richmond-Adelaide Centre. There were two desks and Figliano's had a typewriter. There was a telephone, but no files. ''We had a lot of applications for all kinds of jobs, including hers and mine,'' Beeston said. ''But we had no name, we had no baseball people, we had no general manager – we were in a holding pattern.''

The next move was to hire a general manager and chief operating officer. Several candidates were suggested for the crucial posting. What was needed was an experienced executive with baseball savvy, someone who could kick-start the new franchise and ride it to major-leaguedom. On June 18, 1976, for better or worse, the owners of the infant team found their man.

His name was Peter Bavasi.

FIFTH

SELLING THE SIZZLE

PETER BAVASI'S TITLE was executive vice-president, general manager, and chief operating officer, a mouthful that reflected something of the diverse, open-ended nature of the job.

It reflected something of the man, too. Bavasi was only 34 years old, bright, ambitious, hard-working, and innovative. And handsome – perhaps a little *too* handsome. Newspaper writers invariably described his impeccably assembled wardrobe, his Gucci loafers, his styled hair, the southern California insouciance he could flick on like a lighter for a great first impression. Some swooned at his "model-perfect good looks."

He had a huge job, no doubt about it. He had to find and hire from a very small pool the most competent baseball people available. He needed a field manager who could work with a team as green as its artificial turf. He needed coaches, marketing specialists, public relations experts, ticket sellers, trainers, batboys, number crunchers, office secretaries, and all the others who toil in the wings of the game within the game. He needed enough good players that the team would not be an embarrassment on the field. He had to start the groundwork for a farm system, so that better players could be developed. He had to scout a warm locale for spring training. Uniforms had to be designed. Someone had to come up with a team name and a snappy team logo. Salary schedules had to be worked out. There were television and broadcast rights to be negotiated. And all the while, Bavasi had to convince the fans, the consumers, that a few hours watching the Blue Jays at play would be a worthwhile experience.

Bavasi was not the first choice for the job. Don McDougall of Labatt's wanted Frank Cashen, an executive with National Brewing in the United States who had been general manager of the Baltimore Orioles. McDougall had met Cashen when the Toronto group was trying to buy the Orioles.

"Cashen was clearly the presidential type," McDougall said. "We started with very much of a wish to get somebody to take it over. None of the board had any baseball experience. Probably the only guy who knew anything about baseball was Webster."

One difference between Cashen and Bavasi, McDougall recalled, was that Cashen had to be sold on the job, while Bavasi indicated early on that he was eager.

"Cashen, I still believe, would have been first class," McDougall said. "We were influenced by him being a person who had a good baseball background and good marketing experience because he had come up through the brewery. And he had beer experience, which we thought would be a bonus."

Cashen, a former sportswriter, decided against moving to Toronto. Eventually he became general manager of the New York Mets and rebuilt them into the 1986 World Series champions. He said one of the main reasons he did not come to the new franchise in Toronto was because he was still working for National Brewery, which had been taken over by Carling O'Keefe. He felt it wouldn't be right to leave them to work for Labatt's.

McDougall was not sorry that he was left with Bavasi: "I think he did a super job in terms of the first five years in keeping life and excitement, and I still think a lot of the values around the organization are the results of his doing – the marketing orientation, the emphasis on promotions, the emphasis on the place being neat and tidy and organized. I'm not saying he was an easy guy to work for, or that I would have liked to have worked for him."

Herb Solway, who remains one of the Blue Jay lawyers, talked frequently to Cashen while he was considering the job. He found Cashen's approach to the new team extremely cautious. While many people in the Blue Jay organization do not have fond memories of Bavasi, Solway thinks he was the better choice.

"Bavasi was very hard on the people that worked for him," Solway said. "I'm not sure that Frank Cashen, for the first three or four or five years, could have come close to doing what Bavasi did. In the long run, no doubt he would have done an excellent job. But Bavasi as a salesman, as a marketing guy – very articulate, very bright – did a very good job. Peter is a very, very charming guy, lots of fun. . . . and I don't think I have ever seen anybody that can work as hard as he can."

Another contender for the job was Bill Giles of the Philadelphia Phillies. He liked Toronto. He had been involved in the analysis of the stadium situation when the city was under consideration for a franchise and in the technicalities of pay television for baseball in the area. At the time of his interview, however, he was suffering from the flu. "They were picking my brain," he remembered years later, when he had become president and part-owner of the Phillies. "I told them I was interested and told them how I would operate it. Evidently, I didn't impress them that much. I was sweating, had a temperature of 104. Maybe the gods were looking out for me. I think I've got the best job in baseball now – well, no, I guess the best job in baseball would be president of the Dodgers."

McDougall said Giles was not hired because his experience had been mostly administrative, which was Paul Beeston's domain. McDougall wanted someone stronger on the baseball side of the business. "We didn't have a hard time deciding Bavasi was our second choice. We were looking for someone who could be compatible with something new in Toronto, be involved in the community, put together a marketing plan, and generate excitement and colour."

Bavasi was the youngest of the candidates, 16 years younger than Cashen, and he had had experience with an expansion team, in San Diego. Bavasi recalled his first meeting with McDougall, who had been delegated to find candidates; the board would make the final decision. Bavasi said he met McDougall on a Sunday morning in 1976 in a "splendiferous suite" at a hotel near the Los Angeles airport. At this initial meeting he was given a list of "qualifications or requirements" for the chief operating officer during the formative years. According to this list, Bavasi recalled, there should not be any name players and the franchise would be going through an image-development process. "The chief operating officer would have to act as, and I remember the term, 'the face' of the franchise." Bavasi liked to call himself "the point man," the one who digs and tussles in the corners and gets the job done but is never the hero.

"One of the up sides to that is if it's done right, you can develop your own people, do what you think is consistent with what the franchise should be on the long term," Bavasi said. "One of the down sides is that it's very difficult on you personally, and your family, because you're taking the blame and the responsibility and the hits. Any move you make you're criticized for. It can be wearisome."

For a time early in his tenure, Bavasi had a room at the Lord Simcoe Hotel, which happened to be owned by R. Howard Webster. Millie Figliano, who had been answering a flood of letters for season tickets and job applications, became Bavasi's secretary. The team had its modest quarters among law offices of Goodman & Goodman, around the corner and down the street from the Lord Simcoe in the Richmond-Adelaide Centre above a mall called The Esplanade. In the early days, the code word for the team's offices in the Goodman & Goodman complex was "Peter, Paul and Mary" for Bavasi, Beeston, and a receptionist who handled the telephones. The first time Bavasi entered these temporary quarters he opened his desk drawer and found two paperclips. Recalling the experience in his own dramatic fashion years later, he said, "That's all Metro Baseball Limited had. And I was thrilled. In that empty drawer were hopes and dreams and the future of a ball team that didn't even have a name."

BAVASI WAS BORN into baseball administration on October 31, 1942. His father E.J. (Buzzie) Bavasi, had been general manager of the Montreal Royals in the International League from 1947 to 1949, then he moved up to be general manager of the Brooklyn Dodgers in the days of Duke Snider, Roy Campanella, and Jackie Robinson.

The Dodgers' repeated World Series frustrations, until they finally won in 1955, helped turn a generation of baseball fans into Yankee haters. From 1947 to 1953, the Damn Yankees won six World Series, four times defeating the lovable Dodgers, often known simply as Dem Bums. Some might have envied Bavasi's easy access to one of the all-time glamour teams of baseball – the Brooklyn Dodgers Roger Kahn enshrined in his book *The Boys of Summer* – but Bavasi had known nothing else and always maintained it was nothing special. It was just his father's job.

Growing up under Buzzie Bavasi instilled in Peter a peculiar appreciation of the game within the game. "In our house, there was an ever-prevailing sense of the business of baseball," he said. "My interest always lay more in the operational part of baseball than in being a true fan. I was always more concerned with how a baseball club was put on the field, what was happening behind the scenes, rather than who was on first or what somebody's batting average was."

He had a friend whose father operated a supermarket: "I thought that was the most fascinating thing going. The checkers and the backroom and all that were really exciting to me."

The Bavasis moved to California in 1958 when Walter O'Malley abruptly pulled the Dodgers out of Ebbets Field and relocated them in Los Angeles, changing major-league baseball forever. After graduating from St. Mary's University in 1964, Peter became the business manager for the Dodger farm team in Albuquerque, then in the Double A Texas League, where the manager was Roy Hartsfield. Bavasi was so impressed with Hartsfield's approach to the game that he began to keep notes on strategy. "During the game he'd teach and talk to the players and tell them strategy and all that," Bavasi said. "When I would finish closing the ticket stands and before opening up the gates in the seventh inning, I would rush down to the runway leading to the dugout, pad and pencil in hand, poised for these pearls of wisdom that Hartsfield served up to his players. I became very impressed by Roy Hartsfield and rightfully so. I became very fond of him not only as a baseball man, but as a person. He was helpful to me in my first year out in helping me to understand the nuances of baseball – the difference between the run and hit and the hit and run, for instance – which I would log religiously on an index card and put away. I had 82 index cards, as a matter of fact."

He told Hartsfield that if he ever had a chance to run his own major-league team, he would hire him as his manager.

When Buzzie Bavasi moved to San Diego in 1968 to be part-owner and chief executive officer of the expansion Padres, he appointed Peter as director of the Padres' minor-league operations. There were ownership problems in San Diego and in 1974 the Padres nearly moved to Washington. That was when Ray Kroc, the McDonald's burger magnate, bought the team to keep it in San Diego. Kroc named Buzzie

Bavasi president of the Padres, and Peter became vice-president and general manager.

Kroc made a lasting impression on Peter. Soon after he arrived in Toronto, he talked about "selling the sight, sound, taste, touch and smells of major-league baseball." It was something Ray Kroc had taught him. "Ray always said to look at a product through the eyes of the consumer. He was a big fan of selling the sizzle if you don't have the steak ready. It works the same with baseball as it does with food."

That was the lexicon Bavasi was most comfortable with, and that was the way he responded to the business of baseball. He called the players "entertainers" and the team "the product," and baseball itself was often "the entertainment experience."

In Toronto, one of the first things Bavasi did was fulfil his old promise to Hartsfield, who was managing the Hawaii Islanders of the Triple A Pacific Coast League. Bavasi refrained from announcing the decision until September, 1976. "He said you're going to hear names like Yogi and Dick Williams and a few other guys who were in between jobs," said Hartsfield, who managed the Islanders to their second successive Pacific Coast League championship in 1976. "But he said, 'The job is yours.' And he even told me what he was going to pay me, so he says, 'You can't say anything about it until the end of the year.' "

It showed another side of Bavasi's personality. He could be loyal, but manipulative as hell. Even though he had virtually handed the field manager's job to Hartsfield early in the summer, at his introductory press conference in Toronto, Bavasi said he would not hire a manager before the end of the 1976 baseball season. He denied any decision had been made until the official announcement on September 22.

Another early Bavasi appointment was 31-year-old Howie Starkman, the director of public relations. Starkman had been director of public relations and administration for the NHL Maple Leafs but quit over a salary dispute. Bavasi interviewed him, then called him the next day to say the job was his for more money than he had been asking from the Leafs. Starkman represented the typical Toronto baseball fan who had grown up in the 1950s and 1960s listening to major-league games on radio, watching them on TV, sometimes catching one live at Tiger Stadium in Detroit or at Municipal Stadium in Cleveland but mostly climbing on streetcars to watch the Maple Leafs at Maple Leaf Stadium. Like thousands of others, Starkman grew up listening to Joe Crysdale and Hal Kelly do the play-by-play live from Maple Leaf Stadium and construct facsimiles of road games using recorded crowd noises at the CKEY studio in Toronto. Soon after he was hired, Starkman was helping with interviews and hiring people in the ticket and group sales area. Among those Starkman interviewed was Catherine Elwood, who is still with the team as the manager of employee compensation. Her husband, Norm, a projectionist at the CBC, was showing films in the tent the team set up to promote itself at the 1976 Canadian National Exhibition. She worked in a bank and Norm told Starkman she might be interested in working for the team.

Starkman would move his office, the group sales and ticket department, to a trailer next to Exhibition Stadium. About a dozen of them worked out of the trailer until February, 1977, when Starkman's Exhibition Stadium office was finally ready on the day before he was to leave for the opening of spring training.

Bavasi is remembered for his mercurial personality. He could shift in an instant from "Mr. Affable" to "Mr. Tense." The office staff found it eerie that Bavasi could be in a rage, yet as soon as a visitor arrived he could charm the stitches off a baseball. "But we had a lot of laughs here," Starkman said. "Bavasi could be fun at parties – he liked to play the drums. From an organizational point of view he did some excellent things. He had been in the business and he spoke well. He had a good mind. He was creative. Sometimes his emotions got away from him – he could be hard on people under him – but the next day he would invariably apologize."

With Beeston aboard, and Hartsfield, Starkman, and a skeletal office staff in place, Bavasi's next major move was to hire someone to assemble the players for Hartsfield to manage. This was a crucial position: the right person would guide the fortunes of the new team for the next decade, and beyond. The vice-president of player personnel would have to be someone who lived and breathed the game, who was exceptionally well connected in baseball, with the nerve of a riverboat gambler and the eye and instinct of a top-ranked scout.

Bavasi relied heavily on recommendations from Tal Smith, who had been with the Houston Astros, and Bob Fontaine, who became general manager of the Padres and was scout during Bavasi's time in San Diego. Both advised Bavasi that he could do no better than try for a former southpaw pitcher with an encyclopedic mind, a college graduate who had flirted with the idea of working for the Federal Bureau of Investigation.

Those were only a few of Pat Gillick's credentials.

AFTER TRYING to pitch his way to the major leagues and not getting beyond Triple A, Gillick worked as a scout for the Houston Astros. He stayed ten years, rising through the ranks to director of scouting. In Houston, Gillick aggressively pursued Canadian talent. The Astros had a higher profile in western Canada than did the Montreal Expos, then the only major-league team in Canada. The Astros signed hockey players Clarke Gillies and Bob Bourne, though the two stuck to hockey and eventually became stars with the New York Islanders. Gillick's persistence in scouring Canada for talent, however, made it possible for Wayne Morgan, then a scout with the Astros and now with the Blue Jays, to sign outfielder Terry Puhl of Melville, Saskatchewan, a consistent standout in the Astrodome since 1977.

Gord Lakey, who worked with Gillick in Houston (and who joined the Blue Jays late in 1985), remembers an afternoon early in the 1970s when he was scouting a college baseball game in a remote part of California. Gillick, in Houston, wanted Lakey to check out Lance Parrish, a high-school player in the area. In the sixth inning, a groundskeeper walked through the stands hollering for anyone named Gord Lakey. There was a long-distance call for him. The groundskeeper told Lakey to go to another field where he would find a small, wooden toolshed behind one of the school buildings. ''With classes out, that's the only phone on campus,'' the groundskeeper told a startled Lakey. ''I didn't think anyone but my wife knew the number but there's some guy named Gillick who has it and he's looking for you.''

In July, 1976, Bavasi knew Gillick was his man. From his room in the Lord Simcoe Hotel, he called Gillick, who was working for the New York Yankees.

''I'm on a mission,'' Bavasi said. ''Got an exciting opportunity here, do you want to join me?''

''Sounds good to me,'' Gillick replied.

Bavasi told him about the city and the fledgling franchise and Gillick asked if he could bring with him an administrative assistant named Elliott Wahle, who was 25.

''Great, you handle that,'' Bavasi said. ''When can you come?''

''My contract doesn't expire until the end of October,'' Gillick said.

''Great, the draft is the fifth of November.''

''Don't worry,'' Gillick said, ''we'll be set and ready to go.''

Gillick had already made a call to the new team, anyway. ''I called McDougall and left word and, of course, he didn't know who I was,'' Gillick recalled.

After Bavasi called him early in July, it took Gillick five or six weeks to free himself from the Yankees. George Steinbrenner didn't want to let Gillick out of his contract. He had told Gillick he would be the next Yankee general manager. "So I asked George to put it in writing," Gillick said. "He didn't feel like he wanted to. So I told him if he can't give me any guarantees, I would take a shot at this job."

Early in August, Steinbrenner allowed Gillick to leave. He joined the Jays on August 16.

Within four months, Bavasi had hired a staff of 32. One of them was George Holm, the ticket manager. Holm had worked in the ticket department of the Cincinnati Reds and then in the athletic department of the University of Cincinnati, where he was in charge of tickets, athletic promotions, concessions, souvenirs, and novelties.

Holm, from Waterloo, Iowa, read *Veeck as in Wreck*, the autobiography of Bill Veeck, the maverick owner of the Cleveland Indians, St. Louis Browns, and Chicago White Sox, in the summer of 1966. When he finished, he read it again. Baseball seemed like fun. So he began writing letters to baseball teams. Two years at the University of Northern Iowa convinced him accounting was not the job for him. He finally got an answer from the Reds requesting a résumé, which he had already sent. Then, after several weeks, he was phoned on New Year's Day to arrange an interview. He worked one year in the operations department "chasing janitors and that stuff" and then four years in the ticket department before moving to the University of Cincinnati.

Holm was in the athletic department at the university one afternoon in October, 1976, when he received a call from Bavasi, who told him that he had been recommended by Dick Wagner of the Reds. At first, Holm was reluctant. He finally agreed to go to Toronto for an interview, on the Thanksgiving weekend as it turned out. "I went there, I had no intention of taking the job," he said. "I was on the cab ride from the airport to downtown, it was just twilight time. By the time I got downtown, I knew I wanted to be in that city."

He married a Canadian from Port Colbourne.

Bavasi could be a stickler for detail, but irritatingly inconsistent. Holm had seven full-time employees in the ticket department then, barely enough to set up a ticket distribution system, handle season-ticket sales, and cope with day-to-day demands. (By 1986 the ticket department would have 13 full-time employees, another 19 on staff full-time during the summer, and another 30 part-timers.)

128

"We'd eat in Monday to Thursday, but on Friday we'd go out," Holm said. "After a couple of beers one Friday, I told them I was giving them each a $50-a-month raise. When I told Bavasi, he said no problem. All he told me was that Beeston signs the cheques." In the first year, when Holm needed a new $4,000 ticket machine he simply bought it and heard no more about it. Everyone reported to Bavasi in the first year. But that was supposed to change in subsequent years. The trouble was, it really didn't.

In 1979, the team's third year, when Holm went to St. Louis to attend a ticket managers' annual meeting, the hotel had been heavily booked and the only room available was a $120-a-night suite. Holm gulped, signed for the suite, and then worried all the way home that Bavasi would be furious.

He was, too.

"But it wasn't over the suite," Holm said. "It was over a $3.20 movie charge! He was *screaming*. He told me to go down to accounts and pay for it myself."

Bavasi made some enemies in the media in the early years. He once threatened to have columnist Christie Blatchford fired from *The Globe and Mail* for stories that were critical of him. He also tried to have *Toronto Sun* reporter Paul Palango fired for writing about a woman in the stands who had been hit by a ball. Bavasi could be cynical about the media, which he described as "the plural of mediocrity." In the early years he referred to Toronto baseball reporters as "the expansion press." He was obsessed with image, and the image he wanted his new Blue Jays to project was squeaky clean, mom-and-apple-pie. On the road there was a strict dress code: players had to wear blazers, grey slacks, and team ties. Jeans were not allowed.

Bavasi was caught by the press on this one – he was wearing "designer" jeans – at the first spring training. "I showed up in Vero Beach, having driven from some other business engagement across the state, about five hours," he said. "I had on a pair of khaki jeans of some sort and went into the clubhouse to change into my street clothes. I was seen. Why ruin a good story with facts?"

Players could not sport beards, moustaches, or long hair. The dress code edict flared into a major issue when *The Sun* carried a readership poll that asked: "Should the players be allowed to wear beards and long hair?" Bavasi suggested that the Blue Jay staff phone in to vote no. At first they thought he was joking, but on February 27, 1977, Bavasi dictated a memo to all staff:

> It would be appreciated if all staff members would call Sherry Johnson at *The Toronto Sun*, 360-8211, between 1:30 p.m. and 3 p.m. today in response to the inquiry of public opinion . . . which appeared on the second page of today's Sun.
> Unless you strongly feel otherwise, please state that you agree with Roy Hartsfield, that players do look better with short hair – clean, wholesome, etc. (family image), but that it would be okay during the off-season to have beards, long hair. . . .
> It might be well to refrain from stating that you work for the Blue Jays in responding.

The memo appeared in *The Globe and Mail* on April 30, 1977, with a story by Christie Blatchford about Bavasi's running of the office: sudden firings and resignations, she wrote, had left employees worried that they might be the next to go. "It's like any other business," Bavasi retorted when the story appeared. "I want results. My board wants results. We want aggressive young men and women . . . to work 24 hours a day, and those who choose not to can work somewhere else."

Ten years later, McDougall could be philosophical about it when asked how the board reacted. "The board people have seen very successful guys who have a lot of faults. Human error is not an unusual trait even in the most successful of people. And I think that was kind of the attitude we took. I don't think anybody saw it as affecting the ultimate image of the Blue Jays. It made things a little hot around here for him and for tough relationships with the press, but I kind of look upon those early stages as being relatively small prices to pay for some of the good things he did.

"Now you've got a different, more mature organization. They've got more qualified people. A lot of the people who were hired then are still here. They stayed with him for five years, including Beeston and Gillick. It's maybe more a credit to them than to him that they stayed."

BY THE END of Bavasi's first summer in Toronto, the new franchise had a name, the Blue Jays. It was a good name. The blue jay is related to the crow and the raven, has a raucous cry, likes to eat seeds and nuts – probably Crackerjacks, too, given a chance – and most ornithologists claim few of the birds winter in the northern ranges. Most travel south about the time the World Series ends.

From the beginning, the new franchise wanted public involvement – and got it. Entry forms for a name-the-team contest were regularly carried in the newspapers during June and July, 1976, to solicit as many entries as possible. The team name was selected from about 4,000 suggested in 30,000 entries. Among the suggested names were the Toronto Exhibitionists, the Bay Street Ballers, the Toronto Island Ferries, Toronto Lumberjacks, Towers, Beavers, Trilliums, Les Battes Bleus, Blue Sox, Blue Bats, Blue Shoes, and Blue Birds. The name "Blue Jays" was on 154 ballots. It became the official team name on August 12, not coincidentally the day team director John Robarts woke up to see a blue jay in his backyard. Board chairman R. Howard Webster thought of the blue jay as "strong, aggressive, inquisitive and it dares to take on all comers. It's down to earth, gutsy and good-looking."

The winner of the contest was Dr. William Mills of Etobicoke, who was rewarded with a pair of season tickets and a trip to spring training in Dunedin, Florida.

Not everyone was happy with the name. Some thought it lacked vitality and appeal, though nobody seemed unhappy with the other two major-league baseball teams named after birds, the Orioles and the Cardinals. There was speculation that the selection of Blue Jays was a clever marketing ploy, that the newspapers probably would shorten it to "Blues," which happened to be the plural form of Labatt's most popular beer. The newspapers chafed under any suggestion of manipulation and decided instead to shorten the name to "Jays."

The next order of business was to design a logo for the Blue Jays. "When I came to Toronto, people were calling me saying they wanted to license a T-shirt or caps or buttons," Bavasi said. "I didn't know what the hell licensing meant. . . . when you wanted to go fishing you got a licence. I called a friend in New York who was head of the LCA (Licencing Corporation of America), which is the biggest licensing agent in the world. He said he'd send a man up from New York to talk to me in the morning. When he said he'd send somebody up I knew there was money in it. We decided if these manufacturers who were coming to us were so interested in having our logo – that was when we didn't even have a name for the team, much less a logo – there must be something in it for us. We decided it was a percentage. The logo was the most important element in the whole merchandising-marketing mix."

Bavasi approached the graphic design firm of Savage Sloan Limited, which, he was told, was the biggest and the best corporate image firm in Canada. (Savage Sloan also created logos for Labatt's and for the Canadian Imperial Bank of Commerce.) Bavasi also felt that some of the best-designed corporate logos were Canadian.

"They came back with all sorts of designs," Bavasi said, "from the funny, almost a Woody Woodpecker cartoon, to the very artsy-craftsy type that was an Eskimo drawing of a thunderbird bursting or something."

Bavasi insisted that the logo graphic form "told our story – who we are, what we do, where we come from." In the end, the logo included the head of a blue jay, in dark and light blue, on a baseball with red stitching, with a red maple leaf near the bird's crest. "I got a lot of hooting and hollering by our Canadian staff," Bavasi said, "but I said watch, some day this ball club is going to be a great ball club and it's going to be very important. Symbolically we have to have the maple leaf in the logo."

There are dissenters on this point. People with the Blue Jays from the beginning say they can't remember laughing at the maple leaf. And some remember Bavasi saying that in five years the maple leaf would be dropped because by then people would know the Blue Jays and where they were from.

As a marketing man, Bavasi may have been inexperienced, probably a bit naive, but he proved to be a quick study. He soon realized it was crucial that the new logo get saturation coverage, that it must come to represent the Blue Jays as effectively as the pinstripes and stylized "NY" represent the Yankees, as the golden arches represent Ray Kroc's hamburgers. It would give the Blue Jays an immediate, recognizable identity, and it would help with ticket sales and negotiations for television and radio rights. There were all sorts of trinkets to sell, money to be made.

Bavasi figured, correctly, that the logo would be a hit with children, so he arranged a deal that made Irwin Toy the Blue Jays' licensing agent, manufacturer, and supplier. Irwin Toy had 26 salesmen in the field and could reach 2,500 retail outlets. In the first two years, Irwin Toy reportedly sold $13 million worth of Blue Jay items; the Blue Jays received 10 per cent of the wholesale price. "We didn't make a lot of money off the deal as it turned out," Bavasi said, "but what we did was have this widespread, walking billboard across the country." Bavasi played down his marketing expertise. "Marketing is selling, selling is hustling," he explained. "That's all it is."

Newspaper and magazine articles often mentioned that the Blue Jays' share of the Irwin Toy deal came to $1 million a year. Irwin Toy had exclusive rights for three years, which was extended to five before the deal ended. Despite the reports of the Blue Jays' inflated income from this source, the fact is the contract had a guarantee of $110,000 a year – and the club's revenue from Irwin never exceeded that.

However, even detractors concede that the marketing of the Blue Jay logo was a huge Bavasi success. Bavasi liked to boast about how many Blue Jay caps were sold: various figures appeared in the press, including an estimate of 2,500,000 caps in the first three years. But no one with the club could confirm the number and it seems Bavasi just pulled it out of nowhere. No matter, the logo could be found on myriad other items ranging from sweaters, jackets, and cushions to hotdog wrappers, frozen pizza packages, ponchos, pennants, baby bibs, and pencils.

It was such a success that Howard Cosell, the television commentator with a voice nearly as raucous as a blue jay in a barn, invited Bavasi to speak at his sports-law course at Yale University. "Peter lectured on how to merchandise an expansion team," Cosell once said on a visit to Toronto. "It was an incredible thing to watch what he did with the Blue Jay logo."

FROM THE BEGINNING, the Blue Jays stuck to sound business principles. The team hired experts and gave them room to operate. The business people interfered as little as possible with the baseball people, though the baseball people had to report to the board of directors. Peter Widdrington of Labatt's explained: "It's the same as any kind of management. You get the most capable people you can find and let them go to work, which means let them make mistakes. That's why there are erasers on pencils. It's not exactly a hands-off approach. We question and pursue things that should have happened and didn't, and we decide policy in terms of how many farm clubs we are going to have and why. We look at the budgets, the salaries. We don't negotiate individual salaries, but we sure as hell know how much they can spend. We leave it to them to work within that thing."

Bavasi knew from the start that the team was expected to be run as a business, not as a hobby for some well-heeled jock *manqué*. "It was not going to be a seat-of-the-pants operation," Bavasi said. "We took the lead from the ownership. It's a corporate ownership. From day one, it was expected that we would operate this franchise as a business. We produced annual operating plans, budgets, cash-flow forecasts, business plans, marketing plans, strategy plans, short-term, long-term, medium-term plans. It disciplined us."

Beeston, the vice-president in charge of the team's business details, agrees with Bavasi on how the operating plans, developed along the same line as any other Labatt's undertaking, brought order and discipline to the new operation. As for the plans, however, Beeston said no operating plan was devised until after the first year. "It was broken down into various areas – public relations, operations, finances, tickets, marketing, player development. There were one-year objectives, three-year objectives. The fact of the matter remains that while they were good, they weren't always used . . . we didn't keep pulling them out to see how we were meeting our objectives. What it boils down to is you can have all the objectives you want but it doesn't make any difference if you have a horseshit team on the field."

Bavasi took great pride in his plans, often labouring late into the night and sleeping on a couch in his office and showering in the washroom in the offices. He regarded his plans as "works of art" and "living documents." Even Beeston, who can detect horseshit in another area code, admitted Bavasi's plans were "masterpieces."

Most major-league teams did not operate this way. But after watching the success, on and off the field, of the teams that did – including the Blue Jays – others are imitating the system in the 1980s. "A lot of clubs are going to business technicians to develop their operations," Bavasi said. Bavasi implemented the same type of planning when he became president of the Cleveland Indians.

Soon after the Blue Jays started their fourth season – they finished dead last in each of the first three – Ewing Kauffman, owner of the Kansas City Royals, noticed something interesting happening in Toronto. "From a business point of view, Toronto has one of the best-managed teams in baseball," he said. "It's one of very few financially solid clubs." Kauffman gave most of the credit to Bavasi.

By sticking to sound but standard business principles, the Blue Jays have been able to cope with difficult financial situations. One of the most difficult was the state of the Canadian dollar, which was worth $1.04 U.S. in 1976 but dwindled to 72 cents, and often lower, by 1986.

Early in 1987 it had gone up to above 74 cents. Given the choice, Bavasi said he decided to take his salary from the Blue Jays in Canadian currency. "I felt I'm a smart guy, I know the Canadian dollar is trading higher, I didn't know the reasons why, I was naive to that extent," he said. "When we first started the club, while we recognized there was going to be an exchange rate implication in terms of managing, we never ever believed or even had a bad dream that the dollar would fall to the level it is currently."

All the Blue Jay front-office people in Toronto are paid in Canadian money. In Montreal, the Expo front-office staff are paid in U.S. funds. The players on Canadian teams are protected: the basic agreement says they are paid in the currency that is the higher, so if the Canadian dollar should leap ahead of its U.S. counterpart they would be paid in Canadian funds.

The Canadian dollar was not a problem at first, but the makeshift stadium that resulted from the conversation between Metro Chairman Paul Godfrey and Premier William Davis before the 1973 Grey Cup game has been a constant concern. Bavasi, on the stadium, was at his flim-flam best: "My job was to say this is a great park. You're close to the field of play, there are no pillars or posts. There was very little in the way of foul territory so you're on top of the action. The concession stands are close by, it's well staffed, it's clean, safe, and neat, blah, blah, blah.

"So it's cold, it doesn't have a cover to it and you get rained on, and it's tough to get in and out and there's limited parking. I never even addressed that because that was our home. People would say, well, what about a domed stadium? Well, if you don't have a domed stadium, there's no use talking about it, so you might as well flog the heck out of the place you're at. It's like your home. If you're inviting folks over you're not going to say this is a lousy place to live but it's the only thing I've got."

LEN BRAMSON, chairman of Telemedia Broadcast Systems, which has the radio rights for the Blue Jays, was in Daytona Beach in March, 1977, when he was told he should get over to Tampa. The American League was meeting to add a team in Toronto. "We owned the French radio rights for the Expos and we'd put together a radio network for both the English and French, even though we didn't own the English rights," he said.

Bramson knew one name, Ed Bradley, who worked for Labatt's. He found Bradley in the ice cream parlour at the hotel where the meeting was being held. "We don't have a team yet," Bradley said when Bramson asked about radio rights.

"You will have in an hour and a half," said Bramson, who had been in the advertising business in Montreal.

Once the franchise has been awarded, Bramson and Foster Hewitt, who, more famous for his hockey broadcasting, would also be involved in the venture, made a presentation. But they were told that nothing could be done on it until the Toronto club had the top man hired, who turned out to be Bavasi. Bramson made his presentation again. He had already talked to radio stations around the province and thought there was potential for a strong Ontario network. Bavasi was receptive.

Bramson then presented a five-year offer of $1 million to the board of directors, at $200,000 per year.

"When it was agreed upon that we could have the rights and we had to provide them a minimum of 14 stations and the Toronto station had to carry all the games, they came back and said they were going to give us a four-year contract for $1 million. At that time we were so anxious to get it, it didn't make a hell of a lot of difference. Then Bavasi said he didn't want $200,000 for the first year, but $150,000."

The four-year deal was split up $150,000, $200,000, $300,000, with the final year of the deal worth $350,000. What it meant, Bramson realized, is that the next contract would be negotiated starting from the final year's price.

In that first year, the network had 28 stations. By 1986 it was up to 54 stations. And the new four-year contract with the Blue Jays started at $850,000 and increased. Advertising, which started at $26,500 for one spot (advertisements are sold in 30-second segments) in every network game, has gone up to $65,000.

LABATT'S BOUGHT the television rights directly from the Blue Jays in the first year and then made an agreement with the CBC. The rights cost just under $1 million, a good sum for an expansion team..

"I was impressed with Bavasi when I first met him," says John Hudson, who was with the CBC then and now is director of media properties for Labatt's. "There was no question in my mind that he understood what had to be done and he obviously had a plan. On the negative side, he took the attitude that he was an American and knew baseball and was going to show Canadians how it's done."

Hudson remembers that Bavasi had some ideas about who should be the commentators and Hudson informed him that it would be the CBC's decision. Don Chevrier, who had done baseball in Edmonton and also some major-league games for an Ottawa station, was one. Hudson told Bavasi that he was the best play-by-play announcer in Canada and that, with the right baseball person, he would form part of a good team.

"Who do you think you're going to have as your colour guy?" Bavasi asked Hudson.

"I think I'll start with Tony Kubek," Hudson said.

Bavasi was shocked. "Tony Kubek!"

"Yeah."

"Do you think you can get him?" Bavasi asked.

"I won't know until we ask him," Hudson said.

Kubek, the former Yankee shortstop and one of the best baseball commentators for NBC, took the job, an instant injection of credibility for the new team.

Don Chevrier recalls that Kubek was to be introduced at spring training in 1977. When he reached the Blue Jays' spring training headquarters, the Ramada Inn Countryside in Clearwater, late the night before, there was no room available – the reservation hadn't been held. Kubek had to sleep in his rental car.

WHEN BAVASI THOUGHT he did something right, he was not one to hide it, and there were times it got him – and other executives – into hot water. At the end of the first season, he said that the Blue Jays had made a profit of $4 million, another instance, it seems, of Bavasi plucking a number out of the air. It has become generally accepted that the first-season profit was about $1.5 million, quite an accomplishment for a rookie season. But, of course, the salaries were low because there were no stars and there was only one farm team to support, not six.

Beeston exacerbated the matter in 1979 when he commented on Bavasi's $4 million figure to the *Professional Sports Journal*: "Anyone who quotes profits of a baseball club is missing the point. Under generally accepted accounting principles, I could turn a $4 million profit into a $2 million loss and I could get every national accounting firm to agree with me."

Beeston's remarks ended up in the *Congressional Record* during hearings into proposed U.S. legislation to be known as the Professional Sports Act of 1982. Beeston admitted later, "I really got it over that. But that was the result of Pete claiming we made a $4 million profit the first year. . . . One thing you don't want to do in this business is brag. Let other people, the ballplayers, take credit for the won-lost record. . . . Whether we make money or lose money, it's really no concern to anybody as long as we're continually providing good entertainment on the field.''

It did not take Bavasi long to realize that Toronto would work as a location for major-league baseball. The ''product'' (team) might be shaky for several years, but the ''entertainment experience'' (baseball) had long been entrenched and appreciated in the city. If not being in the National League meant losing a rivalry with Montreal, being in the American League meant developing fresh rivalries with New York, Boston, and especially Detroit. Because of its proximity to the Canadian border, Detroit had been a favourite visiting spot for Ontario fans before the birth of the Blue Jays. Early on, Bavasi was impressed by a report that Toronto ranked ''second or third'' in North America in terms of movie-going: this meant Torontonians liked going out and were willing to spend money on entertainment.

There was much speculation on the impact of major-league baseball on Toronto. Some was official speculation, done by experts, based on demographics and experience in other cities. For example, McDougall predicted in 1976 that a major-league team would pump $50 million into the city. This was based on a study conducted by William Schaffer of the College of Industrial Management of the Georgia Institute of Technology in Atlanta. Professor Schaffer had conducted economic studies of Atlanta's baseball and football teams and of the impact of the 1969 expansion Expos on Montreal. His study estimated that major-league baseball in Toronto would attract more than 400,000 people from outside the city who would spend $7 million on food, lodging, transportation, and services. Home fans would spend another $6 million at the stadium. Visiting teams and associated personnel would spend $1 million. Schaffer's study also forecast that the average fan in Toronto would be married, 30 per cent of them would be women, 30 per cent in the 18-to-29 age group, 16 per cent would have university degrees, and 30 per cent would have attended university.

Surprisingly, there is no known study on the actual impact of the Blue Jays on Toronto. Perhaps that is an indication of their success – no one needs to justify their presence.

After settling his family in Toronto and enrolling his children in Toronto schools, Bavasi also discovered that Canadians are a more patient folk than his fellow Americans, ideal fans for a slowly building, respectable team. "The U.S. media and ticket-buying public want to see things change immediately," Bavasi said. "If this doesn't work, do that. If that button doesn't work, push this button. Do this! Do that! Quick fixes. If the sports mentality of Canada was like it is in the United States – people are shot over high-school Friday-night football in the south – it would have been much more difficult."

He sensed something in the Canadian personality and Canadian business community – patience, tolerance, stability – that would accept some losing seasons while a farm system could be established, while better players could be scouted. He knew the best course for an expansion franchise was to develop its own players and not rely too heavily on free agents. "I know I've been accused of using American tactics, hell-bent for leather. But I found Canadian people to be more patient, more tolerant. . . . Early in the first year I asked Beeston, 'Why don't people here get uptight?' He said, 'Canadians just don't get uptight.' "

However, even Canadians would not put up with a loser forever. "I saw the honeymoon over after three years," Bavasi said. "You get into that fourth year and it's really hard slugging. By the fifth and sixth years, I was worn out physically and emotionally."

Bavasi actually never made it to the sixth season in Toronto. He could see it coming during the fifth year, the 1981 season, when the Blue Jays finished last again in both halves of the strike-shortened split season. "You could see it in their eyes," he said. "You know when it's coming down to closing time."

When it came, it came swiftly. Peter Hardy, the vice-chairman, chief executive officer, and *eminence grise* of the Blue Jays, told Bavasi, "It might be time for you to consider making a change."

"Does that mean I'm being fired?" Bavasi asked.

"No," Hardy said, "that's not what it means. We don't work that way."

Bavasi understood.

Key people in the organization were ready to quit because they could not work with Bavasi. Beeston had put in his resignation. Hardy, investigating why Beeston wanted to leave, found out the problems Bavasi was creating for the employees. Beeston was resigning not only for what was happening to him, but because of the treatment of others. Bavasi also had run-ins with Gillick. One involved hiring a new manager to replace Bob Mattick, who had guided the team on the field in 1980 and 1981. Although Mattick lacked managing experience, he was regarded as a good teacher for the young, developing players, many of whom he had scouted and signed and had watched mature in the minor leagues. The third manager would have to be someone who could lead the Blue Jays into contention. George Bamberger, formerly of the Milwaukee Brewers, was the first choice because he had been a pitching coach, but he decided instead to work for the New York Mets. Next choice was Bob Cox, a fierce competitor who had been fired by the Atlanta Braves. Gillick liked Cox, had known him when they were both in the Yankee system, and wanted him. Bavasi demurred. They argued.

"He's a friend of yours. That's why you want him," Bavasi told Gillick.

"The hell it is," Gillick shot back angrily. "He's the best guy around and if we don't hire him we're going to lose him."

They finally agreed Cox was the man, but Gillick would not speak to Bavasi for three days.

Bavasi had been made the Blue Jays' first and so far only president on November 24, 1977, after the first season that had at least been a grand success at the gate. Beeston became vice-president, business operations, and Gillick vice-president of baseball operations at the same time. Instead of delegating authority, Bavasi became a meddler. "Bavasi was like a government employee who thinks the easiest way to avoid getting into trouble is to say no," Gillick said. "You can't get your ass in a wringer if you say no, so anything you went to Bavasi for you'd have to fight him to make him say yes. It really got to be very tiring."

Bavasi's intransigence cost the Blue Jays the left-handed pitcher Ron Guidry. Even before the Blue Jays had played a game, Gillick was trying to convince the Yankees' Gabe Paul to take Bill Singer in exchange for Guidry. "Finally we got an agreement on it," Gillick said. But Bavasi didn't want to do it. "He said Singer was one of only a few recognizable names on the roster and from a marketing standpoint we needed the guy," Gillick said.

Gillick didn't think Bavasi's attitude was harmful to the development of the minor-league system, or the scouts. "They're pretty well insulated from a problem like that," Gillick said. "I think in the office it tended to pull everyone together, but we probably weren't as productive as we could have been. The thing about Bavasi is that he's a brilliant guy. You weren't dealing with a stupid guy."

But a perplexing guy. He might veto a trade, but then he would want to do something to create the impression of action. "Bavasi was always the marketing type guy," Gillick said. "And he would say, 'We've got to do something to make them believe we're doing something.' We've got to give them a sham, make it appear we're doing something. Quick fix. 'This will buy us 30 days,' or something like that."

In the winter of 1981, the Blue Jays were allegedly chasing "seriously" after Carlton Fisk, the free-agent catcher. It was a marketing quick fix, good for a headline or two. They really weren't.

Bavasi admitted he was getting on people's nerves. "I had done what they had hired me to do," he said. "Anybody who takes on a job like this is just kidding themselves if they think they are going to stay on for the long, long term . . . unless the guy is a great politician. I was a young guy. My idea was to wind myself up as tight as I could and hope that the spring would not give out until we got the thing completed."

The following Tuesday, November 24, 1981 – four years to the day that he had been promoted to club president – Bavasi arranged his own elaborate good-bye at a press conference at the Sheraton Centre.

That morning, he had set up chairs theatre style in the board room at the Blue Jay offices to explain to the office staff that he was leaving. He asked them if they would attend the press conference. There, Bavasi told the assembly, "The thrill is gone. For eighteen years I've been a snake-oil salesman for clubs, selling wares, broadcasting rights and licensing rights and advertising and blocks of tickets." He said he planned to use all he had learned during those years and go into business as a sports consultant. He thought there might be good opportunities for him in Florida. "I've played one side of the checker board this long, now I'll play the other side."

By coincidence, that same evening there had been a staff party planned for His Majesty's Feast, which some of the former employees attended. For some of them, Bavasi had been the cause of the departure. "It was a reunion party," said Judy Van Zutphen, Howie Starkman's secretary. "We'd planned it for about a month." It became more of a celebration, and the event was repeated for the next few years.

Several years later, Hardy talked about Bavasi's leavetaking. "I could tell you he was fired and I could justify it," he said. "I could tell you it was a mutual understanding and justify it. When this thing came up, the other directors were away or weren't available. It was left to me

141

to decide what the decision might be. Peter was affected by his drive for success and the pressures. He was never pressured by the board. I think the outside pressures, trying to field a contending team, just wore him down. Any of us would have had the same problem. We had pretty well determined to sit back and suffer with non-success for a long period of time. Peter was not the most patient person in the world.''

From his first interview for the job, Bavasi seemed obsessed with the idea of a five-year time limit. ''He said there had never been a president of a new franchise who lasted more than five years,'' McDougall said. ''He said, 'That's my time frame and I've got to know you'll probably be replacing me in five years and you'll probably be replacing the manager in two.' I think he had a fatalistic mentality about the thing.''

Bavasi probably said it best to Allen Abel, former sports columnist for *The Globe and Mail.* ''I left because of illness,'' Bavasi said. ''They were sick of me and I was sick of them.''

EARLY IN THE 1986 SEASON, on a warm, bright, Saturday afternoon, the Blue Jays were in Cleveland to play the Indians, one of the hottest stories in baseball. The Indians were winning games, and people actually were crowding into cavernous Cleveland (formerly Municipal) Stadium. The night before had been ''Citizens' Night'' and 61,340 fans cheered themselves hoarse watching the Indians defeat the Blue Jays 3–1.

For more than fifteen years the Indians had fielded lacklustre teams that looked all the more miserable in their enormous stadium. Cleveland Stadium is the largest stadium in baseball, with seats for 76,685, but on most nights – unless the Browns of the National Football League are playing–there are only a few thousand fans in the vast, drab expanse, shivering in the stiff winds off Lake Erie. And almost every game, it seems, there are two guys who show up in the bleachers and pound away on drums, making like tom-toms for the whole game.

It was not always such a lonely place. In the late 1940s and early 1950s Cleveland had some great teams and great players. The Indians made it to the World Series in 1948 and won; they made it again in 1954, and though they lost the Series they had won 111 games of a 154-game schedule, the most wins of any team in major-league base-ball history. Those were the days of the fastball of Bob Feller, who toiled with distinction for 18 seasons in Cleveland Stadium.

After a noisy Friday night gathering, there was a smaller crowd Saturday as Dave Stieb, so long the ace of the Jays but now struggling, took to the mound. Stieb quickly fell behind 4-0. Watching with mixed emotions from a private box at the stadium was Peter Bavasi, the newest president of the Indians. After leaving Toronto, Bavasi worked as a sports consultant in Tampa, representing such groups as the Pinellas Sports Authority, which planned to bring a major-league team to St. Petersburg. According to *Forbes Magazine*, Bavasi's income as a consultant was $325,000 a year.

Watching the game, satisfied with things in Cleveland, Bavasi reminisced about his days in Toronto. He often said "we" when talking about Stieb and Damaso Garcia and Lloyd Moseby and Jim Clancy and Garth Iorg and Ernie Whitt and Willie Upshaw and the newest bullpen hero, Mark Eichhorn.

While Bavasi was president of the Blue Jays, Stieb quickly established himself as one of the team's first true stars. He had started only 19 games in the minors and in 1979 leapt from Class A to Triple A to the majors, where his record was a respectable 8-8. Watching the game, Bavasi sympathized with Stieb, who was having a difficult time early in the 1986 season. With the Indians still ahead 5-3 – oops, a Chris Bando homer made it 6-3 – he could afford to be magnanimous.

"When we were really going bad in those early years, Stieb set a certain standard for himself," Bavasi said, keeping a close eye on the action and applauding Bando's home run. "That standard flowed down to the rest of the players. Too often in this game it's what-have-you-done-for-me-lately? When he came up to the big club, we didn't have the hitting, or the defence, or the relief pitching. It was Dave Stieb against the rest of the world. He set a very high standard for that ball club and for himself, and others on the team began to emulate him. He was hard on his teammates, but never harder than he was on himself. He'll work himself out of this. Most intense competitors find a way."

A foul ball sailed toward the stands, then bounced back onto the field, where the ballboy struggled for it with a fan. "Oh no," Bavasi said. "What kind of style is that? Give it to him!"

In the top of the fifth an error left two Blue Jays on base with one out. Bavasi talked about Clancy and Iorg and Whitt, the three originals. "We were all charter members of the firm," he said. A single loaded the bases. Bavasi said he gave a speech earlier in the week and kept saying the "Blue Jays" when he meant to refer to the Indians. Knuckleballer Phil Niekro, Cleveland's starting pitcher, was replaced by Jamie Easterly. A fielder's choice and the Indians' lead slipped to 6–4. Bavasi became expansive about what causes such dramatic turnabouts in the standings. "Here we are watching the Indians, in first place, against the Blue Jays, who won the American League East last year . . ."

George Bell dug in at the plate.

"Oh, oh. Good-bye, see you later," Bavasi erupted. "They go out fast when he hits them."

Bell had stroked a three-run homer, putting the Jays ahead 7–6. Bavasi's generous mood changed as mercurially as a tropical storm. As Easterly trudged off the mound to be replaced by another reliever, Bavasi switched to a new subject – long-term contracts.

"That guy Easterly, for instance," he said. "He's on a two-year contract, one of the few on our club. We've got only three with long-term contracts. What does he care? It's been this way all season. Pluntsing around. I'm not doing any more long-term contracts, fuck them. That's why this club plays pretty well, it's all year to year. That's why Toronto may have difficulty."

Bavasi had arrived in Cleveland a year and a half earlier all smiles and charm. In his second season, he was at the centre of a controversy: the press was on his tail again. First there was an article in the *Plain Dealer* on the Indians' debt of $11.5 million. There was no criticism of Bavasi in the article, which detailed the Indians' long-established practice of borrowing against future income. No matter, Bavasi bristled, claiming the reporter had obtained a financial statement and did not know how to handle it. The reporter, Russell Schneider, had obtained a financial statement on the Indians; he had also had it examined by an accountant.

A month after the Blue Jays' game, Schneider wrote another article, under the headline "Bavasi's charm wears thin." It reviewed criticisms of Bavasi since he came to Cleveland, which included his firing of long-time employees, closing the bleachers for night games, designing new uniforms that had no mention of Cleveland, not even the letter C on the cap, and ticket-selling snafus under a system Bavasi had introduced. Most extreme and damaging was an accusation that Bavasi was a double agent, alienating fans and undermining interest in the Indians in order to clear the way to relocate the franchise, probably in Florida.

In reply, he said the uniforms had been designed by the *players*. As for closing down the bleachers, he explained that on some nights fewer than twenty fans bought bleacher tickets, and the stadium seemed hugely empty. He said he had to do some housecleaning – firing – to get the team operating like a business. As for being a double agent, Bavasi said: "That accusation should have been made a year and a half ago when I came to Cleveland, because the club was in great peril then. It is hardly in peril now. We're playing well, drawing well, and we have capable ownership. If the club is sold, it will be sold to local owners. If my intention was to steal this franchise, would I have sold my house in Tampa and moved my family here? Would I have enrolled my daughter in school here?"

Bavasi had discovered that Schneider was digging for a series of stories about him. When Schneider asked for an interview, he was reluctant. Bavasi insisted that a third party from the paper be present. Columnist Bob Dolgan accompanied Schneider. According to Schneider, Bavasi tried to be intimidating throughout the interview, raising his voice. Schneider asked his final question – about whether he had been asked to leave Toronto because Beeston and Gillick would have left otherwise – and Bavasi began cursing and making threats. Bavasi reached for Schneider's tape recorder, but Schneider retained it. Schneider said that Bavasi threatened to call the police. Later, Bavasi came to the *Plain Dealer*'s office and engaged in a shouting and cursing match with the sports editor, Thom Greer. Schneider said he left before the conclusion of this exchange, which lasted about 45 minutes, but when the argument was over he was told that they went out for a drink. After Bavasi had resigned from the Indians in January, 1987, Bavasi came to Schneider and told him, "Let's bury the hatchet; let's be friends."

Bavasi's storming had not prevented the series from appearing. In one of the articles, former Blue Jay employees such as Ron Millichamp, a marketing man Bavasi hired and fired before opening day in 1977, and Millie Figliano, Bavasi's first secretary who also did not survive until opening day, were quoted on their former boss's deficiencies.

Actually, Figliano said Bavasi had made her assistant director of operations to Terry Barthelmas, now with the Cleveland Indians. Figliano said it was Barthelmas who fired her because "there was a personality conflict; the chemistry wasn't right." It was two weeks before opening day.

"Outsiders were all fooled by him," Figliano said of Bavasi. "There's a press conference on TV and there he was with this beautiful smile and kibitzing around and even after I got fired my own mother asked me, 'How could you not like that man?' I told her, 'It's easy, very easy.' "

IF THERE IS a bottom line to the Bavasi story – business stories always love bottom lines – it is that he might well have been the right man in Toronto at the right time; he also left at the right time. The style that might have worked in the early going to attract attention to the new franchise was beginning to hold it back. That he made an impact on the new club cannot be denied. More than five years after his leaving, he still remains a somewhat controversial figure in the club's lore, still talked about.

Bavasi also demonstrated that he was no dud when it came to some of the finer points of the game. He had always stressed the importance of scouting, of building a team from the ground up the way the Dodgers and most other great teams had. Bavasi's shrewdest baseball move was bringing in Pat Gillick, the most scout-oriented general manager in baseball. From being "nuisance opponents" in the late 1970s, the Blue Jays grew into one of the most formidable teams in major-league baseball.

Before he was fired in the autumn of 1981, Bavasi had coined a new slogan for 1982. It was "The New Jays." He had it printed on the team stationery, but after his awkward leavetaking the slogan was junked and the stationery was used for scrap. Yet, with Bavasi gone and Bob Cox aboard, and with Gillick and Beeston at the helm, the slogan would have been just about perfect.

S I X T H

THEY CALL US
THE KGB

AT 3 A.M. THE TELEPHONE RANG in Epy Guerrero's house. Guerrero is the scout on whom the Blue Jays rely for their top Hispanic prospects in the hot, tropical fields of the Caribbean. He lives in Santo Domingo, capital of the Dominican Republic. Over the years, with the Houston Astros, the New York Yankees, and now the Blue Jays, he has had uncanny success, discovering such players as Cesar Cedeno, Damaso Garcia, and Tony Fernandez – and others ripening on the minor-league vine.

Guerrero roused himself, pushed open his eyes, and reached for the telephone. It was Pat Gillick calling from Toronto.

"Did I wake you?" Gillick asked.

"No," Guerrero said, "I was waiting for your call."

ANY TIME, day or night, Gillick telephones – New York or San Francisco or Santo Domingo. Driving home late at night he might stop and talk for half an hour from a lighted telephone booth on the shoulder of a highway, or from a service station. Reporters from smaller centres in both Canada and the United States, places that don't have major-league teams, have expressed surprise and pleasure that he has taken time to return their calls. Gillick estimates that he spends from $40,000 to $50,000 a year on telephone calls. "He's got a disease called telephonitis," says Gabe Paul, Gillick's boss when they were with the Yankees. Paul once told Gillick that baseball executives should be accessible, and Gillick's telephone numbers are always listed in the phone book, for both his Mississauga home near Metropolitan Toronto and his Dunedin Beach condominium in Florida.

It is not idle chatter. There are trade talks, contract negotiations with player agents, questions from the press, the plotting of scouting strategy. Most teams have a director of scouting in their front office, but Gillick acts as his own, creating one less bureaucratic layer. He understands scouts (yes, there have been some scouting directors who have not done much scouting themselves); he listens to his scouts; he seeks their opinion in the decision-making process, and that is not always the case in some baseball organizations. Sometimes he'll check out prospects himself. He has not forgotten his beginnings in baseball management; he retains a firm belief in scouting's importance. And the Blue Jays scout aggressively and imaginatively wherever baseball is played.

"Scouts are really the backbone of an organization," Gillick says. "If you've got a good one, you'd better hold on to him."

"There is no substitute for a good scouting staff," says Lou Gorman of the Red Sox. "Nobody, including Branch Rickey and Frank Lane, or anyone else who has been considered a genius in this game, can function without a good scouting staff. You've got to have people who know the game well and can help you find and develop talent."

Gillick believes that, but he also keeps himself involved in the process. On New Year's Day, 1986, Gillick was in Puerto Rico with Epy Guerrero and together they worked out some prospects. One player in which they were particularly interested eventually signed with another team. But Guerrero remembers it for another reason. "He asked me if I think he lost some aggressiveness," Guerrero said. "On January 1, he made me fly from Santo Domingo to Puerto Rico for scouting and we worked so hard going all over the island looking for players – and we found one. And he's asking me if he's lost any aggressiveness?"

GILLICK IS BRIGHT and inquisitive, moody and emotional. At first glance, he looks a little too refined, a little too sensitive – an effect heightened by incredibly long eyelashes – to be a career baseball man, unless perhaps as the team treasurer. He has a round face; his thinning hair is carefully combed. On duty he likes to wear a droopy cowboy hat, a Shady Brady he bought in Lakeland, Florida, and cowboy boots, which he often swings onto a convenient desk or table.

A master of the conversational non sequitur, he frequently interrupts a rambling discourse on baseball strategy or fiscal policy to inquire about some unresolved issue. One morning during spring training in the Blue Jays' trailer at Dunedin, he spoke at length to Martin O'Malley, a Toronto writer, about the art of drafting. At one point, Gillick swung his boots off the table in the trailer office, hunched forward, and said, "Martin, I can never get this straight – who came first, Plato or Socrates? And did one actually teach the other?" O'Malley had no reply.

Gillick's parents split up when he was less than a year old. During the early thirties, his father, Larry, pitched for Sacramento in the Pacific Coast League; he was an average pitcher who, Gillick says, had little influence on his own athletic endeavours. A Marine in the Second World War, Larry had a 40-year career in law enforcement, retiring as sheriff of Butte County in California a few years ago. Gillick's mother was an actress in silent movies. "When they got into speaking, things didn't work out for her," he said. He lived with his mother, his grandparents, and a great aunt in Los Angeles. He was eight or nine years old when his mother remarried; he remained with his grandparents. He attended military school from grade 4 to grade 11, then attended Notre Dame High School in Sherman Oaks, where he played baseball and football. On the football team, he snapped the ball for quarterback Bob Beathard, later the general manager of the Washington Redskins of the National Football League. Gillick's grandfather died when he was 14, so he spent his high school years with his grandmother and great aunt.

Gillick graduated from high school when he was 16 and graduated from the University of Southern California, with a bachelor of science degree in business, when he was 20. In college, he excelled in and enjoyed business and finance subjects. A 1985 story in *Sports Illustrated* said that Gillick's IQ was 169. "I read it, but I don't know where they got it," he said.

His memory is the stuff of legend, earning him the nickname "Wolley Segap" ("yellow pages" spelled backwards) because of his recall of telephone numbers. Although Gillick says the memory is not so keen as it used to be, it would be hard to convince *Globe and Mail* columnist

Trent Frayne. At a Blue Jay spring training game in West Palm Beach (eventually rained out), Frayne needed to reach Bobby Doerr, the former Boston Red Sox second baseman. Doerr had worked as the Blue Jays' batting instructor and had just been named to the Hall of Fame. Frayne tried Howie Starkman, who didn't have Doerr's number with him but suggested he try Gillick. Frayne found Gillick sitting in the stands next to broadcaster Curt Gowdy. Gillick recited Doerr's home number, and added a second number in case Doerr wasn't home.

Gillick says he developed his memory while in military school, learning the various regulations. "If you were on guard duty," he said, "one of the officers would come up and ask what was the fifth rule on guard duty and you'd have to rattle it off – 'TO WALK MY POST IN AN ORDERLY MANNER KEEPING ON THE ALERT blah blah blah . . . . . SIR!' " He also found that in the peculiar rhythm of baseball there was lots of off-time for reading and digesting odd bits of information that might prove useful later. The yellow pages of the telephone book interested him because they helped him find out something about the business of a city.

Despite his academic credentials and class-treasurer demeanour, Gillick nearly made it to the major leagues as a left-handed pitcher. In sports he was a late bloomer, not showing much promise until his late teens. Instead of going directly to university from high school, he attended junior college on a partial baseball scholarship. After junior college he had more scholarship offers, including ones from UCLA and Washington State. He chose the University of Southern California, where he played for the Trojan's famed baseball coach, Rod Dedeaux. The team won the College World Series in 1958.

Gillick did not sign a professional baseball contract when he finished university because he intended to go to law school in order to join the FBI. In the summer of 1958 he played semipro in Edmonton. "If you were going into the FBI, you were looked more favourably upon if you had a law degree," he said. "I had an opportunity to go to law school in Los Angeles, at Loyola University Law School, and then all of a sudden, when I came back from Canada at the end of the summer in 1958, a guy approached me about signing a contract. I thought, hell, I'm 20 years old and if I'm not going to do it now I'm never going to do it. So I signed the contract."

Gillick wanted to study law during the baseball off-season of 1958–59, but the law school would not take him on a semester basis. So he decided to work toward a Master's degree in business, playing some winter baseball and pitching professionally in the summers. He had a wicked curveball, a reliable fastball, a changeup, and good control. He gave himself five years to make the majors. In his second professional season, in Class B at Fox Cities, he was 11–2 with an ERA of 1.91, before being promoted to Triple A in Vancouver. The next three years he played in Elmira (Class A), Little Rock (Double A), and Rochester (Triple A). His career minor-league record was 45–32, ERA 3.42. Twice in the minors he played under Earl Weaver, who became manager of the Orioles. Cal Ripken, who took over from Weaver as the Oriole manager in 1987, was a catcher for Gillick for one season and remembers him as intelligent, with a big leaguer's pitching ability.

Weaver says that Gillick had a major-league curveball. "He was a hard worker and loved to study the game. His fastball wasn't a Nolan Ryan fastball or a Jim Palmer fastball. We didn't have the radar gun then, but I'd say he threw as hard as Dave McNally or Scott McGregor. He threw that hard."

One thing that puzzled Weaver was Gillick's stubborn refusal to learn to throw the slider. Years later, Gillick explained: "Sometimes if you have a real good curve, it takes away from it if you start throwing the slider. I'd rather have one good pitch than two lousy ones."

Gillick's voracious appetite for baseball knowledge impressed Weaver. "He had a lot of nervous energy," Weaver said. "He wanted to know *everything* that was going on in baseball, in every league – and there were a lot of leagues back then. He'd be the guy who was first to get *The Sporting News* and wanted to pass all the information on to everybody. If anybody knew something before him, he got a little disturbed."

In 1963, when five years had passed and he had not made it to the majors, the 26-year-old Gillick, who had pitched through some pain in his arm, decided to try something else. Weaver still felt he might have made the majors and had submitted his name to the Orioles as a chance prospect. Gillick considered going back to school or getting a non-playing job in baseball. The possibility of a job with the Orioles was suggested by their general manager, Harry Dalton, but while Gillick waited for an answer he received an offer to scout for Houston. Gillick had known Eddie Robinson as a batting instructor and Paul Richards as a manager for the Orioles. They had moved to Houston to work for the expansion franchise. Gillick was reluctant, but just when he had decided to go back to school, Robinson called from Houston and asked, "Why don't you give it a shot for a year and see if you like it?"

Gillick, still single, agreed to give it a try. He stayed 10 years, rising to director of scouting. From Houston he went to New York to work for the Yankees, and from New York he went to Toronto to breathe life into the expansion Blue Jays, where his background in judging playing talent would serve him well.

Gillick's tenure in Toronto coincided with baseball's emergence as more of a business and less a toy for wealthy entrepreneurs happy to buy their way into the glory and the smell of sports. The decade from 1976 to 1986 brought free agents, salary arbitration (actually begun in 1973), escalating salaries, multi-year contracts, player agents, deferred compensation, guaranteed contracts, incentive clauses, and player strikes. For a time the pendulum swung heavily to the players' side, as they wrung concessions from team owners and salaries topping $1 million a year. By the mid-1980s the pendulum began to swing back to the owners' side, provoking complaints from players and agents of retrenchment, conspiracy, and collusion.

The job of baseball general manager has become immensely more complicated. Lou Gorman, general manager of the Boston Red Sox, described a baseball general manager as having "the worst job in baseball today, bar none. You negotiate contracts, make major player decisions, handle the trades. It has become the most difficult, most complex, and most multifaceted job in the game today."

Gillick, one of the new-breed general managers, thrives on the pressures, complications, and caterwauling. The difficulties seem a satisfying creative outlet. His wife Doris says he often appears to be in a better mood when things are going badly for the team and seems worried when things are going well.

Tom Grieve, the young general manager of the Texas Rangers, sees Gillick as a role model. "I've learned from a lot of good people over the years – Whitey Herzog, Billy Martin, Joe Klein," Grieve said. "But I think the prototype for the way an organization should be run is Toronto, and the reason is Pat Gillick."

Gillick is a creative general manager. He marches to his own drum, which sometimes ruffles less imaginative baseball executives. He believes in innovative scouting, using some of the wily techniques of the old days before the annual drafts that now bring in busloads of fresh-faced prospects looking like new arrivals at a summer camp – all checked out, new undershorts, no cavities.

On free agency, which many owners and general managers feel obligated to rail against, Gillick believes that no matter how difficult it makes his job, it has been good for the game by doing away with baseball dynasties such as the old Murderers-Row Yankees. "I think free agency is good," he says, "but there has to be some restrictions on it so it won't put financially strapped clubs out of business."

On expansion teams: "It's good for the league, good for everyone. But I think we should try to make the players and teams as competitive as possible as soon as possible. I'd like to reduce the number of players under control. We have 40 now on major-league rosters, but I'd like to reduce it to 35."

On long-term contracts: "Fans would get a better product if we went to one-year contracts. Fans would get more for their money. You'd probably get a better product, and you'd get it at cheaper dollars."

YOUNG PLAYERS are the raw material of a major-league baseball club. A steady stream of talent rising through the minor-league system sustains the major-league team. When the flow is interrupted, performance at the major-league level suffers; when the top team suffers, the entire organization suffers. Attendance drops, radio and television ratings go down, revenue shrinks. What sustains the flow and replenishes the complex support system is good scouting.

Pat Gillick learned early on that the cheapest dollars in baseball are spent on scouting and developing players. The Blue Jays' owners accepted this as a given from the start. Gillick also learned during the heyday of free agents that a successful team cannot necessarily be bought. The teams that buy might fly high for a year or two, but tend to drop from sight. Teams can buy spare parts, sometimes a vital cog; but many players, when they become free agents, are at their physical peak and usually showing the first subtle signs of decline. The nucleus of a team must be developed and nurtured through the farm system, supplemented by acquisitions. One problem Gillick finds with signing the top-rank free agents is that it means surrendering a No. 1 draft choice. Give away enough draft choices and you may be giving away a team's future.

The analogy might not be perfect, but Gillick says scouting and player development are comparable to research and development for a business. He feels that the money is well spent if the organization is constantly restocked with good young players and, every once in a while, with players of a quality that cannot be bought, such as a Tony Fernandez. There can be safety in numbers, too. One high-profile free agent could cost a million dollars a season, almost half the scouting budget, and might well be a flop or provide only short-term benefits. Besides, to stock a 24- or 25-man roster with high-priced free agents would put the payroll beyond the resources of the team. Homegrown players come more cheaply initially and must play in the majors for three years before they are eligible for arbitration, which is the first time the player has any real bargaining leverage. There is value in having players who have come up through the team's system and know what is expected of them. This process also allows the team to thoroughly know its players.

The first amateur draft was held in 1965 with the intention of keeping bonus payments down by restricting the prospects' negotiating power, leaving them with one team with which to bargain. It changed scouting, as well. Before the draft, a scout could be compared to a travelling salesman. After finding a prospect, the scout would have to sell himself to the player and his family to sign him. And there might be several other scouts doing the same thing.

Mel Queen, now a minor-league pitching instructor with the Blue Jays, was signed for an $87,000 bonus for the Cincinnati Reds by Bob Mattick in 1960. Queen was a shortstop when Mattick scouted him but played third base, outfield, and finally pitcher in the major leagues. "He established a real good rapport," Queen said. "There was no draft so there was a real knack to scouting; you got the player to know you and believe you were really interested in him. Bobby was great at that. Whoever Bobby scouted for I probably would have signed with that team because of him."

With the coming of the draft a scout's job now entailed selling the prospect to the organization, to get the club to consider the player as a draft choice. The process would become more bureaucratic with other scouts, cross-checkers, also looking at a top prospect. It became more difficult for a scout to home in on a few prospects because, come draft day, his team might find the player taken when its turn came to select.

Kevin Kerrane, in his book about scouting, *Dollar Sign on the Muscle,* wrote: "A scout's primary job now would be to give advice without making decisions – the way an investment analyst might pass along opinion on new properties that the corporation might or might not be able to acquire. Then the scout would try to sign draftees by persuading them that the club's offer was preferable to college or to waiting . . . until the next draft, when another club could similarly constrain them."

If business analogies are to be used, Gord Lakey, a scout for the Blue Jays, suggests that a scout could be compared with a stockbroker "who can actually go out and do something for a client and see whether it's a win or lose situation. There's a certain amount of risk taken in a stock brokerage and a certain amount taken in scouting."

With the Blue Jays, scouting remains an area where there is room for individuality. "Pat gives a scout a lot of leeway," Lakey said.

"When you're out in the field, you get to meet people from 25 other organizations almost every other day," says eastern regional scouting director Bob Engle. "People talk a lot about the industry and it seems like we are given more freedom to express ourselves and I think the organization realizes what's going on out here in the field."

There is room for individualism on the scouting staff because Gillick believes in exploring all available sources of talent, not relying solely on trades or the amateur draft or free agents. The Blue Jays are strong in Latin America, particularly in the Dominican Republic because of Epy Guerrero, whom Gillick met when he was with the Astros. With no draft in Latin America, more of the old-style techniques can be used. The Blue Jays have exploited the Rule 5 draft, which makes available players who have three years in the pros and are not on a team's 40-man roster at the December deadline. Their success in this draft has been a result of meticulous scouting, and that success has affected the way some teams draw up their rosters. In fact, the Blue Jays are better known for their picks in this draft and their signings in Latin America than they are for their top picks in the June draft, although they have had some spectacular results with lower draft choices.

"You've got to explore every avenue to develop a club," Gillick says. "If you just concentrate on the amateur draft in June and you don't do well there, it's really a crap shoot. If you concentrate on just trades or the free agents, you're in trouble. You have to be able to use the amateur draft, the Rule 5 draft, trades, and free agency. And you have to use Latin America. Some clubs have a preponderance of white players, but if you decide what colour your team's supposed to be you're limiting yourself. You have to use all the tools available. If you don't, you're short-changing your employer and you're short-changing the fans."

GORD LAKEY WORKED as a scout with Gillick in Houston and joined the Blue Jays in 1985. He remembers how aggressively Gillick pursued talent, how he would charge off to any corner of the continent if he thought he could find some rawboned kid with major-league talent. "Pat's going to be the first guy to go to the moon looking for players," Lakey said.

Bill Giles, now Philadelphia Phillies president and part-owner, was working for the Astros when Gillick signed on. If Giles had been successful in landing the Toronto job that went to Bavasi, Gillick would not have been his choice as general manager. Giles's first impression of Gillick was that he was a bit odd in his thinking. He would not elaborate, but added, "I wasn't too high on him at the time, I remember. But over the past four or five years, I've really come to like Pat. He had theories which, I don't know if they were right or wrong, but they were different. He still is a bit different. . . ."

When Lakey and Gillick worked for the Astros, they did considerable scouting in Canada as part of this philosophy of searching for talent in all areas. "There were some camps where we had only five people show up," Lakey said. "If there was a kid in Canada who aspired to be a ballplayer, he knew the Houston Astros would be close enough so he could attend a tryout camp. We had a kid from the Northwest Territories at one camp."

On the way to Peace River, Alberta, Gillick and Lakey stopped at a garbage dump late one night because they had heard a bear was on the prowl. They waited, but the bear didn't show. They shrugged and went on their way. The bear probably couldn't hit the slider anyway.

There was the expedition to Okotoks, Alberta, a rural community just south of Calgary that is so small it often is omitted from maps of the province. Gillick and Lakey were working with scouts Epy Guerrero and John Jemison. They had heard of a strong young man who might have a major-league arm. The four scouts drove to the boy's home; his mother told them he was working as a carpenter for the summer and was fixing the roof of a barn down the road. The scouts pulled up at the barn, shouted hello to the boy working on the roof, and said they would like to watch him throw some baseballs.

"It was a little muddy and we didn't even have a catcher's mitt," Lakey said. "We got the kid to throw inside the barn he was working on. Epy used a fielder's glove, which he stuffed with some insulation he found on the floor of the barn. And the kid's throwing *bullets*."

The four scouts were impressed enough that Gillick decided they would watch the boy pitch in a game scheduled for Sunday afternoon in

Okotoks. On the day of the game, Gillick did the driving – he is an impatient driver – and as they neared the playing field he got lost and kept complaining he couldn't see anything.

"I don't know about the field, Pat," Jemison shouted from the back seat, "but I think you just ran over second base."

"We were in the middle of the ballpark," Lakey said. "It was just an open field."

They watched the young pitcher but decided not to sign him. He was not as impressive in the game as he had been in the barn two days earlier.

IN SEPTEMBER, 1974, Gillick moved to New York, where he joined the Yankees as co-ordinator of scouting and player development. There he met Elliott Wahle, an accountant who was born in The Bronx, grew up in New York City, and was a staunch Yankee fan. Wahle worked for nine months as an auditor but decided it would be more fun to try the business of baseball. He got on with the Yankees, he says, "by being a pest." He was 23.

"The Yankees had been taken over by George Steinbrenner in the early 1970s and he had made a number of moves to dramatically change the franchise," Wahle said. "Steinbrenner brought in Gabe Paul as president. Paul brought in Tal Smith from Houston as executive vice-president. When I saw Tal's name in the newspaper I decided to write him a cold letter. He wrote back and asked me to give him a call. When I called him, he said there were no jobs available but to try some of the other clubs."

Wahle wrote to all the clubs Smith mentioned but received negative answers or no answers at all. He called Smith again and told him nothing happened, so Smith agreed to meet him. He handed Wahle the Blue Book, baseball's bible, setting out all the rules and regulations governing a baseball organization.

"Only a few people in baseball really understand the rules," Smith told Wahle. "Learn this and let's see where it goes."

Two months later, Wahle sprained his ankle and stayed home from work one day to recuperate. As it turned out, Smith only had Wahle's home number and he chose that day to call.

"Are you still interested in working for the Yankees?" Smith asked.

"Very much," Wahle said.

Smith met Wahle and his wife for dinner and hired him. He warned

Wahle that he would face some resentment as an outsider and that he should be a good listener and should refrain from offering opinions on player evaluation.

Wahle was most impressed with Gillick, whom Smith had brought in from Houston. "We became very close, very quickly," Wahle said. "One of Pat's greatest skills is that he makes sure everybody participates in decisions. He puts people at ease and he's probably the best information-gatherer I've ever met. And he's loyal to his people."

Gillick is a scout's general manager. Six or eight of the general managers may fit that category. Among them are Al Campanis of the Los Angeles Dodgers, John Schuerholz of the Kansas City Royals, Lou Gorman of the Boston Red Sox, Dallas Green of the Chicago Cubs, and Bill Bergesch of the Cincinnati Reds.

Gillick co-ordinates the scouting and makes the final decisions. The scouts who pursue the amateur free agents report to the team's two regional scouting directors, Bob Engle in the East and Wayne Morgan in the West; they report to Gillick.

Gillick deals directly with the major-league scouts: Al LaMacchia, who covers the National League; Gord Lakey, who covers the American League; and Moose Johnson, who covers both the free-agent amateurs and the major leagues. Advance scout Dave Yoakum reports mostly to manager Jimy Williams.

DAVE YOAKUM is boyish looking, with blond hair in a youthful cut and casual dress; he looks as if he should be on the Professional Golfers' Association tour.

He seldom sees the results of his assessments or if they were of any use, though he might get a clue from the box scores. Once he relays his information to Jimy Williams, he is usually on to the next city scouting the upcoming Blue Jay opponent. Sitting behind home plate with a pencil and chart, he tries to assess how to pitch to a batter, where to play him in the field, what to look for in a pitcher. He also keeps the manager updated on injuries and what plays an opposing manager is favouring – any little thing that can help the Blue Jays' manager and his coaches. Yoakum carries a lap-top computer – like those that newspaper reporters favour – for updating scouting reports; he sends the printout to Williams. "I used to carry a typewriter. I'd make some minor changes on a guy and I'd have to retype the entire report," Yoakum said.

In 1987, the other scouts also were being equipped with lap-top computers so they could file reports through a modem to the office instead of dictating them. With the capability of the office to receive these transmissions, Yoakum should be saved some problems, at least when the Blue Jays are at home.

Usually, Yoakum will try to send his reports to Williams by Federal Express. "But most often it seems like I've had to put it on the plane physically and have someone pick it up at the airport," he said. "The problem we've run into in the past is that when it goes into Toronto it has to clear customs and if it's a 1:30 game time, sometimes it won't clear customs until two o'clock, so we'd have to go over the entire club by telephone." Yoakum backs up his report with a phone call anyway.

"It's exciting when you do get to see a Blue Jays' game on television, or if I do stay over to watch a game," he said. "Most times it's like being a photographer taking pictures but never getting to see the print. There's so many things involved; there's interpretation. I might say you can pitch a guy a certain way and get him with breaking stuff, but our pitcher that night might not have a good breaking ball. That's part of the job of the manager to interpret the information I give him for the particular case involved."

Usually, by a quirk of the schedule, Yoakum will see one team more than the others. In 1986, it was the American League East champion Red Sox. He saw them play 35 times, including Roger Clemens's major-league-record 20 strikeouts against the Mariners at Fenway Park, April 29.

"I think about the third inning there was just a feeling in the air," he said. "There was somebody out in right field putting the Ks up for the first time as if he had some premonition. . . . There was the usher who took Clemens's wife down to a better seat, which happened to be directly in front of me. About the seventh inning she turned around and asked me how close he was to the record."

Yoakum saw a lot of strikeouts. Ten days before that historic game, he watched the Mariners and the Oakland A's combine for 30 strikeouts, a major-league record for a nine-inning game.

Soon after, he was in Chicago behind home plate. He turned in his seat, trying politely to shrug off a fan who was persistent in his questioning. As he looked up he saw a man fall from the upper deck at Comiskey Park. The man died.

Yoakum was signed out of high school by the Detroit Tigers, went to the Houston organization on a loan basis, and eventually was signed as a scout by the Astros. He left Houston with Tal Smith and Pat Gillick, when they joined the Yankees, and came with Gillick to the Blue Jays.

He did see the results of his work in September, 1985, when the Blue Jays won three of four games against the Yankees to take a major step toward their division title. He had been following the Yankees and had flown to New York with his reports for a special meeting with Gillick, manager Bob Cox, and the coaching staff. The Yankees had had a staff of three scouting the Blue Jays. "Yank scouting hokum, Jays relied on Yoakum," read a *Globe and Mail* headline.

AS AN EXPANSION TEAM, the Blue Jays had to have more resourceful and aggressive scouting than the established teams. Early on, Gillick hired veteran scouts Bob Mattick and Al LaMacchia to work with him in Toronto. Most of the recent staff additions have come at the major-league level as the team progressed. In 1986, the Blue Jays spent $2.1 million on scouting salaries and expenses. The Blue Jays and Dodgers spend the most on scouting of any of the major-league teams; several teams have found scouting to be a convenient place to cut costs. The Jays have 20 full-time scouts and 43 part-time scouts, known as "commission scouts" or "bird dogs." Of those, there are 13 in Canada, three in Puerto Rico, two in the Dominican Republic, and one each in Mexico, Venezuela, Guam, and Australia. The rest are in the United States. If they find a prospect, the bird dogs report him to one of the area scouts, who investigates personally. The players are graded on various skills under a system known as the OFP (Overall Future Potential), which produces a certain grade number for each prospect. Much cross-checking is done of top prospects as scouts compare notes. The bird dogs are paid bonuses based on how far their players go in the system and, of course, the highest reward is for a discovery making the majors.

At one time the Blue Jays did not belong to the Major League Scouting Bureau, which provides information to all members. At the 1983 winter meetings in Nashville, major-league general managers decided to make membership in the scouting bureau mandatory. Gillick fought it vehemently, arguing that the four divisional winners in 1983 and the previous four World Series winners had not belonged. For Gillick, mandatory membership in the scouting bureau was another erosion of team identity and scouting initiative.

Gillick sees scouting as a science and an art, something that some people are naturally better at than others. "A lot is instinct. It's just like with ballplayers who have the talent to be successful, but if they had a little more instinct, a little more *feel* for their work, they could be better. Some people have the talent to look at somebody and project him into the future. A lot of scouts do all the right things, but they have a hard time *projecting* the player – visualizing him a year, two, three, four years from now."

The scout knows that most of the players he sees will never make it to the professional ranks, let alone the major leagues. Of 100 players who sign professional contracts, perhaps seven or eight will spend even one day in the majors. With those odds, it is easy for a scout to be overly cautious and make negative judgements. He would be right most of the time, but he would not find many major-league players.

Mattick and LaMacchia, now vice-presidents with the Blue Jays, are known as positive scouts. They stand by their beliefs. They play hunches. They take chances. When LaMacchia was working for the Atlanta Braves he scouted Dale Murphy as a catcher. He argued strenuously to convince the Braves to draft him over another player. Murphy wound up becoming the Braves' centre fielder and the National League's Most Valuable Player in 1982 and 1983.

"When I started scouting, the older guys I had respect for told me always to go with a positive approach – to look for pluses," LaMacchia said. "Don't look for minuses because you're going to find enough minuses. If you go looking for minuses, you're going to find it hard to like a ballplayer."

When Mattick was head of player development for the Milwaukee Brewers, the name George Brett first came up. It was the early 1970s, at a meeting to discuss the amateur draft. Brett was listed as a shortstop. "They said he'd go in the draft, but he's too slow and can't play shortstop," Mattick recalled, "instead of going out and looking at a guy and saying he can't play short but he's got a good bat and maybe can play the outfield or third." Brett, of course, went on to become one of the game's top players as the Kansas City Royals' third baseman. In nine of his first ten seasons, he hit over .300, and he is a certainty for the Hall of Fame.

Mistakes have ruined scouts. They find a prospect, pay him lots of money, and he never amounts to anything. It happens all the time, and it can make some scouts gun shy. When Mattick arrived in Toronto, one of the first things he told Gillick was not to be afraid of making mistakes. "It's a game of mistakes," he said. "Don't pull in your horns. Keep firing."

The Blue Jays misfired a few times, gloriously. In going for top athletes, they drafted Danny Ainge, knowing he was an outstanding college basketball player. And they drafted Jay Schroeder, a quarterback at UCLA. After three seasons with the Blue Jays, Ainge left baseball to play guard for the Boston Celtics. Schroeder was tried as an outfielder, then as a catcher. He had trouble hitting the breaking ball. When the Blue Jays wanted to try his strong right arm as a pitcher, he decided to return to football and now is the quarterback for the Washington Redskins.

There is an interesting sidelight to Ainge's situation. Gillick asked lawyer Gord Kirke if he could put a clause in Ainge's contract that would prevent him from playing professional basketball. Kirke drafted the clause on a napkin over dinner with Gillick and said he wasn't sure that the clause would stand up in court.

The clause was structured so that the $300,000 signing bonus was stipulated as consideration for not playing basketball and that he would agree in advance that if he tried to play basketball he would consent to a court injunction to prohibit him from doing so. The contract was signed September 15, 1980. Kirke wrote the general manager of each National Basketball Association team, informing them about the clause and that if a club drafted Ainge, the Blue Jays would consider it an attempt to breach contract and would sue. The Celtics drafted Ainge and started negotiations. The Blue Jays went to the Supreme Court of New York to restrain the Celtics and won the case. A deal was then worked out with the Celtics. The clause is now used in law schools as a model of restrictive covenant for sports.

AS IMPORTANT AS THEIR WORK IS, scouts are generally underappreciated and underpaid. But the Blue Jays are more supportive than most teams. As a result they obtained 25-year Philadelphia Phillie scout Moose Johnson early in 1985. Johnson was 54 when he made the move, seeking an organization that had a superior pension plan and benefits. Toronto's attitude toward scouts is the result of Gillick having been there himself and of the people-oriented philosophy of Peter Hardy.

"I looked for an organization that had good benefits and Toronto was right up there with the top five or six organizations," Johnson said. "I knew the Toronto organization and I knew where they were headed and I liked their philosophy."

When he was with Philadelphia, he noticed some things he liked about a relief pitcher in the Texas Rangers' organization – Tom Henke. Johnson first saw him pitch in Triple A. In his trials with the Rangers, the intimidating personality of manager Doug Rader, a former Blue Jay player, had eroded Henke's confidence. Rader kicked garbage cans and cursed when Henke made a mistake. "When he was in Triple A before he had ever been in the big leagues, he showed a very good arm with great potential as a short man," Johnson said. "But for whatever the reasons, personality conflict or something to do with Rader, he could never relax up there. I knew his arm was sound, it was just that maybe he needed a change of scenery."

Johnson had unsuccessfully pestered the Phillies to obtain Henke. In January, 1985, when Henke was available in the now-discontinued free-agent compensation draft, Johnson talked highly of him to his new employers. The Blue Jays had third choice of the three teams entitled to draft from the pool of unprotected players as compensation for losing a Type A free agent (a player ranking in the top 20 per cent of his category). The Rangers had signed Cliff Johnson from the Jays as a free agent, but it was mere coincidence that the Jays chose a player from the Rangers as compensation. The Blue Jays' first choice had been Donnie Moore, a good relief pitcher for Atlanta who was taken by the California Angels. The next team, the St. Louis Cardinals, took shortstop Angel Salazar from the Montreal Expos. There was another advantage in Henke. He had one option remaining, which meant he could be sent to the minor leagues once more without passing through waivers. The Blue Jays used this to advantage, and when Henke was overpowering in Syracuse in the first half of 1985 and Bill Caudill was disappointing with the major-league team, Henke came to the rescue during the second half of the season.

ELLIOTT WAHLE had grown accustomed to Gillick's calls at all hours of the day. "In most families if the phone rings at three in the morning, you'd think that somebody had died. In our house, we knew it was Pat."

One summer when Gillick was with the Blue Jays in California, he called Wahle in Toronto. It was 3 a.m. One of the Blue Jay pitchers had hurt his arm and Gillick needed a replacement from Syracuse.

"Elliott, we want to bring Dave Wallace up from Syracuse," Gillick said.

"Pat, it's three o'clock in the morning," Wahle replied.

"I don't care, call Vern Benson and tell him to get Wallace on a plane."

"It's three in the morning."

"I don't care, we've got to have him."

Wahle said good night, put the phone down, and went back to sleep. He woke at eight, called Syracuse, and spoke to Benson, the manager, and Wallace made it to California in time for the evening game.

Gillick's scouts fan out across North America to South America, the islands of the Caribbean, and Mexico. They have gone on hunting expeditions to Alaska, Australia, Europe, Taiwan, Korea, and Cuba. They attend the palmy ritual of spring training, usually sitting in chatty clusters with scouts from other teams behind home plate with clipboards, charts, stopwatches, and radar guns. Many of the older scouts think the radar gun, used to measure the speed of pitches, is often over-rated and overused as an evaluation tool. It makes it easy to forget about control and location and how the ball moves, which can be as important as pure speed.

The annual June draft yields the biggest and best crop of young players, though it has taken some of the old competitive edge from scouting. Scouts used to have to develop ingenious methods of ingratiating themselves to players and players' families. They had to be part *pater familias*, part Willy Loman – getting by on a smile and a shoeshine. Now the competition rears its head only when a young prospect faces the choice between baseball and football, or baseball and basketball, or baseball and basketball *and* football (Dave Winfield comes to mind), or baseball and a college athletic scholarship. "It's kind of tough to try to tell a kid not to take a full scholarship to Stanford," Morgan said.

Top draft choices, sometimes still in their teens, may be offered signing bonuses of $100,000 or more. (That is one figure that has not changed much during the time in which major-league salaries have soared.) The bonuses are driven up if the prospect can play off a football bonus against a baseball bonus.

"With the draft being the way it is, scouts don't always know whether they are going to get a guy, so they don't dig in enough on the kid's makeup," Mattick said. "The crutch scouts use is, 'I'm not going to spend a lot of time and have somebody else take him before we get a chance to take him.' To me, ability is important, but makeup is more important."

Even with the draft, the good scouts can still use initiative, which is how Mattick landed outfielder Jesse Barfield. In 1977, Mattick took in a local high-school game in Joliet, Illinois. Bill Gullickson was pitching for Joliet Catholic High School and was rated as one of the top picks for the coming June draft. Because the Blue Jays were picking 25th in the draft – the established teams did the expansion franchises no favours – Mattick knew he would have no chance at Gullickson. During the warmup, Mattick noticed a young Joliet Central High School outfielder who had a good arm; Jesse Barfield wasn't even listed by the scouting bureau. He hit a double off Gullickson in the seventh inning to win the game, a drive that went through the picket fence in left field.

As expected, Montreal picked Gullickson in the first round, second overall. The Blue Jays picked Barfield in the ninth round, 233rd overall. A routine scouting assignment had uncovered gold.

In Latin America, where players are not subject to the draft, baseball scouts can use the old methods. In countries such as the Dominican Republic, bonuses might range from $3,000 to $6,000 (U.S.) – three times the annual income of the average Dominican. A signing-age minimum of 17 years was recently introduced to prevent undue exploitation of young Latinos.

Gillick moves his scouts around, sometimes bringing one in to provide a fresh perspective on the Blue Jays. Scouts constantly roam the Blue Jays' farm system – and those of other major-league teams – to glean valuable information for the Rule 5 draft picks. LaMacchia will see each National League team play about 20 times. He will watch them at home and on the road, on natural grass and artificial turf. He prepares a report on every player in the league, which is used when a player becomes available in a draft or becomes a free agent or is offered in a trade. Gord Lakey does the same thing in the American League.

If the Blue Jays are hot and heading for post-season play, scouts travel to the American League and National League cities to check out teams most likely to be their opponents in the divisional playoffs and the World Series.

AL LAMACCHIA, the son of an Italian immigrant, had been a pitcher. In 1903, his father came from the Calabrian town of Spezzano Piccolo to Carnegie, Pennsylvania, and worked in the coal mines. Not appreciative of the constant darkness, of entering the shaft in the gloom of morning and emerging at night, he moved to Vancouver to work in the lumber mills, then to Portland, Oregon, and finally to St. Louis, where he worked on the railroad. LaMacchia was born in St. Louis. Between 1943 and 1946 he pitched a total of 30 innings for the hometown Browns and Washington Senators. When he was out of baseball, living in San Antonio, a friend scouting for the Cincinnati Reds asked LaMacchia to scout part-time. He did, and then joined the Philadelphia Phillies as a scout. He worked 16 years for the Braves in Milwaukee and Atlanta. While with the Braves, LaMacchia met Gillick, who had just started as an Astro scout.

"He kind of impressed me as a young, energetic guy who was listening and asking questions," LaMacchia said. "You could sense he was going somewhere in the game. We'd always talk at games and he'd always drop by my house in San Antonio."

When Gillick had moved to New York, LaMacchia helped him sign Willie Upshaw for the Yankees. Upshaw had grown up in Blanco, Texas, about 35 miles from San Antonio. LaMacchia and another scout planned to work out Upshaw one Sunday and Gillick happened to be in town to inspect another prospect. Gillick came along and watched the scouts work with Upshaw, who was still in high school. Upshaw had the build, the tools, but he was raw. He leaned toward college football. LaMacchia says the Braves were prepared to take him in the 12th or 14th round. The Yankees, however, on Gillick's recommendation, took him in the fifth round.

LaMacchia had followed Upshaw in high school and knew his family. Gillick asked LaMacchia to accompany him and Dave Yoakum, also with the Yankees then, on a visit to the Upshaw home. As Gillick talked, Upshaw looked down and scuffed the ground with his foot. LaMacchia joined in. Although his team did not draft him, there is a sense of loyalty to the game of baseball that takes over if a prospect is considering another sport. LaMacchia told Upshaw that the Yankees had bonus money for him and he would have a better chance to earn a living and support a family in baseball.

Upshaw's father, who had been listening to the discussion outside the house, nodded in agreement. About 10 minutes later, Upshaw signed the contract. In 1977, the year after Gillick quit the Yankees to join the Blue Jays, the Yankees left Upshaw unprotected in the Rule 5 draft in December. The Blue Jays quickly snapped him up.

Mattick and LaMacchia teamed up for Dave Stieb, who had been found and turned in as an outfielder by local scout Tom Welke. Stieb played centre field at Southern Illinois University and would be named to *The Sporting News* All America team as an outfielder. "We had gone there to look at him and a shortstop on another club," LaMacchia said. "During batting practice, we didn't like Stieb's swing, but we liked his outfield play. He had a good arm and he could run. You could tell he was a good athlete. In the fifth inning, lo and behold, they bring him in to pitch. Nobody's warming up, a couple of men get on base, and they call in the centre fielder. What happens after that is he just opens our eyes."

There were five other scouts, LaMacchia said, and between the games of the doubleheader they went to the concession stands for a soft drink. LaMacchia went down to talk to Stieb.

"Have you ever pitched before?" he asked.

"Naw," Stieb said. "We've just got some tired arms and the coach wanted me to help out. I'm a pretty good hitter. I didn't hit this first game, but I'll show you I can hit. You stick around for the second game and I'll show you some hitting."

"I'm sure you will," LaMacchia said, "but if you don't hit, would you consider pitching?"

Stieb kept insisting he was a hitter.

Finally, LaMacchia said, "I'm going to ask you a question, and before you answer I want you to think it out." Stieb listened carefully. "If you were drafted and given every opportunity to hit and didn't make it, would you go to the mound and give it the maximum effort?"

"I'd have to be the one to decide I couldn't hit," Stieb said.

In August, 1978, Stieb began his professional career in Class A in Dunedin as an outfielder and designated hitter – and pitcher. By June the next season he was with the Blue Jays and within two years he was regarded as one of the best pitchers in the majors.

In his 66th year, LaMacchia, who is bald, took to wearing a moustache. LaMacchia, who has two children and three grandchildren, had seen a picture of his father with one, and his family found a striking resemblance. When his daughter first saw him with it she said, "Nonno (grandfather)." But the clincher was from six-year-old Andrew, his grandson. "When he said he liked it, I said it stays."

IN THE FIRST MONTHS of the Blue Jays' existence, the team had only five scouts covering the United States – Mattick, LaMacchia, John McLaren, Duane Larson, and Bob Engle. Bob Prentice was working out of Toronto, covering Canada.

Engle came from the Baltimore Orioles, where he was scouting supervisor for Ohio, Michigan, Indiana, and Kentucky. Engle's father was in the military and he spent four years in Puerto Rico as a boy doing nothing but attending school and playing baseball. After a stint in the military during the Vietnam era, Engle was a catcher and whatever else his team needed first at junior college and then at the University of Colorado. Upon graduation he stayed in baseball as a coach and then, after working for the Orioles, he joined Gillick and the Blue Jays in November, 1976.

Engle, trim, with carefully combed blond hair, could pass for a youngish college professor. He began as an area scout for the Blue Jays, covering an enormous territory that included all of the northeastern states and most of the midwest. "I think Virginia was my cutoff," he said. "We all had large areas, other than Mattick and LaMacchia, who did all the cross-checking for us. We were dashing around. We'd try to set up some kind of itinerary and see our priority players. We knew we could get a phone call from Gillick any time asking us to hop a plane to check out a player."

Engle had one last-minute scouting assignment that didn't get him back home until Christmas Eve. But he did it, he said, because he knew Gillick would have done it in the same situation. "You know that and so you tend to go a little further for him."

In 1985 the Blue Jays hired a new scout, a former professional player named Chris Bourjos of Des Plaines, Illinois. The Blue Jays sent him to cover part of the Class A Midwest League. Other scouts asked Bourjos why he was wasting time covering the league, especially since the Blue Jays had no team in it. Bourjos called Engle. "I told him to look at the Rule 5 draft and the selections we've made," Engle said. "It's the whole key. This is where it starts and we think it's of great value."

Engle's most hectic time is from February until the June draft. He zigzags across the East, starting in Florida, catching a high-school game in the afternoon and perhaps a college team at night. Many northern colleges have spring training and an exhibition schedule in Florida. As unpredictable as his schedule is during this period, his wife knows exactly where he is so that Gillick can reach him.

Once the June draft is done, Engle can set up his own schedule for the rest of the summer as he scouts the Blue Jay farm system. His family accompanies him on some trips.

While the Blue Jays have excelled at drafting from other teams and in their late-round amateur draft picks, their No. 1 selections have often gone wrong. One reason for this is that they'll often use the first pick to gamble on taking the best athlete available.

In 1982 the Blue Jays bypassed Dwight Gooden for Augie Schmidt, a shortstop from the University of New Orleans. Schmidt had been named college player of the year, and the Blue Jays projected him as a third baseman. He was traded to San Francisco in the deal that brought Gary Lavelle to Toronto. Gooden won the National League Cy Young Award in 1985, and in 1986 Schmidt was playing with Kenosha of the Class A Midwest League, batting .226.

"We had strong reports on Gooden," Engle said. "But we had stronger reports on Augie Schmidt. The thing about a high-school player versus a college player is that you're getting a 17-year-old or an 18-year-old versus a 21-year-old who's just a little more mature. Many times college players don't realize there's still a big change from college baseball to professional baseball. Some of them have trouble making the adjustment – physically and mentally. You've heard a million times about the adjustment from the aluminum bats to the wooden bat, but it goes further than that. In college, there's 60 or 70 games. And it's not only the number of games, but the instruction they're getting. They don't get as much in-depth instruction in college. The college coach's job is to win. The job in the farm system is to develop players and get them to the big leagues."

Not all the Blue Jays' top picks in the June draft have been duds. In 1978 they selected Lloyd Moseby, an All-America in baseball and basketball at Oakland High School. In 1981 the Blue Jays selected pitcher John Cerutti with in an additional first-round pick they were given for losing third baseman Roy Howell as a free agent. The Jays' first-round pick was pitcher Matt Williams, one of the players traded to Texas to reacquire Cliff Johnson.

Engle's western counterpart, Wayne Morgan, was born in Saskatoon and raised in Kindersley, Saskatchewan. He has taken his family on an Australian vacation so he could scout a player there. He has been to Cuba and Belgium to check out international amateur baseball tournaments. Gillick wants to be prepared in case Cuban talent once again becomes available to the major leagues.

Once, in a playful mood at the winter meetings, Engle called over to Morgan, "They call us the KGB."

169

IN 1962, WAYNE MORGAN packed up his fond memories of long hours of skating in the cold Saskatchewan air and headed for California. He played baseball first at the College of the Sequoias in Visalia and then at San Francisco State College. He was an infielder, called Peewee back home, who lacked range and speed. "Not a bad amateur hitter," Morgan the scout says of Morgan the player.

After earning a Master's degree in physical education, he coached at a Los Angeles high school and in a junior college in Menlo Park. He'd play baseball in the summers in western Canada. He became a part-time scout for the Expos – winters in California and summers in western Canada. Gillick hired him for Houston. "He needed a guy to scout Canada, coast to coast," Morgan said, "that's what he was doing."

Morgan went to the Yankees with Gillick and came to the Blue Jays in 1977. While with the Yankees he scouted and signed Willie McGee, who won the National League's Most Valuable Player Award in 1985 for the St. Louis Cardinals.

Morgan likes a player with speed and strength – not to be confused with bulk – and follows a simple philosophy: "The pluses got to carry the minuses."

In the pursuit of Gillick's philosophy of exploring all avenues, Morgan has become a world traveller. A last-minute assignment of Gillick's sent Morgan to the other side of the world in search of a baseball pitcher. During the 1981 players' strike, Gillick called Morgan in California and suggested he cover the Intercontinental Cup, a baseball tournament in Edmonton. It was ten in the morning; Gillick told Morgan there was a game he should see in Edmonton at six o'clock that night.

Morgan made it and caught sight of Dong-Won Choi, a pitcher for the Korean team. Morgan knew at once he was a major-league prospect. "The Dodgers offered him $150,000 right there at Edmonton," he said. "But he would have had to go to the minors, and he wouldn't."

Morgan found a Korean university student to act as interpreter and talked to Choi in the stands during practice. The Korean coach took one look and pulled the entire team out of the stadium and put them on the bus. However, Morgan's brief chat confirmed that Choi was interested in signing with the Blue Jays.

"He wasn't a real big guy," Elliott Wahle said, "and unless you saw him, you'd never believe the stuff that came out of his arm. There was no doubt in our minds that he could pitch in the majors right away."

Morgan would make four trips to Seoul. "At that time they had a curfew. A city of millions and at midnight everything stops. If the taxi-cab was on the street, you had to stop and sleep in the car. Right there, that's it. They were prepared to go to war every day."

Morgan and Wahle negotiated with Choi's father through an interpreter in Seoul, after they had watched Choi throw on a baseball field on a military base. As a favour to the man who arranged the session, they worked out his 15-year-old son as well. "I was pitching the guy batting practice and I can't throw worth a darn," Wahle recalled. "The kid hits a liner back at me and nearly splits my index finger. I went to a military hospital and they fixed me up, but it just about tore my nail off."

The negotiations continued. Late one night, about half an hour before curfew, they agreed on a major-league contract. Choi would start with the big-league team. Wahle was the only one who could type. He produced the contract on the hotel typewriter, pecking at the machine with his finger sticking in the air. Choi signed the contract and rushed home.

In major-league baseball, two contracts must be submitted for approval. The next morning, Wahle typed the second one, his injured finger still held at an awkward angle, and telephoned for Choi to come sign it. He refused. They were being advised to sign not with the Blue Jays but with the Dodgers. As Morgan recalls it, one of Choi's advisers, who had acted as the interpreter for the team in Edmonton, had businesses in Los Angeles.

Wahle and Morgan feared they would not be able to leave the country with the contract – threats to that effect were made and they were concerned they might have trouble with customs at the airport – so they made several photocopies of the original and mailed them to different North American destinations, including the commissioner's office, the league office, the player relations committee's office, and the Blue Jay office. As a further precaution, they mailed them from different mailboxes near the hotel. Wahle stuffed the original contract in his pants and they flew home that night.

Choi never made it to the Blue Jays. A Korean professional league was started the next year. "And the agreement was made with Korea, the same as it is with Japan, that you can't sign those players," Morgan said. "He was a national hero and they put up enough red tape so he couldn't leave."

Morgan soon had another Asian project. This one took him to Taiwan to try to sign a pitcher whom he and Gillick had seen in the 1982 Intercontinental Cup in Edmonton. He'd been clocked on the radar gun at 94 miles an hour and before attending the 1982 winter meetings in Hawaii, Morgan flew to Taiwan. "I got to meet the father and it was a completely different situation than the Korean deal," Morgan said. "The Korean father ran the whole show. In fact, the boy cried when his father said he couldn't go to the States but he didn't say a word. In Taiwan, the father told me it was completely up to his son. Entirely his decision. The only catch was the boy didn't get out of the military until June of 1984 and he wasn't allowed to sign until then. We couldn't really do much, but we did look at other players in the country."

In 1984, baseball was a demonstration sport at the Los Angeles-Ueberroth Olympics. The year before the Olympics, Morgan travelled to Belgium, where Cuba and Taiwan had teams playing in a tournament. It was a chance to make points with Taiwan's coach, in case he could help in the signing.

"Early in 1984, the coach sent me their summer schedule," Morgan said. "They were going to be in the United States for about three months prior to the Olympics. And this guy's going to be eligible in June, right before the Olympics. So we thought at that time we'd better get over there and try to make a deal before everybody in the United States sees him. They were going to Michigan and to southern California and we figured, heck, everybody's going to see this guy. So it was probably February and I jumped a flight to Taiwan and offered him a lot of money. I spent 10 days with them when they were training at a little town. I mean I just lived with the guy. They'd go out at night and play this game, mahjong, with little tiles. One day after practice he said to c'mon, he was going to play some mahjong. We were there for seven hours straight, the pitcher and the coach, in this little room about three floors up in some old factory that they rent out to these guys."

The pitcher told Morgan that his first choice was to play in Japan, because it was close to home. But he said the Blue Jays would be his first choice if he decided to play in North America.

Fortuitously, Blue Jay manager Bob Cox and pitching coach Al Widmar could join LaMacchia, Mattick, and Gillick in observing the pitcher: the Taiwan team was training at the University of California at Berkeley, the major-league All Star game was being played in San Francisco, and the Blue Jays were resuming their schedule in Oakland. Morgan arranged for the pitcher to throw a couple of innings of a simulated game. "He threw good, real good in the bullpen," Morgan said. "But when he went into the game he kind of threw like he was in a workout. He didn't cut loose. So he looked just okay. Good enough that you wanted him but nothing like I'd seen him."

In his team's first game of the Olympics at Dodger Stadium he pitched against the U.S. team, which was loaded with top college stars. On the 20-man roster, 18 of them were or would be No. 1 draft choices. The pitcher struck out 12 and threw a fastball at 95 miles per hour. LaMacchia came in to watch the game and confirmed that he would be a first round draft pick in the United States.

"The second game he pitched, in the first two innings he's throwing like 93, 94, 95, the third inning he pitched 88, 89, 90," Morgan said. "I'd seen this guy pitch a lot. He might pitch nine innings and come back a day later and throw 94. I mean that never bothered him because they throw a lot. Something was the matter with him so I asked the kids I knew with the team who were charting the games in the stands and the next day I asked him. He had hurt his elbow in the third inning. I got scared for the kind of money we were talking about and we kind of drew back on the deal because of the injury. But if I hadn't known these people so well from my times over there, I wouldn't have been able to find that out."

The pitcher eventually signed with Seibu of the Japanese League for $250,000 even though other teams were interested and probably would have paid more. Seibu had made a deal with the pitcher's brother, Morgan says. He had heard that the father had died – the mother had died earlier – and the brother was in charge of the family. If he didn't sign with Seibu he would be banished from the family. "And he cried, the coach told me, because he could have got about $400,000," Morgan said. The Blue Jays also were prepared to go that high and, as encouragement, were considering signing a friend they judged had the ability to pitch in Double A or Triple A. That didn't work out, either. In 1985, his first season in Japan, where he is known as Taigen Kaku, he pitched well before developing an arm problem.

The effort, time, and expense of these exercises are worthwhile only for a premium player who is about ready to step into the major leagues, Morgan says. It's not worth it for a fringe player. If Morgan's Taiwan excursion accomplished nothing else, some future prospects may be wearing the Blue Jay ties and pins Morgan gave out or they may have committed to memory an old Blue Jay highlight film. There was no television of major-league games there, so he took a Blue Jay promotional film. Sounds easy, but it wasn't.

First, no projector was available at the college where the team was working out. The coach found someone downtown who could convert the film to videotape and Morgan was given a lift on the back of a moped. Morgan has seen whole families on one moped. "We go into a little shop and this guy has a small projector and he can show it on the screen and he has this thing that takes it off the screen and puts it onto a VHS tape."

The man wanted only cash, no traveller's cheques, and thus phoned his bank so that Morgan could cash the cheques. Morgan rode the moped to the baseball park, where it was discovered that the VCR was for Beta. Morgan was back on the moped to the little shop downtown.

Morgan enjoys the cloak-and-dagger stuff; he looks and talks a little like he could be a movie detective who has seen everything. Before 1985, Canadian players did not have to go through the amateur draft and there was a place for the intrigue and creativity of the old-time scouting even though there wasn't an abundance of talent.

Gordon Pladson, a pitcher from New Westminster, B.C., pitched briefly with the Astros during four seasons. In what became an exercise in espionage, he was scouted in Vancouver for the Astros by Gillick and Morgan. "We flew a scout in from Arkansas to Vancouver just because he was a new face that nobody knew in town," Morgan said. "We'd rent a different car every day so nobody would be able to recognize our car. This guy went in and watched the kid pitch. Gillick and I were across the street in a coffee shop – then we couldn't stand it any longer. We decided to go out to the right-field line out in the bushes there. We're going up this bank to look at the field and there are three guys hiding there already. We still don't know who they were."

Because Canadian amateurs usually play a shorter schedule than their U.S. counterparts, it is sometimes advantageous to find a younger player who can be groomed. A couple of years' delay could be too late. Morgan was thinking this way when he strayed from the easy path and ignored a semipro tournament in Kamloops, B.C., where the accommodations were good, Instead, he attended the Canadian Midget Tournament in Barrhead, Alberta, a small community north of Edmonton. He took his wife and two children and stayed at the best available accommodations – a cabin with no running water. "It wasn't real convenient," Morgan said.

But he figured it was better to scout younger talent, players with a chance to develop. He noticed a pitcher, but Morgan didn't like his delivery and he didn't throw hard. "But he was big and he could run," Morgan said. "Then he played the outfield, but because he had pitched he didn't throw that well from the outfield when we saw him."

The player went home to Melville, Saskatchewan, about 500 miles away, but Morgan kept in contact. After his arm had a chance to rest, Morgan drove to Melville and had the player make some throws from right field to third base. The arm was fine. The Astros signed the outfielder, Terry Puhl, who would serve them so well in the majors.

"That's what keeps you going, looking for that diamond in the rough," Morgan said.

GORD LAKEY ARRIVED at work in the Astrodome one winter morning when the call from Pat Gillick came. "Get some warm clothes and meet me in Minneapolis," Gillick told Lakey. They were going to western Canada to try to sign a junior hockey player, Bob Bourne, the future New York Islander, to a baseball contract. Lakey had few warm clothes. The best he could do was a trench coat.

From Minneapolis, where it was nine degrees below zero, Lakey and Gillick caught a plane to Winnipeg. The jet had a scheduled stop in Grand Forks, North Dakota, but because of the cold there was concern about the landing gear. "They pulled the rug back, looked down this little inverted periscope type thing to check to see whether the wheels were in place," Lakey recalled. "It was so cold, the bay had frozen shut a little. They got the wheels down and we landed at the airport in Grand Forks, in the middle of nowhere, and naturally the plane couldn't fly on to Winnipeg."

It was 10 p.m. Lakey noted there were not a lot of rental cars in Grand Forks. "There were seven cars available, so they had everybody going to Winnipeg pair up. The first thing the guy we were with said was to put some alcohol in the gas tank so it wouldn't freeze up. We get to Winnipeg and it's colder than I can believe. The plastic buttons on my trench coat pop off. We got in at about 3:30 in the morning and slept on a bench in the Winnipeg airport until about six and took the first plane to Saskatoon."

Gillick rented a car in Saskatoon; it spun in circles in the parking lot of the Holiday Inn. They looked around and saw a young boy with skates on holding onto the back of the bumper. Lakey was learning quickly about Canadian winters. They already had signed Clarke Gillies,

175

Bourne's teammate on the Regina Pats junior hockey team and also a future Islander. Gillick and Lakey watched Bourne play a hockey game in Saskatoon. "We walked to the arena and we couldn't even breathe," Lakey said. "It was so cold, you couldn't walk more than about 50 yards without having to go into a building."

They signed Bourne the next morning. Both would play briefly in the lower minor leagues for manager Billy Smith, who would become the Blue Jays' first-base coach in 1984.

After Bourne was signed, Gillick and Lakey could not fly out of Saskatoon because of an air-traffic controllers' strike. They took a bus to Minneapolis. "We were sitting at the back of the bus," Lakey recalled, "and Pat says, 'I smell smoke.' The bus caught on fire. . . ."

S E V E N T H

CULTIVATING THE FUTURE DOWN ON THE FARM

THEY COME TO STRANGE TOWNS AND CITIES in states and provinces – and sometimes countries – they have never seen and probably know little about.

They are lonely, perhaps frightened. Some of them cannot speak English, and many must adjust to a new culture. A few carry the burden of ''unlimited potential'' and must deliver on the promise of a $100,000 bonus. The odds are they never will.

Jesse Barfield experienced the loneliness but none of the high expectations when he arrived in Utica, New York, in June, 1977, to play professional baseball. He was a skinny homesick 17-year-old, fresh from high school in Joliet, Illinois, near Chicago. He lived on the east side of Joliet, population 78,000. ''It was one of the worst sides – the south side was by far the worst – and the east side and the south side were next door to each other,'' he said. ''It was rough; it wasn't a jungle but there were a lot of mischievous things you could get into. My mom was strict and I appreciate the way she moulded me. She told me, 'You don't have to hang around with the crowd.' ''

The Utica Blue Jays of the New York-Penn League, a short-season

Class A league, were the fledgling Toronto Blue Jays' only farm team that year. Barfield had signed for a bonus of $7,500 with another $7,500 if he made the major leagues. The best thing about him at this stage was his right arm. It was a bazooka. And he grew. From a six-foot, 168 pounder, he developed into a muscular six-foot one-inch, 200 pounder who would become the 1986 major-league home-run champion, bound to earn more than a million dollars in 1987. But he wasn't always so potent at the plate.

"The first time I saw a slider, I couldn't hit it," Barfield said. "I just made a half swing. You don't see any sliders in high school.

"When I was hitting .226 and .206 in A ball, I believe my fielding is what kept me in the game until I learned how to hit. If it wasn't for my defence, I wouldn't be here right now."

Barfield had seven home runs and 69 runs batted in combined in his first two seasons in Class A, at Utica and Dunedin. He was seriously considering going back to school. If the Blue Jays had not drafted him, he was set to go to college and major in architectural drawing; he had won two statewide contests in high school. Barfield didn't have the stamina for the length of a professional season and his manager at Dunedin, Denis Menke, a former major-leaguer, suggested he try a weight program.

Barfield's mother, Annie, had lost her job at the Caterpillar Tractor factory in Illinois and moved to Houston in 1979, where there was a job opportunity. In the off-season there, Barfield augmented his minor-league salary by working for What A Burger, answering the telephone, "Thank you for calling What A Burger San Felipe, may I help you."

In the 1979 season, Barfield's third as a professional, he exceeded the total of the previous two years with eight homers and 71 RBIs for the Class A team at Kinston, when he improved his batting average to .264. In 1980, he advanced to Knoxville, a Double A team, and batted .240 with 14 homers and 65 RBIs. In 1981, he was batting .261 with 16 homers and 70 RBIs when he was called up to the major-league team to stay in September after Pat Gillick had heard the persistent requests of Blue Jay manager Bob Mattick, who had spotted Barfield as a high-schooler.

"We were playing so horseshit and we didn't have anybody," manager Mattick said, "so I went up to the office, I don't know how many times, three or four, and said, 'Pat, get me Barfield, I'll play him.' "

Barfield is still teased about the way Mattick stood up for him. "George Bell calls Mattick my daddy," Barfield said.

Barfield, then 21, joined two other outfielders of the same age, Bell and Lloyd Moseby; in a few years they would be considered the best outfield in baseball.

But in 1977, Barfield was young and vulnerable. His parents had separated when he was less than two years old and his mother raised four children. "She did a tremendous job; I owe her a lot," Barfield says. It was only in his mid-twenties that Barfield, who has become a devout Christian since joining the Blue Jays, began to establish a relationship with his father.

John McLaren, his playing career over at the age of 25, was Utica's coach. McLaren remembers a day Barfield arrived at the park depressed.

"Jesse James, what's bothering you?" McLaren said.

"I'm a little homesick; I'm just not feeling right," Barfield answered.

McLaren took the teenager into his office and had him call his mother. "He felt real good about it," McLaren said.

A little more than four years later, Barfield was in the major leagues. When he joined the Blue Jays in Chicago there was no uniform with his number on it, because he was in Double A and they didn't expect him to be called up. "I was so fresh," Barfield said, "that they had to staple my number to my uniform. I said, 'So this is the big leagues.' "

PETER HARDY, the chief executive officer of the Blue Jays, tries to visit each of the organization's six minor-league teams during the season, always aware of the potential problems. "We're giving a little bit, but not enough, in the guidance and interest we're showing in these young people," Hardy said. "They come from the Dominican Republic and it's a whole new culture. And language is another problem."

The concern includes the players from the United States and Canada. "We bring them in, we give them money that many of them have never had before, leave them on their own, let them get exposed to a lot of outside distractions," he said. "We try to encourage . . . our coaches or managers on the minor-league teams to consider themselves surrogate parents to these young people. Let's make sure they're living in decent places . . . that they're not running wild or loose. I'm also concerned about drugs. These kids are open to temptation. The only way is to portray an honest and concerned interest in them."

Hardy is concerned with nutrition and has asked to see what the organization can do about making sure the minor-leaguers eat properly.

"It might cost a little more, but when you take a youngster at 18 or

20 and put them in the environment we do, then you have a responsibility to them," Hardy said. "And we have a long way to go on that one."

BARFIELD SORT OF EASED into the big-league picture, but there were high expectations for Lloyd Moseby. And no one had higher expectations than Moseby himself. He was 18 years old when the Blue Jays took him in the first round of the June, 1978, free-agent draft. He was the second pick in the whole country, behind Bob Horner, who was drafted by the Atlanta Braves.

Born in Portland, Arkansas, Moseby was a preschooler when his family – like generations of "Arkies" and "Okies" before them – headed to California. He grew up in Oakland, started baseball as a catcher, but was cut from his Little League team. At high school, he was a superb athlete, making All-America in baseball and basketball. He was big, strong, and fast. Moseby grew up with Rickey Henderson, the prodigious base stealer for the Oakland A's and New York Yankees. They played baseball together from Babe Ruth League up to Oakland Technical High School before Moseby transferred to Oakland High. Moseby's basketball teammates called him "Shaker" for the way he could move on the court, and he is still called that to this day. He was gregarious and fun-loving, full of life and jive.

Moseby soon found himself in Medicine Hat, a city of 40,000 in southeastern Alberta, hard by the Saskatchewan border. Medicine Hat started as a tent town on the flat, treeless prairies when the railroad pushed through the Canadian West. According to Indian legend, the name comes from a Cree medicine man who lost his headdress fleeing the Blackfoot across the South Saskatchewan River. It is a friendly, pretty place, surrounded by sprawling ranches and wheat farms, but when Moseby arrived in the summer of 1978 he was frightened and lonely . . . culture shock. His friend Henderson had been drafted by the hometown Oakland A's, another friend had been drafted by the Houston Astros. Moseby knew nothing about Toronto or the Blue Jays, but when they told him they would make him their top pick he heeded the advice of his high-school coach. "He said I'd get a better chance with them because they were losing a hundred games a year," Moseby said.

On his arrival in Medicine Hat, he saw a family of Hutterites come to town in a horse-drawn wagon to pick up provisions. "I'd never been anywhere outside of California or Arkansas," he said. "I'd never seen anything like that."

Medicine Hat plays in the Pioneer League, for rookie professionals. Sometimes the young players arrive in June bringing ski jackets and fur-lined mitts, the price tags still attached. It's Canada, after all. They carry their own luggage, do their own laundry. They get by on $700 a month, for two and a half months and a 70-game schedule. They eat together and bunk together at the Silver Buckle Inn. They will have a chance to marvel at a man named Larry Plante, who actually eats glass. All summer long they travel on buses from southern Alberta across the border into Montana and along 800 miles of dusty highways to play the Salt Lake City Trappers. They dream of some day making The Show, which is what they call major-league baseball, but the odds are dismal. Some are signed merely to fill out team rosters, to act as the supporting cast to players with real potential.

Moseby adapted quickly to Medicine Hat. Before long, he was chatting up the locals, visiting shops and stores on Third Street, and passing out his business cards. ''Hi! I'm Lloyd Moseby. Come on out to the park tonight and I'll hit a dinger for you.'' He says it's been his favourite place to play baseball.

People invited the irrepressible young outfielder, and the other players, to their homes for dinner. In Medicine Hat they still talk about Lloyd Moseby. ''He was such a good guy. He basically likes people,'' said Russ Williams, the team's vice-president. Moseby played in 67 games, batted .310, hit 10 home runs, stole 20 bases. Two years later, after a season in the Florida State League and a few weeks in Syracuse, Moseby was with the Blue Jays in Toronto. (''I was in Syracuse for a cup of coffee,'' he says, ''but I was on my way out before I got a chance to put in the cream.'') Moseby, Garth Iorg, and Luis Leal were called up from Syracuse on May 24, the day Moseby's good friend Willie Upshaw and infielder Domingo Ramos were demoted. Aided by a police escort, they arrived at Exhibition Stadium 25 minutes before game time after playing in Pawtucket, Rhode Island, the previous night. Moseby went 2-for-4, including a double, and Iorg had a pinch-hit double. The next day, Moseby went 3-for-5 and hit a homer against Yankee pitcher Tommy John.

Because the Blue Jays were so weak and the talent was spread so thinly – both on the farm and in The Show – Moseby did most of his apprenticeship in the majors. After the quick start at the plate and a batting average of better than .300 in his short minor-league career, he struggled for the first three seasons, inching his average up from

.229 in 1980 to .233 in 1981, to .236 in 1982. In each of his first three seasons he hit nine home runs. Sceptics began to regard him as a bust, a wasted first-round draft choice. Moseby wasn't a natural outfielder, so he had to work at his defensive play. On many spring training days manager Bob Mattick spent time showing him how to execute the sliding catch. Mattick would drop the ball; Moseby, in a grass-stained uniform, would slide for it, keeping the ball in front of him if he didn't catch it and avoiding a shoulder injury that could result from a diving attempt. Finally, in 1981, Moseby's defence and throwing had improved enough to use him regularly in centre field. It was a luxury a developing team could afford, but the move was not popular with incumbent centre fielder Rick Bosetti, who was sent to Oakland in June.

"When we signed Moseby a lot of people in the organization thought he should be a first baseman because of his arm," Mattick said. "He worked hard. He rebelled down there in the Instructional League. But he was good. It doesn't bother me if the guys piss and moan as long as they do the job. He really strengthened his arm. When I managed, we all thought he should lower his hands when he hit. But we never could get him to do it. I guess he'd had so much success in high school and the minor leagues that way.

"Probably one of the reasons they appointed me manager, maybe *the* reason, you could stay with the kids and work with them. I don't think you can do the thing that we did then in New York City, or in California, or in Kansas City, or even in Toronto *now*."

At the beginning of the 1983 season, Bob Cox started to platoon Moseby, but not for long. Moseby broke through and batted .315, with 18 home runs, 81 runs batted in, and 27 stolen bases.

At last, he belonged in The Show.

"MOST PEOPLE SUFFERED from the misconception that we started out 25 players behind," said Elliott Wahle, administrator of player personnel for the first six years. "What they didn't realize is that we started out about 150 players behind because everybody else had developed a minor-league system."

A flow of talent is to a major-league team what a flow of cash is to any other business. Without a productive farm system, long-range planning is futile, and there can be no long-term goals. The farm system is where the raw material, mined by the scouts, is processed. There are risks and disappointments. The Blue Jays spent $4.5 million (Cdn.) in

1986 on their minor-league system, including $1.1 million to buy U.S. dollars. The total does not include scouting or signing bonuses for amateurs.

Minor-league salaries, all in U.S. funds, were nearly $2.4 million for the year; players were paid $1.6 million; another $800,000 went to managers, coaches, trainers, and administrative staff. Travel cost about $420,000. Uniforms, medical insurance, and the special considerations that must be paid to the minor-league teams came to $557,000.

It is expensive, but it would be more expensive to ignore the farm system and try to fuel the major-league team with free agents and trades, which do not guarantee even short-term success. "The farm and scouting are two areas that are as important as any in the organization," Paul Beeston says, "because they distinguish a competitive club from a non-competitive club. You have to develop players for the major-league club. You can make judicious trades, you can go into the free-agent market, you can get released players like Doyle Alexander – but look at the players we've developed. Even players we got from other organizations – Willie Upshaw, George Bell – they've gone back to the minor leagues to be taught."

Teams that have prospered in recent years have strong, well-financed farm systems. The New York Mets showed the promise of their 1986 World Series victory years earlier by scouting and developing superb young players such as Dwight Gooden and Darryl Strawberry. A healthy and extensive farm system also creates a depth of talent that allows the parent team to trade for specific needs. Established but aging regulars can be traded because there are young players ready to replace them, at considerably lower salaries. Sometimes a package of young players can be traded for a crucial acquisition, which is how the Mets obtained catcher Gary Carter from the Montreal Expos and, two years later, outfielder Kevin McReynolds from the San Diego Padres. From 1982 to 1985, the four World Series champions had a total of two free agents, Darrell Porter with the 1982 St. Louis Cardinals and Darrell Evans with the 1984 Detroit Tigers.

From one minor-league team, the Blue Jays had expanded their system to six teams. In 1986 they had one in Triple A, one in Double A, three in Class A, and the rookie team in Medicine Hat. The Blue Jays had originally planned on only one Class A team, but that proved unworkable because it forced decisions on players to be made too quickly.

At the lowest level is the rookie league team, owned in Medicine

Hat by Bill Yuill, who owns radio and television stations as well as other minor-league teams. Medicine Hat, which plays in the Pioneer League, has been connected with the Blue Jays since 1978. Moving up in the hierarchy is Class A, which has two levels. The short-season Class A team is similar in calibre and length of season to the rookie league, but it allows players with up to four years' professional experience. The Blue Jays' short-season Class A team is based in St. Catharines, Ontario, a 90-minute drive from Toronto. It played a 78-game schedule in 1986. The franchise used to be based in Niagara Falls, N.Y., until purchased by the Jays before the 1986 season. It won the New York-Penn League championship in its first year in St. Catharines. The St. Catharines franchise took the place of a rookie team the Blue Jays operated in Bradenton, Florida, in the Gulf Coast League, which is like the Instructional League, with games starting at noon, practices before and after the games, and no attempt to augment the microscopic attendance.

The other Blue Jays' Class A teams in 1986 were the Ventura County Gulls of the California League, where the teams played 142 games, and the Florence, South Carolina, Blue Jays of the South Atlantic League, in which the teams played from 132 to 140 games. The Florence team also was owned by Yuill but after the 1986 season was sold to Baltimore businessman Winston Blenckstone and moved to Myrtle Beach, South Carolina, about 50 miles away.

Ventura, which replaced Kinston, North Carolina, for the 1986 season, was a one-year location until the Blue Jays were able to activate their Class A Florida State League franchise at Dunedin, using Grant Field, where the Blue Jays play their home games in spring training.

At the Double A level the Blue Jays have a team at Knoxville, Tennessee, in the Southern League, which has a 144-game schedule. The Blue Jays bought the Knoxville franchise in 1985 and installed Gillick as chairman and Beeston as president. The Blue Jays also own the St. Catharines and Dunedin franchises. "They have to exist on their own merit," Ash said, "but it's still a little easier when you run your own ball club."

The prices of minor-league teams have been increasing. The Blue Jays paid $90,000 for St. Catharines and now a comparable franchise could go for twice that much. When the Blue Jays bought Knoxville, the price was about $250,000. A couple of years later, Reading in the Double A Eastern League sold for $1 million.

The Blue Jays' top minor-league team is the Syracuse Chiefs, who play in the venerable Triple A International League, in which the Toronto Maple Leafs once toiled with distinction. The Blue Jays decided on Syracuse, which had been a New York Yankee farm team, in 1978. It has a couple of advantages: it is only a four-hour drive from Toronto, ballpark to ballpark. The International League parks are closer to major-league dimensions, which give a more accurate reading of individual heroics. Moreover, the climate in Syracuse is similar to that of Toronto.

Promising players might be signed to bonuses as low as $2,000 or as high as $200,000. But there is little variation in salaries in the lower minors. Compared to the six- and seven-figure paycheques in the majors, salaries are paltry. Most players must work at odd jobs in the off-season to make ends meet, though once they have progressed to the higher minors some can polish their skills and earn money playing winter baseball in Latin America.

Rookies in the Pioneer League earn $700 a month. All drafted first-year players must be paid that amount although usually the non-drafted players are as well. The pay is $825 a month in the short-season Class A level, about $900 a month in the long-season Class A, which is five months. First-year players in Double A get $1,000 a month, second-year players between $1,200 and $1,500, and players who have been around longer at that level make up to $1,800. First-year players in Triple A make $1,500 to $2,000 a month and in subsequent seasons can make $4,000 to $5,000 a month.

Some players on major-league contracts but playing for Triple A teams earn much more, of course. Luis Leal, once a regular in the Blue Jays' pitching rotation, made $400,000 playing for Syracuse in 1986.

Meal money for road games, as stipulated in the Player Development Contract between the minor-league teams and their parent major-league clubs, barely covers a hamburger, fries, and a Coke – $11 a day in Class A, $12 in Double A, and $14 in Triple A. The major-league club reimburses its minor-league affiliate a portion of the meal money – $8 per day at Class A and Double A and $6.50 at Triple A. If a team is able to commute to and from a road game, requiring no overnight stop, then half the meal money may be paid. The minor-league team pays hotel and transportation on road trips for the first 20 players at Triple A, the first 19 at Double A, and the first 18 at Class A. The major-league teams pick up the tabs for the others.

The Player Development Contract, a standard working agreement between major-league clubs and their affiliates, was worked out late in

1985. Prior to the standardized agreement, the farm teams and the parent clubs would negotiate their own deals. The major-league teams covered all spring-training expenses, for instance, and still do under the new agreement. That includes the players' travel to spring training and for the teams from there to the season-opening games.

The standardized PDC has its drawbacks. Teams that were affiliated with the more generous major-league clubs – including the Jays – actually receive less under the standardized agreement than they were previously receiving from their parent clubs.

It's all spelled out. Under the agreement, for instance, the major-league team must provide the following equipment to its Triple A, Double A, and full-season Class A teams: 25 dozen bats, 100 dozen game balls, and 20 dozen sanitary socks. For short-season Class A teams, the totals are 15 dozen bats, 50 dozen game balls, and 10 dozen sanitary socks. (The equipment remains the property of the major-league team.)

The major-league team also provides each team with 18 assorted-sized batting helmets, three sets of catching equipment (including throat guard and catcher's helmet), and sufficient jackets for the pitching staff. Damaged helmets are to be replaced by the big-league team during the season.

The major-league team must provide each team with one set of uniforms in "good condition," which includes six uniforms more than the active playing limit, plus four extra sets of pants. A uniform includes two caps.

The major-league team must pick up all the salaries of its Class A and Double A players. It pays salaries in excess of $200 per month ($6.66 per day) for the first 20 players on a Triple A club and all the salaries of any players over that limit.

Bats, balls, equipment, and shipping to the Blue Jays' Triple A team costs about $16,000. One set of uniforms costs about $3,000 for a team in the lower classifications, $6,000 at Triple A. (The lower minor-league teams usually get uniforms worn the previous season by the major-leaguers.)

The Blue Jays give each of their affiliates two sets of uniforms, rather than the one required, and pick up all salaries at their Syracuse farm after the first $100 per month on the first 20 players – a break of $100 per player per month for the Chiefs. The Blue Jays and Chiefs signed their agreement before the new standardized PDC came into effect; it runs for three years with an option for a fourth, in 1989.

The managers, coaches, and trainers for each team are selected and paid for by the parent club; however, a Triple A team has a say in the choice of its manager. The Blue Jays pay above the industry average for trainers, who work from March 1 until September 1 (or until the playoffs are finished). A Triple A trainer with the Blue Jays would earn about $16,000.

John McLaren says the Blue Jays try to do extra things for their minor-league people. "They give allowances for apartments," McLaren said. "I talked to a lot of minor-league managers, and none of them had anything like that. Some of them do, but a lot don't."

Major-league teams also have roving minor-league instructors in addition to the coaches on each team. Bob Mattick runs the Blue Jays' minor-league system and visits each team and sometimes offers advice to players. Roving coaches John Mayberry, who instructs the hitters, and Mel Queen, who tutors the pitchers, also work at the major-league camp during spring training to maintain a consistent philosophy. During the season they make regular visits throughout the minor-league system.

The Blue Jays, like the Dodgers, believe in developing continuity and loyalty in their system. And, following the Dodger example, the Blue Jays are hiring more and more of their former players for their system. Mattick joined the Blue Jays as scouting supervisor in 1976 and served two years as field manager. Mayberry played for the Blue Jays for five seasons before being traded to the New York Yankees early in the 1982 season. Bob Bailor, the first player picked by the Jays in the 1976 expansion draft, joined the Blue Jays as manager of their Class A team in Dunedin for the 1987 season. He played four seasons in Toronto and was traded to the Mets for pitcher Roy Lee Jackson and then to the Dodgers, who released him in 1986. Other former Blue Jay players, survivors of that snowy 1977 opener, who have found jobs in the system are Doug Ault, the manager in Syracuse, and Hector Torres, who was the field manager in Florence before becoming a coach at Syracuse in 1987. Eddie Dennis, from the Dominican Republic, had played in the Jay farm system from 1978 until 1984 without rising above Double A; in 1986 he was the coach at St. Catharines and in 1987 the manager at Medicine Hat.

Having six farm teams gives the Blue Jays the flexibility to develop players. Many have not mastered all the fundamentals; others may need grooming to play an unfamiliar position. Some players have been ruined by being promoted too soon – there was fear during his first few seasons that this had happened to Moseby.

AS THE TORONTO organization matured, as more and better players were signed, the results trickled up from the minor-league teams, first in Medicine Hat, then up through the system to Syracuse. In the early years, the Blue Jay farm teams were as pathetic as the senior team in Toronto. Gradually that changed, too. Medicine Hat won the 1982 Pioneer League championship, but the real winning did not begin until the summer of 1985. Knoxville had made the Southern League finals in 1984 but lost in the playoffs. In 1985, Knoxville finished first in its division in the split season and had the best overall record in the league; but it lost in the playoffs. Kinston finished first in the second half of the season in the Carolina League but also lost in the playoffs. Florence won the championship in the South Atlantic League after finishing first overall in the split-season schedule. Syracuse won the International League pennant in 1985, as the major-league Blue Jays were charging to their AL East championship. Badly weakened by call-ups to Toronto, the Chiefs lost in the playoffs.

Fans of minor-league teams often find it frustrating because they know the emphasis is on developing players, not on winning games. Still, winning is important. "I think you have to learn how to win," says Gord Ash. "Winning creates a better atmosphere on the club. You can get more things done than you can when everybody's down all the time."

Not only players can be groomed in the farm system. It is also where field managers, coaches, and trainers learn their crafts. Like any pitcher or shortstop, Doug Ault and Hector Torres and the others wait for the call to move to the big team. It happened to John McLaren in 1986. When Jimy Williams took over from Bob Cox as field manager of the Blue Jays, McLaren replaced Williams as the third-base coach.

McLaren, a catcher in the Houston Astros organization (he was signed by Gord Lakey, now with the Jays), developed shoulder problems; he became a backup catcher in Memphis, a Triple A team. Pat Gillick, who knew McLaren from his Houston days, offered him a job with the expansion Blue Jays as a minor-league coach and scout. "I still have the letter Peter Bavasi sent me telling me that we'd start from the ground up and hope we can all grow together," McLaren said. "He was right. We started on the ground floor and came a long way. Every now and then I'll look at it because it makes me feel good."

188

He managed Medicine Hat in 1978, Utica in 1979, Medicine Hat in 1980, Kinston in 1981 and 1982, then Knoxville from 1983 to 1985. He also managed winter baseball for two years in Colombia and coached for three years in Venezuela, working with Lara, a team with many Blue Jay prospects.

Ault, who manages in Syracuse, says a good farm-team manager must be a mother, father, priest, and psychologist to the players. After his opening-day heroics with the Blue Jays in 1977, Ault settled in as an average-to-mediocre player with a hitch in his swing. He stayed three years in Toronto, drifted back to Triple A, then played in Japan and returned to play for Syracuse. When he stopped playing the Blue Jays hired him as a coach in Knoxville, then moved him to be manager in Kinston with three weeks to go in the 1983 season. He learned that managing at the Class A level means more than trying to win games. "Some of these guys you see are not doing too good, but they've got the potential to be good players and you've got to sacrifice wins to develop them," he said. "If there's somebody you feel could play in the big leagues some day, you could hurt his confidence if you pinch hit for him or take him out for a defensive replacement. You stick with a guy and he comes through a couple of times, his confidence goes up."

After each game the minor-league managers send a report on the game back to the office in Toronto. For home games they send it over a telecopier – except for Medicine Hat and St. Catharines, neither of which has one – and on road games they dictate it over the telephone into a tape machine and Ken Fry, who works in the office part-time, types it onto the forms. The game report consists of statistics from the game, with some comments.

Ault said the first time he took the lineup card to home plate he felt the same excitement he did on the day he hit the two opening-day homers. By 1985, Ault was managing in Syracuse. "Managing is never easy, no matter where you go," Ault said. "You've always got problems, whether it's A ball, where the guys are fighting homesickness, or Triple A, where the guys coming down don't think they should be there. It's not easy managing more than twenty different personalities, coming in every day in different moods, not to mention your own moods."

IN 1980, THE BLUE JAYS had the first pick in the first round of the free-agent draft in January. (This draft was discontinued in 1987.) The January draft was not as bountiful as the June draft, consisting mainly of college dropouts, junior-college players, and players selected in the June draft but not signed. However, it has yielded some good players, among them Tom Seaver.

The Blue Jays selected Colin McLaughlin, a lean six-foot, six-inch right-handed pitcher from the University of Connecticut. Seven years later, McLaughlin had yet to throw a ball in the majors, but he was still regarded as a prospect – one does not give up on a pitcher easily.

"Sometimes I look back and wonder if maybe it would have been better for me to have stayed another year in school – especially this winter," he said, pulling on his uniform at the minor-league spring training camp in March of 1986. He was starting his seventh season in the minors. In three months he would be 27.

"I didn't get to play winter ball and I had a couple of bad jobs because I don't really have any skills," McLaughlin said. "I have a year and a half or two years' worth of college. I have no degree. Who's going to hire me other than Mr. McDonald's or Mr. Burger King or something like that? I know I've got a brain in my head but I don't have any skills. I worked for a fence builder and for an apartment complex this winter. Just manual labour that anybody can do. We were in Marietta, Georgia. My wife went to the National Centre for Para-Legal Training. I worked out, hoping I'd get a job in winter ball. I told them I didn't want to go Venezuela again. I'd been there three times. I thought maybe I could get a job in the Dominican Republic or Puerto Rico but nothing ever came through."

In an age when the big stars can say they are insulted by an offer of $1 million a year, players such as McLaughlin would like to know what it's like to earn even the major-league minimum. McLaughlin would earn close to $17,000 in 1986. Out of this the player must pay for an apartment in the city in which he plays. And in the nomadic life of the minor leagues, there sometimes can be more than one move – up or down. Winter baseball can help provide year-round employment, but without it McLaughlin had to search elsewhere.

"I had to get a *real* job," McLaughlin said. "It was just brutal. Jobs that you would do for the summer in high school. Here I am 26 years old, I've got a wife and now I've got a baby on the way. I'm working for five dollars an hour. How am I going to survive, especially if this is my last year playing baseball? I might have to go four years in college again depending on my credits . . . I could be up shit creek in a hurry if

190

I don't have a very good year. Sometimes I look back and say, 'Well, you might have made the wrong decision.' But I don't regret it. If I have a tough time in the future it's because I made a choice. I've just got to pay for that. It's not like somebody tricked me. You know, when you get to be 20 or 21 years old you want to run your own life and that's why I did it.''

McLaughlin is intelligent, thoughtful, scholarly looking, and very much still like a college student searching for answers. His attitude toward baseball might be considered different from those who share the clubhouse, but he has the same dream. He admits that one of his problems as a pitcher is ''a wavering concentration level. I just don't have a 162-game face. Some nights I go out there and I really don't pay attention.''

McLaughlin had attended Amherst College in Massachusetts – the same school as John Cerutti – and then moved to the University of Connecticut. In a 1985 list of the most difficult schools to enter, Amherst ranked ninth in the United States with an acceptance rate of 21.8 per cent, not far behind such schools as Stanford, Harvard, Princeton, and Yale. Among the courses McLaughlin tried in his college career was chemistry, which he found difficult, and business administration, mainly because he didn't know what he wanted to do. ''That was as boring as could be,'' he said.

At Connecticut, he helped the Huskies into the 1979 College World Series, then did not to continue in school. ''I thought it was really a waste of my time to be in school and not give it too much of an effort. Or only give it an effort just to play baseball. If I wanted to play baseball a lot I could play for money.''

His one regret was not getting a provision put in his contract that would have the Jays pay his college tuition. There is now such a plan available for players; Lou Thornton, McLaughlin's teammate on the 1986 Syracuse Chiefs, took advantage of it when he signed with the Mets in 1981.

''It's kind of funny,'' McLaughlin said. ''The rest of my family is kind of an achieving family. Seven children in the family and pretty soon I'm going to be the only one without a degree. My father always said, 'Those goddamn aptitude tests say you're the smartest of the bunch.' ''

In 1981, his second professional season, McLaughlin was shuttled between the Double A team at Knoxville and the Triple A team at Syracuse. In 1986 he was still being shuttled between those two teams.

As a reliever in Knoxville he made 31 appearances and was 2–1 with an earned run average of 3.20 and eight saves. At Syracuse, he made six appearances and had one save and an ERA of 0.79. He was eligible to become a minor-league free agent after the 1986 season. Before that season began, he suggested to the team that perhaps a change of organizations might help him find that missing ingredient. But he was promoted to the Blue Jays' major-league roster in the fall, signed to a major-league contract, and then returned to the Triple A roster. He would be invited to the major-league spring training camp as a non-roster player.

"Toronto as an organization has more patience than I do as an individual," McLaughlin said.

Making the major leagues would bring him considerably more money. In 1987, the major-league minimum was $62,500, increased by $2,500 over 1986 because of a cost of living clause in the basic agreement between the players and owners. McLaughlin has yet to earn even half of that for a baseball season. A good Triple A salary might be $30,000 but it's likely to be less.

Angry? Hurt? Despondent? "I don't approach the game from the perspective of wanting to get rich," McLaughlin said. "But I sure would like to have a little bit more money than I have right now. I'm not really interested in a million dollars. I'm not saying I should be paid a lot, but I should be paid more."

What rankles minor-leaguers is that they are expected to prepare themselves for each season by working out during the winter, which means expending time and effort for the organization with no remuneration. "When Gord Ash sends out a letter and says you better be ready to go three innings when you get to minor-league camp, I think Gord Ash should be sending you a cheque for the winter so that you can work out instead of having to work at some job. Minor-league training camp is short, so you have long preparation on your own before you get there. All right, so compensate the individual for the work you're expected to do."

In 1985, McLaughlin attended the major-league camp but thinks his attitude hurt him. He was told that if he worked hard he might have a chance at a bullpen job. "But I didn't really believe that when I got there. I looked around and saw all the people they had acquired and I said I don't have a snowball's chance."

What if he did quit baseball? "That's the thing, I don't know what I want to do," he said, tying the laces of his shoes. He straightened up, grabbed his glove, and walked toward the field. "Sometimes I think I want to continue being a gypsy. Maybe join the merchant marine for a while. When I signed I said I'm not in it to be a career minor-leaguer. Here I am in my seventh year."

SITTING IN HIS OFFICE in front of the big board that shows the status of every player the Blue Jays control, Gord Ash handles the administrative work of the minor-league system. Between his office and Pat Gillick's there are three secretaries. Fran Brown, Gillick's secretary, and Ellen Harrigan and Sue Allen. When administrative assistant Carolyn Thiers left in late 1986 her duties were spread among the others with Janet Donaldson coming in from marketing. This office staff, equipped with computer terminals, handles the administrative paperwork, details, and assorted odds and ends. Harrigan does most of the work involving immigration.

Ash has orchestrated the shifting of three franchises. The constants for the past several years have been the Triple A team in Syracuse, the Double A team in Knoxville, and the rookie league team in Medicine Hat.

In each of the past three seasons, the Blue Jays have taken over ownership of a minor-league team: Knoxville in 1985, St. Catharines in 1986, and Dunedin for 1987. (The last time the Blue Jays had a minor-league team in Dunedin the ownership ran into financial difficulties.)

The addition of St. Catharines gives the Blue Jays two Canadian teams in their farm system, which is good business from a Canadian market standpoint and helps the Blue Jays circumvent visa restrictions limiting the number of foreign players on U.S.-based teams. Visas have been limited to a total of 500 for the 26 major-league teams, which works out to an average of 19 per team.

The Blue Jays can stock the teams in Medicine Hat and St. Catharines with players from Latin America, and even Canadian or Australian players, and stay within their U.S. quota.

Ash logged many miles on the Queen Elizabeth Way between Toronto, St. Catharines, and other interested cities while working on the deal – Welland, Niagara Falls, and Hamilton also wanted a Blue Jay farm team. If the decision had been based strictly on the baseball facilities, St. Catharines would have been last on the list. In fact, it would not have been considered but for the enthusiasm of Bill Lefebvre, the city's business and development officer. The St. Catharines team plays in Community Park, next to Merritton High School. For their first season, the park had a covered grandstand with 530 seats, all down the first-base line; temporary bleacher seats were installed around the rest of the field. The players used dressing rooms in the high school, but they stayed in comfortable rooms at a nurses' residence on the campus of Brock University. For the 1987 season, St. Catharines agreed to build new clubhouse facilities – which also can be used for local amateur baseball – and stands that would hold 2,000. The Blue Jays contributed $80,000 toward the renovation costs; Labatt's added $80,000 and another $20,000 for promotion and fund-raising; the city of St. Catharines paid $168,000; and a grant from the Wintario lottery added $191,000. Local citizens pitched in, donating their time to upgrade the stadium; a steel company donated construction material. So, although the total estimate for work was $750,000, it actually cost less.

The St. Catharines team drew about 46,000 in its first season, and broke about even on its $250,000 budget, including startup costs. Rick Amos, who became the team's general manager at the age of 24, was voted the league's executive of the year. He accepted his award at baseball's winter meetings with his arm in a sling after undergoing surgery on his rotator cuff; it had been torn playing hockey. Amos went to high school in Winnipeg, attended Toronto's York University, and started with the Blue Jays as a mail-room clerk, turning down a chance to work for the Canadian Imperial Bank of Commerce. After a part-time stint on the ground crew, he worked his way up to assistant director of operations.

Amos said the St. Catharines players were treated "like celebrities" and that the blacks and Latins found the atmosphere more comfortable than that of the southern U.S. cities. "There they would walk into a store and be refused service," Amos said, "or they would be there before a white person, but the white person would be served first." Eddie Dennis told Amos how he enjoyed St. Catharines. "He loved the people because there wasn't the prejudice," Amos said.

Besides wanting another Canadian team, the Blue Jays were anxious to sever their ties with Kinston, a small tobacco, timber, and cotton city in North Carolina. They entered into a one-season agreement with the California League team in Ventura (they used the field of a community college and played all day games at home), biding their time until the Florida State League could activate their Dunedin franchise and keep the divisions balanced.

Doug Ault managed the Kinston Blue Jays for part of 1983 and all of the 1984 season. There was trouble finding places for his players to live, particularly the blacks and the Latins. "Not all the people were that way," Ault said. "One guy had a big five-bedroom house in the old style, and he'd always have a few guys who'd stay there. If it hadn't been for him, it would really have been bad. Some of them don't speak English, they're 17, 18, and it would have been difficult to separate them."

Most players lived in trailer parks, which are plentiful throughout the Carolinas; there is one across from Florence's American Legion Field, where the team played. Two players usually shared a trailer. Ron Shepherd remembers the utilities bill came to about $90 a month, almost as high as the rent, which was between $130 and $140.

Another problem in Kinston was keeping the players from getting bored and restless. Only two fast-food places were open after night games, a Pizza Hut and a Hardee's hamburger joint. "It's a very strange city," Ault said. "Everything closes down at nine o'clock." The only hotel was a Holiday Inn, which was almost always filled. This made it inconvenient for anyone from Toronto to visit. Kinston also happens to be in the heart of Ku Klux Klan territory.

Florence was better than Kinston, but not much. There were a few more hotels and restaurants, but boredom could be a problem. Yuill and Russ Williams, the business manager of his minor-league empire, finally sold it because the team wasn't making money. The franchise was moved to Myrtle Beach, partly because of the abundance of Canadian tourists in the area.

"We contemplated buying the club ourselves," Ash said. "We had no place to take it. Russ and Yuill tried for a long time to take that club to Myrtle Beach. Going back two years ago, we provided a letter of agreement to Russ that the Blue Jays would go with him to Myrtle Beach, but they could never get a deal over there."

But Blenckstone has a condominium in Myrtle Beach and was able to work a deal to use the baseball park at nearby Coastal Carolina College, which officially is in Conway. There's a football stadium behind the baseball park that will be remodelled and renovated for the baseball team's exclusive use during the summer – there is no overlap with the football season. The lease ensures that the Blue Jays have use of the field for morning workouts, an important aspect of life in the low minors. The general manager, Burl Yarborough, who also was the general manager when the team was in Florence, says the hard core of 50 or 60 fans that followed the team would probably make the drive to Myrtle Beach for games. Ash says the Blue Jays are comfortable with the new owner. ''He seems like he's a businessman, which is important for the operation of the franchise,'' Ash said. ''He made a very good move in keeping the general manager from Florence so he knows our organization and we know how he operates. It's a difficult process to own all your own clubs.''

With a team in Myrtle Beach and another back in Dunedin, the farm system again becomes more compact. Only Medicine Hat is not in the East. There is another advantage to Dunedin. It becomes an important cog in the Blue Jays' minor-league system, particularly as it's also the Blue Jays' spring-training and Instructional League headquarters. Also, except for Medicine Hat, there is a steady progression of the farm teams northward, which allows for more convenient transfer of players from team to team – the three-hour time difference between Toronto and Ventura sometimes proved a problem in trying to contact someone with the team.

Another plus is that Grant Field, improved as part of the renovations done in 1984 and 1985 on the Jays' spring-training facilities, gets more use. Having a team there fulfils a commitment the Blue Jays made to Dunedin to have the park as active as possible. It also can act as a depot for the U.S. teams in the Jays' minor-league system. ''It's tough to bring equipment back and forth over the border,'' Ash said. ''It's easier being based in Dunedin and able to service all the clubs out of there – and make use of the employees and the facilities we have there. It allows us to establish, from a minor-league perspective, almost a central warehouse of equipment and supplies and inventories. I hate to use the term, but it's almost like an American headquarters.''

It should make things easier for Jody Pucello, the minor-league equipment co-ordinator who also looks after the visitors' clubhouse at MacArthur Stadium in Syracuse. When it was time to leave for Syracuse (Pucello is from Syracuse and has worked for the Chiefs for 14 years) at the end of spring training, he'd pack what he thought would be the season's equipment requirements for the minor-league system and take everything to Syracuse. Some of the equipment wouldn't be needed, so at season's end he'd have to take it back to Dunedin. With the Dunedin team in operation, much of the extra equipment can stay there and, when needed, can be shipped from there.

At one time, Florida was a handy starting point for Latin American players. The team at Bradenton was largely Latin, but many Latins start with Canadian teams now. While the Blue Jays do not have a formal program to teach the young Latin players English – an area Ash would like to improve – they try to use as many Spanish-speaking coaches as possible. Ramon Webster, a Panamanian who played for the A's (Kansas City and Oakland), Padres, and Cubs in five major-league seasons, went to Kinston as a coach in 1985 when there were mid-season language problems. The team's performance improved dramatically. The Dominican Eddie Dennis worked with manager Cloyd Boyer in St. Catharines, where a dozen of the players were Hispanic. And Hector Torres was a minor-league instructor for several years in the Blue Jay organization and managed Florence in 1985 and 1986 before being named to coach at Syracuse in 1987.

"The first year is most important. Once they play here a year, they pick up a few words, at least the words they use in a game," Torres said. "The second year, it becomes easier. When I was in school I liked English, but I can relate to these kids. I was 16 years old when I signed and I got real homesick when I was struggling my first year. I just wanted to go home. In those days there was only tne manager – no coach, no trainer. Sometimes you need somebody you can talk to in your own language, a shoulder to cry on."

Hector Epitacio Torres was born in Monterrey, Mexico, on September 14, 1945. After his purgatory in the minors, he made it to the big leagues in 1968 as a shortstop for the Houston Astros. After three seasons he moved to the Chicago Cubs, the Montreal Expos, back to Houston, and then to the San Diego Padres. Toronto picked him up in a trade for John Lowenstein late in spring training of their first season. He was in the lineup for the opener in the snow at Exhibition Stadium. He remembers the "sucker thing sucking up the snow" – the Zamboni that usually sucks up the water in rain delays – and being so cold that he was "shaking like a leaf" standing for the U.S. anthem, then turning around to face home plate to ready for the game to start, forgetting that there must be one more anthem, the Canadian, to shiver through before the game would start. He played one season for the Blue Jays, filling in at short, second, and third. He batted .241 and hit five home runs – including the first grand slam in club history, against Ron Guidry

197

of the Yankees on June 27 – and then was released in March, 1978. He played for Columbus and Syracuse in the International League before being hired by the Jays as a minor-league instructor.

Down on the farm, he tells the young players what it was like when he broke in, long before anyone bothered with the delicacies of language, racism, and loneliness. "I have never forgotten the hotel in Dubuque, Iowa. There were railroad tracks right outside the windows and every night a train rattled by about midnight. It was a rough hotel. We didn't have bathrooms in the rooms – there was one for the whole floor and I was scared because of the people who stayed there. When I had to go in the middle of the night I was so scared I used to go out the window."

The hotels had no room service, no television, no air-conditioning. Torres remembers the hot, muggy summer when he would open all the windows in his room to get some air. "One night I heard this noise – *whish, whish, whish.* I turned the lights on and there was a bat. It was unbelievable. I chased it all over, trying to kill it with my pillows."

When Torres played in the minors, there was no morning practice during the season, just the usual batting practice before games. Now that Mattick runs the Blue Jays' minor-league system there are practices all the time. It's not so unusual any more for minor-league teams to hold workouts during the day, but no one is more demanding than Mattick. He is known for his long, arduous drills at minor-league camp during spring training. Mattick turned 71 in December, 1986, but he works tirelessly with the young players on the farm. A towel around his neck, wearing a track suit, he cracks out hard grounders or rolls baseballs repeatedly to an infielder to work on his throw, offering encouragement and explaining the fundamentals of the game again and again until they become instinctive. He firmly believes that baseball is a game of repetition.

"We practise a lot," Torres said. "Bobby believes in it and I agree with him. If we make a mental mistake on a certain play, we go over it the next morning. You've got to walk through it, so they get the idea. At first they hate to get up in the morning – they were barking about it the first couple of weeks – but once they get there they get going and they tell me they feel stronger than if they had slept in."

Rob Ducey, the Canadian outfielder, appreciates the work. "He's pretty strict," Ducey assesses Mattick. "We're like his kids out there and he wants the best for us but he wants the best from us, too. I would rather have someone who's going to work us hard than someone who's not going to."

Ducey grinned. "We're young, we're not supposed to get tired."

MATTICK GREW UP with baseball. His father, Chick Mattick, had a brief stint as a major-league player – in 1912 and 1913 with the Chicago White Sox, before Mattick was born, and in 1918 with the St. Louis Cardinals, when Mattick was too young to remember. "After he got through playing, he managed in the minor leagues and owned minor-league clubs," said Mattick, who was born in Sioux City, Iowa, in 1915 and grew up in St. Louis. "He had 50 per cent in Dallas, he had Sioux City. I used to go on trips with him. I'd hang around the ballplayers' hotels. I guess I took an interest and used to like doing something in the summertime. In those days you could let kids to go out on the field in batting practice. The field was loaded with kids shagging."

He learned by playing, by watching the little things, and by constantly practising, even if there was only one other person to hit ground balls to him. Scouts like Mattick claim that modern children do not practise enough or play enough. They just do what's organized by the teams they play for.

Mattick had a chance to sign with the Cardinals at 16 but waited until he was 18 and signed with the Chicago Cubs. His father had been out of professional baseball since he was 12.

"He had about 10 acres and he planted apple trees and he was more or less retired when the Depression came along," Mattick said. "We lived on this place, we had chickens and apple trees and one cow and we had the gardens. He used to love to hunt, so we didn't have any problems with food. There were times when we had fried chicken for breakfast, lunch, and dinner but it was always fresh and my mother was a good cook."

From 1934 to 1937, Mattick played for the Los Angeles Angels of the Pacific Coast League. He was a shortstop – Gabe Paul remembers him having a very good arm – but he never reached his potential because a batting-practice foul ball fractured his skull above the right eye in 1936 (he was hitting .363). The accident left him with double vision and he must wear prism glasses. He never hit well after that, his best year being 1939, when he batted .287 in 51 games with the Cubs. He was with Cincinnati in 1941 and 1942, but hardly played. He was finished playing at 27.

"Certain doctors told me they could straighten this double vision up," Mattick said. "Others said you couldn't do it. So I went to the one that said he could because I was so damn down. That just threw it off worse."

He was out of baseball in 1943, working in the Navy shipyards in Los Angeles, in the gas-rationing department, while keeping up his baseball contacts.

"There's an old Chicago Cub scout, Jack Doyle, who knew my dad and when he'd come to Los Angeles I'd drive him around," Mattick said. "He asked me if I wanted to get back into baseball and I said I sure do. I said I wanted to be a manager."

Doyle gave Mattick some advice. "He said the best thing to do is to get in the front office. There you won't have to take all the heat that you do in managing. But if you go into managing, be sure you get a good club the first year or two in order to establish yourself. He said to go into scouting for longevity, but if I ever went into managing to be sure of one thing: Don't overmanage. There's a tendency of guys who break in to overmanage and to stress so many things that aren't important."

Mattick returned to baseball as travelling secretary and coach with Birmingham of the Southern League, scouted a year for the Yankees, then worked for the Cincinnati Reds. The manager of the Reds' Ogden club was fired and Mattick took over, moving the team from last to third. But he returned to scouting, staying with the Reds until 1961, when he moved to Houston's expansion team. He was with Cleveland, Baltimore, and the Seattle Pilots (moving with them to Milwaukee). He spent five years with the Montreal Expos before joining Toronto in 1976. When the Blue Jays offered him the managing job for 1980, he was surprised. In retrospect, he would have liked to have managed earlier and moved around less.

"I was always the fortunate type of guy, maybe too fortunate in that I could always get a job," Mattick said. "If things didn't go right, I just pulled the pin and said to hell with it and go somewhere else. I guess you could say I was strong-willed, bull-headed. Like my wife said, 'The only time you'll be happy is if you own a ball club.' "

THE BLUE JAYS have had only four Canadians on their major-league roster. The first was Dave McKay, the infielder, who went on to play and then coach for the Oakland A's. Another was Paul Hodgson. In a brief stint with the Blue Jays he hit a home run in Baltimore in 1980, but then shoulder injuries ended a promising career. Dave Shipanoff pitched in the Blue Jay minor-league system; he finally made it to the majors late in the 1985 season with the Philadelphia Phillies, where he had been traded in spring training. The fourth Canadian to make the roster was Rob Ducey, an outfielder who made an impressive transition from Class A to Double A in 1986 and played well in centre field in the Venezuelan winter league. There were five other Canadians in the Blue Jay system in 1986: right-handed pitchers John Bilawey of Mississauga and Rob Guenther of Surrey, British Columbia; left-handed pitchers Alan Butler of Toronto and Vince Horsman of Dartmouth, Nova Scotia; outfielder Winston Brown of Truro, Nova Scotia.

Bob Prentice is the Blue Jays' scouting supervisor for Canada. He oversees a dozen part-time scouts from Prince Edward Island to British Columbia. He crosses the country at least once a year to attend major tournaments and compare notes with local scouts. He helps with spring training and tryout camps. Occasionally he wanders south of the border to check out Canadians playing in U.S. colleges.

Prentice knows what it takes, having played in the minors for years but never quite making it to the majors. He thinks Canadian players have a better chance at the major leagues today than when he started out on the sandlots of Toronto. "There are twenty-six major-league teams now," he said. "When I started out there were only sixteen. And there were a lot more minor leagues to go through. When I was in the Cleveland organization there were fourteen minor-league teams. They had four Class D teams, three Class C teams, so you had to work your way through a lot more players to get to the top. I know a lot of people who played Triple A and Double A who would have been major-league players today."

Prentice grew up in Toronto's east end in a cosy area known as The Beach. He attended Riverdale Collegiate and started playing at Riverdale Park, a sprawling verdant stretch near what is now the Don Valley Parkway. Some summers, in his mid-teens, he played on four teams – both junior and senior teams, baseball and fastball, including a team in The Beach sponsored by Tip Top Tailors. He played fastball Monday, Wednesday, and Friday, baseball Tuesday, Thursday, and Saturday. On Sundays he practised.

He first signed with the St. Louis Cardinals organization in 1947 and attended a camp in Georgia. (Jimmy Williams, the Toronto-born first-base coach of the Baltimore Orioles, signed with the Dodgers at about the same time.) Prentice was released after two weeks and given a ticket home. Not wanting to return a failure, he cashed it in and he and a friend from Windsor bought bus tickets to South Carolina, where there was a Boston Red Sox farm team.

"We asked for a tryout and they said, 'Okay, but we're only here for 13 more days.' They worked us out, gave us a little meal money and put us up in a rooming house." Prentice played well at the tryout camp and was offered a chance to play in New Orleans, where he got room and board and $5 a day meal money.

Prentice worked out with a Double A team in New Orleans until the manager suggested he move on because older players were returning from the war and deserved a chance to play professional baseball. Prentice grudgingly returned home, still convinced he could make it to the major leagues. "I left Toronto with $50 and came home with $25," he said. Later in the summer he attended a tournament in Baltimore, where he caught the eye of someone from the Cleveland Indians, then a power in the American League. The Indians signed Prentice to a contract worth $250 a month, with a $2,000 signing bonus. He played short-stop for a team in Batavia that year and hit 13 home runs.

"I went on from there and never missed a step," he said, "from D to C to B, until I finally got to the major-league roster with Cleveland in 1954. But I didn't stay. I think I should have. The year before I hit 24 home runs in Double A, which isn't bad for an infielder."

The 1954 Indians had such players as infielders as Al Rosen and Bobby Avila. Prentice hit 151 home runs in his career; in Tulsa, in 1957, he hit grand-slam home runs in consecutive at-bats. Prentice became a full-time scout with the Detroit Tigers for 17 years, signing three Canadian pitchers who made the big team – John Hiller, Mike Kilkenny, and George Korince. He joined the Blue Jays in 1976. Paul Hodgson was signed in 1977 out of Marysville, New Brunswick. He could run and hit for power and Prentice is convinced that if he had not injured both shoulders – one impairing his throwing and the other his swing – he would be with the Blue Jays today.

ANTHONY SIMONE, called Tex by everyone, was a Syracuse accountant who loved baseball so much that when the team regained an International League franchise in 1961 he took a job with the ground crew. Syracuse has a rich minor-league baseball history that goes back to

1885, but the city was abandoned in 1957 in favour of Miami. When the Dodgers wanted their Triple A franchise closer to their new West Coast home, their Montreal franchise was sold to the Community Baseball Club of Syracuse. The official price was $50,000, but payments were made when money became available. The Dodgers eventually called it a deal nine years later, after receiving $37,000. The price of a Triple A franchise has increased dramatically in recent years. In 1974, for instance, the Pawtucket Red Sox sold for $25,000 – $5,000 a year for five years. Late in the 1986 season, the Maine Guides were sold for $2.4 million to a group in Scranton, Pennsylvania.

Simone, grey-haired, slight and wiry, had been a frustrated semipro player. Halfway through the 1961 season, the Syracuse trainer suffered a heart attack and Simone, who had some training background, took over. After six years, he tried the front office, progressing from business manager in 1968 to assistant general manager in 1969 and general manager in 1970. Today he is the general manager and executive vice-president; his son, John, is director of operations.

Simone calls the Chiefs a "pure community-owned" team. "A lot of clubs like to have the community-owned image, okay, but somebody within that concept owns 51 per cent share of the stock," he explained. "Our club is pure community-owned; you can own all the stock you want but you cannot vote more than 500 shares' worth at the annual meeting. It was set up that way so nobody could get control of the club."

In the first year, 1961, 1,100 shareholders paid $10 a share. A dividend of 25 cents was paid that year, but none has been paid since. At the end of 1986 there were about 4,000 shareholders in the Syracuse Chiefs owning a total of 16,832 shares. "I would say 75 per cent of them own one share," Simone said. "Me, I own 10 shares."

Simone was chatting in the press box at Exhibition Stadium, sitting up in the third row down toward the right-field corner. It was late September, and the Blue Jay minor-league organization was having its annual gathering in Toronto to discuss the business of baseball.

"Funny thing, they just had an article in *Money* magazine on the Syracuse Chiefs that there was stock available," Simone said. "I'm getting calls from California, San Diego, Connecticut. I lay it on the line to them, you know, that we're not listed in the newspapers, we are a corporation but I am the broker dealer, I handle all the transactions. They say they would like to own a share of the Syracuse Chiefs, these people. Just before I came up here, a guy from San Diego called me and bought four shares, one for himself, one for his wife, and one each for his two children. Finally I asked him why he was doing it and he says, 'Well, we want to be part-owners of a professional baseball team.' So I sent him some team colours and a souvenir list.''

The budget for a Triple A team is upwards of $600,000, depending on the stadium rental deal. Ed Mapstone, the team's assistant general manager, says the Chiefs have an excellent deal on MacArthur Stadium. ''Basically, it doesn't cost us anything other than we maintain it annually for the county,'' he said.

When Simone took over as general manager in 1970, the team had a $200,000 deficit. ''We haven't lost a dime since 1970 and that's with eighth-place ball clubs, too. That cliché about you've got to have a winner doesn't prove out in my mind. It depends on the job you do within your facility of promoting and providing entertainment. At our level it's constant promoting every night. I budget on the basis of an eighth-place club and if you have a winning team it's frosting on the cake.'' In 1985 the Chiefs won the pennant and drew 222,000 fans to MacArthur Stadium; they missed the playoffs in 1986 and drew 187,000.

Profits are put back into the team, with some money invested so the team makes something from interest. ''We've built up stockholders' equity over the past 16 years,'' Simone said. ''In 1970 our stock had a $7.77 deficit. They call it the book value. Now the book value of the stock sold at $10 is $23.65. Now the remaining shares are selling at $20 a share. If we were to liquidate tomorrow, they'd get $23.65 a share.'' As of October 31, 1986, the book value of the stock increased to $24.08 and the price of the shares was increased to $25.

The Chiefs were a Yankee farm team, and the Yankees are still the big team in upper New York State. But the Chiefs dropped the Yankees, who moved their team to Columbus, and joined with the Blue Jays. Simone said there was some consternation with the Yankees: in two years, the parent club's moves resulted in the Triple A team losing 26 players. The Blue Jays presented an opportunity to grow with a major league team. In their first year with the Blue Jays, Syracuse came closest to a loss in any time since 1970, when it made $1,400.

Simone said the relationship between the Chiefs and the Blue Jays has been such that their three-year agreements are virtually automatically renewed. ''It's because of the people that we are dealing with. Let me put it this way – and it doesn't exist in professional baseball –

they are concerned. They've always been concerned. They are always asking, 'Is everything all right? Is there anything else we can do?' That doesn't exist in professional baseball. Usually they don't want to hear from you once the season starts. We've always had good rapport.''

RUSS WILLIAMS was running a contracting business when he met Bill Yuill in a bar in Medicine Hat in 1979. ''We got along good. The rest is history,'' Williams said.

At that time, Yuill was the owner of the Pioneer League franchise in his home town of Medicine Hat. The team became connected with the Blue Jays in 1978. The history Williams mentions is the building of a minor-league empire that makes a profit.

Williams, who is from Saskatoon, looks after the business end of Yuill's baseball teams. For fun and profit, Yuill added the Blue Jays' team in Florence to his collection: Fort Myers, a Class A team in the Kansas City Royals' chain; Chattanooga, in the Double A Southern League, an affiliate of the Seattle Mariners; and Tucson in the Triple A Pacific Coast League, an affiliate of the Houston Astros. They also owned the spring-training concessions rights for the Fort Myers park.

Williams said that they were able to make some good buys. ''The trouble is getting in,'' he said. ''It's a closed game. We snuck up on everybody, got in at the right time.''

The total of the purchases came to about $2.5 million (Cdn.). They bought Florence for $100,000 and sold it for $200,000. They bought Fort Meyers in 1985 for $225,000 and sold it for $461,000.

Williams is stocky, with dark hair and moustache; he is in his mid-thirties and quick to laugh – and 1986 gave Williams something to laugh about. The profit was close to $500,000 (Cdn.). He says it was their best season by far. However, they decided to divest themselves of the Florence team, a consistent money loser, and of the Fort Myers team, which in 1988 will be moved to Haines City, a new spring-training site for the Royals. ''The first year in Florence we lost about $60,000, then $40,000, and in 1986 about $25,000,'' Williams said.

Despite a slow start, 3–17, and less than ideal weather, Medicine Hat still made about $40,000, drawing 42,000 fans. The team's best year was 1982, the championship season and one of good weather, when they drew 57,000 fans to the 3,200-seat park and made $100,000. Attendance was 55,000 in 1985, when the Blue Jays' major-league club was becoming Canada's team. The budget for Medicine Hat is about $150,000.

"Work hard," Williams says, explaining the profits. "Sell a lot of advertising, season's tickets, promotions. We're big on promotions at our ballparks. That's where we make most of our money. Giving away stuff. All you have to do to break even in operations the size of Medicine Hat is to draw about 800 people. When you start drawing 2,500–3,000 a night you're talking about fairly serious dollars. You're talking $4.50 a head and they're going to eat and drink and buy souvenirs."

In the hospitality trailer at the Blue Jays' spring-training camp, Williams said, "This is not political at all and I say this to other organizations – you put Toronto up here and you go about 10 country miles to find number two. They do absolutely everything first class in the minor leagues. There's also intangibles. Toronto took its entire minor-league system – the coaches, the general managers, owners – up to Toronto for the playoffs in 1985. We're also with Kansas City and they didn't even send me an order form for tickets. Toronto not only sent me an order form, they sent us a plane ticket and said come on down. And every year, they bring in the general managers and the owners of every one of their minor-league clubs, their expenses paid, to Toronto. Nobody else we deal with is even close."

JOHN MCLAREN CHUCKLES when he looks back on the summer he managed Lloyd Moseby at Medicine Hat. Moseby would come up with schemes to make money for the Blue Jays; one time he told McLaren to get Peter Bavasi to order 15,000 Lloyd Moseby bats. He would get his friends to sell them outside the Oakland Alameda County Stadium. Or the time he was going to buy a purple Corvette like basketball star Darryl Dawkins's and put "Shaker" on the licence plates.

"You can't get those plates," McLaren told him. "I saw them on the freeway in California when I was scouting."

"I guess I've got to go with Plan B," said the crestfallen 18-year-old. "What's that?"

"Bavasi. I'm going to get plates with Bavasi on them."

Before one game, Moseby told McLaren he would not be able to play that day. "I can't go today, Mac, I'm beat. My body's tired."

"Lloyd, how can that body of yours be tired? What have you been eating?"

Moseby said he hadn't eaten anything because he ran out of money. McLaren bought him two hot dogs and two Cokes. In the game, Moseby hit two home runs, two doubles, and drove in seven runs.

A week later, same thing. "Can't go today, Mac," Moseby told McLaren. "My body's hurting."

"Are we going to go through that *again*?" McLaren asked.

After two hot dogs and two Cokes, Moseby struck out four times.

E I G H T H

THE LATIN CONNECTION

IT IS DECEMBER. The air is warm and charged with excitement. The outfield bleachers, set well back from the foul lines, are packed. A couple of skirmishes erupt in the left-field seats half an hour before game time and are quickly extinguished. For the rest of the night the crowd behaves, unless you count the time in the early innings when the security guards in military garb have to settle an argument in the boxes behind home plate about who belongs in what seat.

In the covered grandstand the seats are reserved, and the people stream in closer to game time – some with radios or ghetto blasters on their shoulders so they can listen to the game as well as watch. The procession continues well after the first pitch. Finally, there is no place to sit except in the aisles. A woman and her young daughter sit on the steps; men beside them occupy the seats. The spaces behind the last row of seats are crammed with standees, and behind them others find positions up beside the bases of the beams that support the grandstand roof. Estadio Quisqueya is literally jammed to the rafters; the crowd is perhaps 17,000. It may still be the regular season of the Dominican Republic's winter league, but this is no ordinary game.

This is Escogido vs. Licey. The old Dodgers and Giants have nothing on these two.

In Latin America the *beisbol* is spiced with passion. For its youthful practitioners in the Dominican Republic, major-league baseball is usually the only hope to escape from extreme poverty. They improvise. Barefoot and tattered, they might use milk cartons for gloves, sticks for bats, tightly packed tin foil or the top of a water pitcher thrown like a Frisbee for a ball. But they play.

A country of great beauty, with dazzling beaches and 1,000 miles of shoreline, the Dominican Republic occupies the eastern two-thirds of the island of Hispaniola, which it shares with Haiti. It has a population of 6.4 million and an unemployment rate estimated at anywhere from 40 to 70 per cent. The per capita income in 1983 was $1,371 (U.S.) and has held steady. Sugar provides employment for 80,000 Dominicans and cutting sugar cane is hard, physical, low-paying work. The country was the hardest hit Latin American country when the United States cut its world sugar importing quota by 41 per cent in December, 1986, to bolster domestic production. It was estimated that the Dominican Republic's earnings from sugar sales to the United States would drop to $60 million from $111 million.

In the Dominican Republic, the Caribbean hotbed of the Summer Game, the game is at its hottest in the six-team winter league when the opponents are the teams representing the capital, Santo Domingo, and its population of 1.5 million. Licey is dressed in Dodger-like white with blue trim, and Escogido has white-and-red uniforms reminiscent of the Philadelphia Phillies. Both teams play their home games at Santo Domingo's Estadio Quisqueya, one of the baseball parks built by the dictator Trujillo in 1955. During the regular winter-league season, a half-empty Estadio Quisqueya can be relaxed, a hint of the late, lamented Maple Leaf Stadium, but with a Latin beat: colourful advertisements on the outfield fences, a plain green wall in straightaway centre field, and the aging, covered stand. There might be a sudden argument or a fight in the stands or the constant buzz of intense involvement; but when Licey is playing Estrellas from San Pedro de Macoris or Azucareros of La Romana, or when Escogido plays Caimanes of San Cristobal or Aguilas of Santiago, there is the idyllic feeling of a warm summer night and of games played long ago on grass.

During the regular-season games at Quisqueya, there is room to stretch out. Money circulates among the cluster of gamblers who occupy seats high up in the stands on the first-base side; ragged urchins chase foul balls hit into the stands and immediately put them up for sale. There is a hole in the screen behind home plate toward first base; sometimes a foul ball rolls through it and drops to the seats to be attacked by a scrambling group of boys.

The parade of vendors is constant, some with ice on their trays. It could be a local beer, Bohemia or Presidente, or Burmudez rum, or soft drinks. It could be peanuts or baseball caps of your favourite Dominican team or noise-makers. An arrangement can be made with the beer vendor for a visit every couple of innings. The beer is cold and poured from bottles into paper cups. If a bottle is left at the seats, an admonition from a security guard accompanies its removal. Some of the vendors tap their hands on their trays as they move through the crowd. Others use their voices. Some both. "Maní, maní, maní, maní," yells the young peanut vendor.

Outside the stadium there are rows of souvenirs for sale – caps, pennants, shirts – before and after the game. And delicious oranges, cheap. Before the games, scalpers sell box seats to unsuspecting tourists even for a game that will fill only half the stadium. Top price for a seat is six pesos ($2 U.S.); a scalper might charge 10 pesos.

Each male entering the stadium is searched by armed guards for bottles and guns. With that formality out of the way, the unofficial greeters, boys, hand out a roster sheet that offers a fascinating array of misspellings. The boys check the ticket stub and scamper to the seat, dust it with a cloth, and linger. A peso tip earns the title of "amigo." During the game, the rascals run through the stadium, hustling what they can – grab a baseball and sell it, go to a concession stand for an "amigo" in the seats – and sometimes, if the boy is very young and the game very long, falling into a sleep so sound that his brother cannot batter him awake with a rolled-up newspaper.

But even during the regular 60-game schedule, there is nothing relaxed about a game between Licey and Escogido. The vendors are as plentiful as ever and run off their feet; the boys still roam as best they can. Regardless of the standing, Licey-Escogido games are of playoff intensity. Even the players imported from the United States, most of them from the major leagues or Triple A, are caught up in the excitement, exchanging high fives in the dugout after an inning-ending double play.

In this game, Licey took a first-inning lead when Blue Jay Tony Fernandez walked and stole second and Houston Astro first baseman

Glenn Davis doubled. A run is greeted with dancing in the seats and joyous taunting of the other team's fans. A sixth-inning triple by Cleveland Indians outfielder Carmelo Castillo tied the game and Jose Rijo replaced Oakland A's teammate Bill Krueger, who had duelled with Mickey Mahler, the left-hander who had finished the 1985 season with the Detroit Tigers.

In the bottom of the eighth the "Lee-say! Lee-say!" chant by fans of Los Tigres reached a crescendo as Jose Uribe of the San Francisco Giants tripled and scored on a sacrifice fly by the Dodgers' Mariano Duncan. As the taut, skilfully played game ended, "Lee-say! Lee-say!" filled the stadium while the fans of Los Leones del Escogido slumped in their seats. Mahler had pitched a four-hitter, but Escogido stranded 11 runners and Krueger yielded eight hits. "Mahler won the game, but Escogido lost it," a dejected red-capped fan said.

"I like that kind of ballgame; everybody is keyed up," said Elvio Jimenez, Licey's third-base coach and a Dominican scout for the Dodgers. "And the directors, as far as they're concerned, if you beat Escogido, it doesn't matter if you lose to the other teams. You beat Escogido and everything will be all right."

Outside the stadium, a tourist goes for a cab and is surrounded by a pack of youths looking for a peso or some loose change. "My mother is starving," says an eight-year-old with sad eyes. Then once more, even more sadly, "My mother is starving."

"THE ATMOSPHERE is like college football in the United States," said Mickey Mahler, who in 1986 pitched for the Texas Rangers, the Oklahoma City 89ers, and the Toronto Blue Jays. He is the winningest pitcher from the United States in the Dominican winter league with a career record of 42–17. "Mom and dad instill a team in their children. Blue is Licey, red is Escogido, yellow is Santiago, green is Estrallas. And the kids say 'I'm red' or 'I'm blue.' Each game is kind of a festival and that's what I think the Americans like there. It's the importance of it to the fans."

The teams are a blend of U.S. imports, Dominican major-leaguers, and young Dominican players who might still be in the lower minor leagues in the United States. The Licey team in 1985–86 included Silvestre Campusano, born New Year's Eve, 1966, who played for the Blue Jays' Double A farm club and was considered a prime prospect.

"Anytime I pitch against Licey, it is the ultimate game," said Mahler. "I am the red pitcher. I really feel the pressure every time I pitch. I know there's a lot of gambling on the game. A place I go to eat has a bar and they have the odds on each game. I like to go in and check out the odds.''

Mahler saw evidence of his own prowess in the Dominican on one visit to his bistro. The odds were 6 to 5 on Escogido. But then word came there had been a change in the rotation, that Mahler would be pitching. The odds dropped suddenly to 12 to 5 – the bettors had to bet 12 pesos instead of six to win five.

''A lot of people have more than their pride on the games,'' Mahler said.

In 1977, Mahler was with Estrellas of San Pedro de Macoris. He did not play in the Dominican in 1978, but has returned each year since to pitch for Escogido (though he left early in the 1986–87 winter season to return home to Salt Lake City).

''It's outstanding,'' he said. ''The only bad thing is that you have to stay in a hotel room. But I have it in my contract that they have to fly me home for Christmas. You can do that as long as you perform. A lot of people think you go there to work on things. You don't. The pressure is to win. One year, we had 14 Americans released. You think you can go there to work on things, but there's so much pressure you don't.''

In Mahler's first year with Estrellas, when he was pitching with his brother, Rick, of the Atlanta Braves, Tony Fernandez was on the ground crew (he hung around the park so much they gave him a job). Ray Knight, then with the Cincinnati Reds, would lend his glove to Fernandez, who would take ground balls with the professionals, clad in jeans.

He remembers Alfredo Griffin as a young player with Estrellas. When Mahler moved to Escogido, George Bell and Juan Samuel were sitting on the bench. ''They were just skinny kids, but they had a lot of ability,'' Mahler said.

THE BLUE JAYS used the rivalry between Licey and Escogido to land one of their best players, left fielder ''Jorge'' Bell. He was known as Jorge (when he was in the Philadelphia Phillie organization a scout allegedly assumed his name was Jorge, not George). In 1980, playing with Reading of the Double A Eastern League, Bell had suffered a stress fracture in his shoulder while swinging a bat. He had reinjured it sliding and had played only 22 games; the rest of the season he was on the disabled list. As a third-year professional, he had to be protected on the 40-man winter major-league roster or be exposed to December's Rule 5 draft, available for $25,000. The Phillies hoped he'd be ignored in the draft because of his injuries and protected players more visible to the scouts. Escogido had a working relationship with the Phillies. There were strict instructions that Bell not play in the winter league.

Al LaMacchia remembered visiting the Dominican Republic in 1979 to watch Tony Fernandez play. The Blue Jays had signed Fernandez earlier that year. An outfielder caught his attention during the game. It was Bell.

Epy Guerrero was working for Licey at that time. After a workout in San Pedro de Macoris, Guerrero had seen a player taking swings at the plate. "This one guy started to hit the ball out of the park," Guerrero said.

Guerrero immediately phoned Gillick. "Pat, there's one guy here who can be a good draft, George Bell."

Gillick hung up the phone and quickly checked what he had on Bell. Five minutes later he called Guerrero back and told him all reports were favourable, except that Bell had been on the disabled list with a back injury.

"If his back is hurt," Guerrero said, "when he don't hurt he might hit the ball three hundred kilometres. You'd better draft him."

Guerrero arranged a morning best-of-three series between the reserve teams of Licey and Escogido.

"You can ask to play pre-season games with the other group. There's nothing wrong with that," Guerrero said. "They don't have to play him. If they make a mistake, that's their problem."

Guerrero has a way with a story. He says he phoned the president of the Escogido club: "I want to beat you bad – use all your players. I'm going to use all the Toronto players."

Guerrero said he had no chance in the series. He had Tony Fernandez but Escogido had such future major-leaguers as second baseman Juan Samuel, shortstop Julio Franco, right fielder Alejandro Sanchez, and the centre fielder, George Bell. LaMacchia was to be in Puerto Rico to check out Candy Maldonado, then of the Dodger organization, and he was to slip over to the Dominican Republic to watch the morning games. "I called Pat and said, if you want to see Bell you better get here today or tomorrow because I might lose in two games," Guerrero recalled.

LaMacchia made it, wearing his hat low so he wouldn't be recognized. "He looks like a Latin anyway," Guerrero said.

When Bell did not arrive for batting and infield practice, LaMacchia was concerned. Guerrero was confident Bell would show. "We're playing this like a championship series," Guerrero told LaMacchia. "He's going to try to beat me." Sure enough, he put him in the lineup, batted him third, and played him in centre field.

They saw what they needed. Licey lost but the Blue Jays won.

LaMacchia remembered the surprised looks on the faces of the Phillies' people after the Blue Jays drafted him for $25,000. The Blue Jays had to keep Bell on the major-league team for all of 1981, the strike-shortened season, because the Phillies surely would have leaped at the chance to get him back for half price.

He returned to the minor leagues in 1982 – and played only 37 games when he had mononucleosis, a knee injury, and a broken jaw when hit by a pitch – and was called up to the Blue Jays in the middle of the 1983 season. In 1986, he batted in 108 runs.

EPY GUERRERO'S PROWESS as sleuth and Wayne Morgan's sharp eyes resulted in the Blue Jays signing a prized prospect from war-torn Nicaragua, population 3.3 million.

Brant Alyea, 19, played first base for the Class A Florence Blue Jays in 1986. He batted .261 in 80 games with eight home runs and 45 runs batted in.

Alyea's father played outfield with the occasional stint at first base for the Washington Senators, Minnesota Twins, St. Louis Cardinals, and Oakland A's from 1965 to 1972. He was born Garrabant Ryerson Alyea III, on December 8, 1940, in Passaic, New Jersey.

At the end of the Nicaraguan winter-league season in February, 1966, Alyea and Auda Medina, a nurse, spent a weekend together. Alyea returned the following November. His son was a week old. Alyea signed a baptismal certificate, naming the baby Brant Alyea; the family added the names Medina and Jose and held a joyous party.

In January, 1967, political problems in Nicaragua forced Alyea to leave the country quickly. He returned in the fall for a brief visit on his way to play winter baseball in Venezuela. After a severe earthquake in 1972, he lost track of Auda Medina and young Brant. He next heard of them in 1976, from a friend, Pancho Herrera, who said the boy was always playing baseball. Several years later, when he was working in a casino at Atlantic City, a clipping from the *Baseball Card News* was left for him. There was a list of sons of former major-leaguers who were playing professional baseball: an outfielder named Brant Alyea was playing in Medicine Hat, Canada.

The Blue Jays first became interested in young Alyea in July, 1984. He was 17 and playing for Nicaragua in the World Youth Baseball Tournament in Kindersley, Saskatchewan. Morgan scouted the tournament and liked Alyea's moves and the way he swung the bat. Morgan suggested that the Blue Jays follow up on him. If he was related to the former major-league player, he might be able to get out of Nicaragua.

Later that year, Morgan went to Cuba as an adviser to Team Canada in the world amateur tournament. He was sure Alyea would be on the Nicaraguan team, but was told Alyea was too young to play in the tournament. Morgan found a Nicaraguan player who spoke English; he knew Alyea and saw him all the time in Managua. "I had one of these player information cards, a postcard type thing," Morgan said. "I said, 'Here's my address on this card. Have him fill it out with his address, phone number and all that and send it to me in the mail.' Sure enough, he did."

The next question was how to sign him and get him out of the country. Alyea's mother and her three daughters by a subsequent marriage had moved to Margarita Island off the coast of Venezuela; but men could not leave Nicaragua.

Nicaragua discourages baseball scouts from entering the country. Dennis Martinez and David Green are two Nicaraguan players who made the major leagues, but no younger players had been able to make it to North America. "They don't let anybody out now, no baseball player, no athlete," Guerrero said. "They are becoming just like Cuba."

He had been to Nicaragua as a trainer with the Dominican Republic national team in 1973 and was regarded as a friend of Nicaraguan baseball. He knew officials who could help him, telling them he was coming to operate some baseball clinics.

"I put my passport in the Nicaragua counsel in the Dominican and tried to get a visa," Guerrero said. "It stayed there for about two weeks. They don't give me an answer. One day they called me, they could give me the visa – no problem."

He obtained a visa and first went to Panama, where he met Blue Jay minor-league coach Ramon Webster, and they went to Nicaragua at the end of January, 1985. He finally met Alyea, his grandmother, and an aunt at a Managua hotel. The hotel made Guerrero nervous. A bomb had gone off not far away one night and knocked all the windows out. Disguised in a Sandanista-type beret and camouflage fatigues, Guerrero left the hotel and took a taxi to their home, despite warnings that he shouldn't. (Guerrero's brother-in-law, a retired general in the Dominican Republic, had provided the uniform.) There is fighting in the streets sometimes and Alyea once saw a couple of friends killed in a crossfire. One time at his house he went to his knees to fix something on the floor and bullets went right where he had been standing. If he wasn't such a good baseball player, Alyea likely would have been in the army. Guerrero made it to the house and signed Alyea to a $6,000 bonus.

"Now we had to get him out of there," Morgan said. "We talked to the people he had stayed with in Saskatchewan and told them our problem."

Alyea had written a thank-you note to Dennis Hyland and his family in Mantario, Saskatchewan, after the 1984 tournament; that started an exchange of letters. The Hylands were asked to send an invitation for him to visit the family again, enclosing a money order for U.S. funds to buy an airplane ticket and to arrange a visa. Given the frequent correspondence, the Blue Jays thought there would be a good chance that the letter with the money order and visa would get through. It did.

Alyea used the money to pay an official, who gave him the passport he had used for previous baseball trips. Guerrero arranged for a Mexican visa. Alyea underwent some anxious questioning at the Nicaragua airport when he said he was going to visit his mother in Venezuela but had to go to Mexico for his visa. He met Guerrero in Mexico City. Guerrero hid him for two days while he arranged a Canadian visa and put him on a flight to Vancouver, where he was met by Blue Jay scout Ozzie Chavarria. Alyea carried only a duffel bag and a scrapbook; tucked in the scrapbook was a picture of his father selecting a bat in the Washington Senators' dugout. The next day he was put on a flight to Calgary, where he was met by Gord Ash and driven to Medicine Hat. There he joined the Pioneer League Blue Jays, batting .337 in 51 games during the 1985 season. He went to the Florida Instructional League, then played winter ball in a Venezuelan rookie league.

During spring training of 1986, Brant Alyea, Sr., went to Florida. On Easter Sunday, at the Ramada Inn Countryside, near where the

Blue Jays conduct their spring training, he saw his son for the first time since he was an infant in Managua and was in his mother's arms.

More than a month later, on May 12, 1986, he saw his son play for the Florence Blue Jays of the South Atlantic League. It was the first professional baseball game Alyea had attended since September, 1972, when he had been placed on the disabled list by the Oakland A's.

EPY GUERRERO never got past the lower minors. "I was a horseshit player," he says. He is stocky, medium height, dark-haired, and has courtly manners with a hint of mischief.

He started out in professional baseball in the United States with another Dominican, Rico Carty. "There were not too many players from here then," he said. "No Spanish instructors at that time. I had to go into a restaurant and buy Rico Carty food because he couldn't get into the restaurant. We were in Waco, Georgia. It was very tough for the black people."

Carty ended a 15-year major-league career, in which be batted .299, when the Blue Jays released him during spring training in 1980. He is still bitter about it; he thinks he still could have played. The deferred payments on his 1979 contract will give him about $30,000 a year until 1990.

Epy's brother, Mario, played shortstop for eight years in the major leagues. "Epy says that in 1960, the blacks had to sleep on the trains and the whites in the hotels," Mario Guerrero said. "Epy said, 'What the hell, I'm going to stay on the train.' And the white people say, 'Hey, you can't go in there.' And Epy told them, 'I don't give a shit.' Epy stayed on the train with the blacks."

While Carty achieved fame in the major leagues, Guerrero became a legendary scout in Latin American baseball. When Pat Gillick was named Houston's Latin American scouting supervisor in 1966 he was introduced to Guerrero, and the two have been inseparable ever since, moving together to New York and then to Toronto. The relationship survived a Blue Jay trade that sent Guerrero's 20-year-old son, Sandy, a second baseman in Class A, to the Milwaukee Brewer organization. And accusations that Epy's brother Mario, a player representative, was working at Guerrero's complex near Santo Domingo to gain access to clients. Epy told Mario to stay away from the complex and meet players elsewhere. Mario represented Tony Fernandez at one time, but after a disagreement with Gillick he decided that it would be better

217

if someone else represented the young shortstop. Mario is acting for Silvestre Campusano.

In Guerrero's first meeting with Gillick he told him of some players that he should see. "One of the guys was Cesar Cedeno," Guerrero said. "We signed Cedeno that year. From there, Gillick named me a scout."

Cesar Cedeno was touted as one of the all-time great prospects, a potential Willie Mays. Cedeno proved an excellent player for the Astros but enjoyed the major-league life too much and never achieved greatness. After playing with Houston, Cincinnati, and St. Louis, and his ability obviously on a decline despite a hot September with the Cardinals, he tried out with the Blue Jays at spring training but was cut.

Epy Guerrero says Gillick taught him how to scout. "He showed me how to work, how to see the pitcher, how to see the player, what kind of body, having a loose arm, who can improve in running."

Guerrero fulfilled a dream when he opened his training complex for young Dominican players a few years ago. It was the first such complex in the Dominican and the idea is being copied by several other major-league teams. "When I started scouting in 1966–67, my purpose was to have my own ballpark," he said. "I bought the land in 1975. It was three cents a metre. Now that land goes for twenty cents a metre."

The drive from Santo Domingo to the Epy Guerrero Complex leads through pockets of poverty, past men pedalling fruit-laden carts and women carrying bundles on their heads. It is not easy to find the complex, tucked away as it is. It might keep the next Tony Fernandez from the prying eyes of a rival scout, although representatives of a few major-league teams have visited it to see how they might build their own. About 45 minutes from downtown Santo Domingo, a left-hand turn past a sign that reads *Complejo Epy Deportivo* leads to a hilly, primitive rocky path with trees on either side and pastures beyond. Cars share this road with cattle. Horses graze at the roadside. The terrain is best suited for grazing and Guerrero glows with pride when it is suggested that it must have been a monumental feat to level this terrain for a baseball field. "That was a hill," he said. "I put a tractor all the way to the back to get the dirt down. Then I levelled it out. Then I started working on the infield. I started working on the ball field when I was with the Yankees, little by little."

He arrived one morning to find that concrete blocks for the walls were lined up from home plate all the way down the left-field line. Damaso Garcia had them delivered. "One day I went to the complex when Epy was trying to put it together and I said I'll pay for the wall," Garcia said. "It wasn't much."

Garcia, even after he was traded to the Atlanta Braves, and Tony Fernandez and other players in the Blue Jay system who live in the Santo Domingo area work out at the complex to prepare for a new season. But the main purpose is to provide a training base for young prospects. They can work all day on fundamentals and game situations and have a good meal, which may be as important to undernourished Dominican youths as the baseball instruction. Besides the baseball field, there are dormitories and a dining room. Some of the teenagers are given a nutritious diet for the first time in their lives. Teachers help with schooling. There are batting cages with pitching machines sitting under palm trees; there are half diamonds and pitching areas with four home plates, similar to a spring-training complex. The coaches, mostly Dominicans who have played in the United States, will instruct the young players in English. One of the coaches is Juan Jose Joa, a Dominican who is part Chinese. He played for two seasons in the Canadian Provincial League, for Sherbrooke, Quebec, and married a local woman. They had a son and a daughter, now in their teens, and they have since divorced. "When we talk on the phone I talk in English and they talk in French," Joa said.

During the off-season many players who have been in the rookie leagues or in Class A, but who are not quite ready for the Dominican winter league, work out during the day. First there are stretching exercises, running, fundamentals, and an infield practice with plenty of chatter. There is the game, which will go all day without a final score, stopping only so that a mistake can be corrected. Other times, a game situation will be set up. The workout begins at about nine in the morning and goes until two or three in the afternoon. Afterwards, there is a meal in the dining area. Some players stay at the dormitory but most will either drive, catch a ride, or walk home.

"People in Canada and the United States, they know they've got food on the table," Mario Guerrero said. "The gang at the complex, they don't know if they're going to have it. They go looking for it. With Epy's complex, the food is there after practice. They've got a bed where they can sleep. All they have to do is work, play baseball. Most of the kids come from poor people and there's nothing they can do, only play baseball. In the United States, there are different ways of making money. Here, the only way they can make money is baseball.''

Baseball America, a nationall baseball newspaper in the United States, surveyed the 26 major-league organizations in June, 1985. It found that there were 349 professional players in major-league organizations from Latin America. Of those, 163 were from the Dominican Republic, 93 from Puerto Rico, 52 from Venezuela, 18 from Mexico, 10 from Panama, nine from Cuba, three from Colombia, and one from Nicaragua. (The survey was done before Brant Alyea joined Medicine Hat Blue Jays in mid-June.)

Of the major-league teams, the Blue Jays had the most players, 34, from Latin America in its organization, 23 from the Dominican Republic. The tally was done as of June 1, which means the short-season Class A teams and the rookie league teams were not counted. (In 1984, the Blue Jays controlled 52 Latin players.) The closest teams to the Blue Jays were the Pittsburgh Pirates with 25 (18 from the Dominican) and the Philadelphia Phillies with 24 (10 from the Dominican). The Minnesota Twins had the fewest, five (including one Dominican.) In addition to their Dominicans, the Blue Jays had one player from Puerto Rico, seven from Venezuela, two from Mexico, and one from Panama.

The U.S. State Department has restricted the total number of foreign professional baseball players to 500 for the 26 major-league teams. Still, the number of Latin players has increased. In 1965 approximately one in every 17 major-league players was from Latin America. At the beginning of the 1985 season, the number had doubled.

Damaso Garcia grew up in Moca, an agricultural city of 70,000. He played soccer for the Dominican team in the Panama Games and was signed by Guerrero for the Yankees. Gillick obtained him for the Jays in 1980 in a trade with the Yankees. With Alfredo Griffin at shortstop and Garcia at second, the Blue Jays had the first Dominican double-play combination in the major leagues. The Blue Jays are probably the most popular major-league team in the Dominican, followed by the Dodgers. The Giants and then the Pirates had gone after Dominican talent long before the Blue Jays were created; but the Blue Jays' success with Dominicans helped make other teams aware of what could be done.

"Almost every club has a scout looking for talent in the Dominican," Garcia says. "With the $200,000 it might take to sign a free agent from the June draft, you can sign 20 Dominicans. From that, you can get three players as good as the free agents.

"Most of these guys are unemployed. If they sign it brings them a job and he supports a lot of people. It's very lucrative if you can make the major leagues."

It can be looked upon as exploitation. A minimum age limit of 17 for signing players was established in 1986; before that teams signed players as young as 14, using the rationale that if they didn't sign him then another team would. Jimy Kelly, the son of a customs broker who speaks English and who has a physical resemblance to Alfredo Griffin, was the shortstop for St. Catharines in 1986. He turned 16 during the season, his second as a professional.

Donald Odermann is a stockbroker and brokerage office manager from San Jose, California, who has a Master's degree from UCLA in Latin American studies. Odermann, who worked in the Peace Corps in Colombia from 1963 to 1965 and as a marketing manager in Puerto Rico, has been a critic of the way major-league teams have dealt with Latin players, particularly Dominicans.

He has set up the Latin Athletic Education Fund to help athletes from Latin American gain an education. He sends them to junior college, where it is hoped their athletic ability and their academic qualifications will bring scholarship offers to four-year universities. "We have had thirty-three kids who have benefitted from what we've been doing," Odermann said. The program is not restricted to Dominicans or baseball, and female athletes have also received grants. But the main thrust has been in the Dominican. "That's where the greatest need is and the greatest poverty," he said. "And that's where the greatest athletic talent is."

The fund has a selection committee of six: Dominican pitching great Juan Marichal, a scout for Oakland, Pablo Cruz, a scout for the Pirates, and Jesus Alou, a scout for the Expos, look for playing talent while three others on the committee check out their academics.

"We have thirteen kids in an intensive English program in the Dominican Republic for at least a year," Odermann said.

He is not quite as critical of major-league teams' exploitation of the Dominican players as he was a few years ago. The teams used to take them to the United States or Canada before they knew any English and without worrying about those who did not make it and were left with no education.

"I've had a little bit of a change of heart," he said. "I'm not quite as opposed to what the major leagues are doing. They're being a little more sensitive to the needs of the kids. Being a little more aware of the damage they can do. They've got these camps where they can work out for 30 or 60 days and stay in the Dominican. . . . But I still think there's some oversigning, too.''

Although major-league baseball itself has not offered financial support for Odermann's foundation, a few individual teams have, including the Blue Jays. ''The Blue Jays have been pretty generous,'' Odermann said. ''They've been giving $3,000 a year for the past couple of years.'' He says he finds Pat Gillick of the Blue Jays ''very easy to deal with.''

Sandy Alderson, general manager of the Oakland A's, and Manny Mota, a coach with the Los Angeles Dodgers and a Dominican, are on the foundation's board of directors. Joan Kroc, owner of the San Diego Padres, also has donated.

''They're using our foundation as a vehicle to put something back into the country,'' Odermann said.

Damaso Garcia, for one, did have a choice between education and baseball. He attended college for two years, intending to become an engineer. ''They needed a shortstop to play one day in my home town,'' he said. ''They asked me if I could help them. I went. There was somebody watching and he told me I had the ability to play the game. He asked, 'Do you mind if I bring someone to see you play?' Here comes Epy.''

Garcia's raw ability was honed by Mike Ferraro, a coach in the Yankee organization. ''I didn't know anything about the game when I came to the United States,'' Garcia said. ''After God, I owe my career to him.''

''Damo was very, very green,'' Ferraro recalled. ''He wanted to learn everything about baseball within two weeks.''

Garcia likes to remind Ferraro how hard he worked him taking ground balls. ''He said he couldn't wait to get to the water fountain after I'd finished hitting those ground balls,'' Ferraro said. ''I used to make him whistle. If he could still whistle, I knew he wasn't tired and I'd keep hitting him ground balls.''

THE BASEBALL TALENT of Tony Fernandez, another Guerrero find, had been apparent early. He thinks Guerrero must have been watching him since he ''was nine or ten.'' Fernandez's home was among the poor dwellings beyond the outfield fences of the Estadio Tetelo Vargas in San Pedro de Macoris. He used to climb the stadium fence and take ground balls, a thin, ragged figure with bare feet, and a right knee that put off the scouts.

"When I signed Fernandez, all the other scouts say I signed a cripple," Guerrero said. "They said the guy can't run."

The knee needed corrective surgery and it was done when Fernandez was 16. "He went all the way down from 7.6 or 7.7 running the 60 yards to 6.5," said Guerrero, who likes to time the players running 60 yards – the equivalent of two bases.

Tony Fernandez is a sensitive person, quieter than teammate George Bell. Fernandez, deeply religious, wept after he had his first major-league hit in September, 1983, because his father had not lived to see it. Like many of the Dominican players, he would send a chunk of his pay home. Fernandez's contract called for a specified amount to be sent to Epy Guerrero, who delivered it to Fernandez's mother. Andrea Fernandez died before the 1986 season began.

EPY GUERRERO BELIEVES in contacts, and that is what helped him find Silvestre Campusano, an outfielder with a strong arm who throws the ball on a low trajectory, like a line drive from a bat. If Cedeno rated highly as a prospect, Guerrero is even more fond of Campusano.

"I think he's got a chance to be a superstar," Guerrero said. "Maybe the Dominican Willie Mays. No, he's going to be like Silvestre Campusano."

Campusano's first baseball glove was a milk carton. And like many before him, he quit high school to play baseball full time. He was signed by the Blue Jays in November, 1983.

"I know the guy who is the keeper of the clubhouse for the Licey baseball club," Guerrero remembers. "He told me he saw a guy hitting the ball the day before. I said okay, bring him tomorrow to the clubhouse and I will take him right down to the complex. He looks like he's quick, his wrists are so strong."

Campusano is from Mano Guayabo, one of six children. His family lived in a three-room dirt-floor dwelling. During Hurricane David in 1979, the roof was ripped off and the walls collapsed. The dwelling was put back together over a period of time but the roof still leaked and there were no windows, so mosquitos were a problem. There are mosquito nets around the beds.

Campusano borrowed a glove and shoes to work out at Guerrero's camp. He was raw but learned quickly, and within two weeks Campusano was offered a contract. He signed for a bonus of $3,500 (U.S.), and all but $250 went to the family to fix up the house – painting, putting in a cement floor, building a sheet-metal roof, and buying furniture.

He quit school in the spring of 1984 and played for Bradenton in the Gulf Coast (rookie) League. He hit .267 and was superb in the field. In 1985, his first full year as a professional, he played for Florence in the Class A South Atlantic League. For the first half of the season he hit .313 with 15 homers, 56 runs batted in, and 21 stolen bases. Managers in the league voted him the league's best batting prospect, best defensive outfielder, and outfielder with the best arm. He was promoted to Knoxville in the Double A Southern League, still 18. At Knoxville he batted .303 with six homers and 29 RBIs. In 1986, back at Knoxville, he batted .256 with 14 homers, 56 RBIs, and 18 stolen bases, playing the outfield with Canadian Rob Ducey and Californian Glenallen Hill.

Guerrero cannot afford the time to admire his finds as they climb toward the majors. He has to continue his quest, wherever it may take him.

"All over," he said. "Bird dogs, contacts. I've got them all over. Like the guy in Aruba."

A friend in Aruba called him to tell him about a 17-year-old. Guerrero was there the next day. "He told me he was very green, green, green. Now, it looks like I am going to have a player out of Aruba. Now, everybody is trying to get into Aruba. I'm going to another place. I move my ass very good. I make people think I am at the complex. I might go there in the morning at seven or eight o'clock, but I have my own program. I might be in Macoris at 10 o'clock the same day."

One day Guerrero had nothing to do. There were no prospects to check, no tips. So he went to a high-school track meet at Santo Domingo's Olympic Stadium. "I went to the running track event, you know, a big tournament," he said. "And I pick three guys out. I said, 'Have you ever played baseball before?' And they said when they were little. So I make them play baseball. They liked it. They run like hell, 3.5 to first base." Two of the three, Junior Felix and Charlie Romero, wound up playing baseball in the Blue Jay organization in 1986.

Guerrero will be out scouting for another scrawny prospect to see what wonders proper feeding will work. "That's a big problem in the whole country," he said. "When the kids start growing, they can't go to school. They have to work to make a living. It's a poor country, but sometimes God gives something to poor countries. He don't give us the black gold, the oil, like he gave to Venezuela, but he gave us the ability to play baseball.''

SAN PEDRO DE MACORIS has become known for producing major-league baseball players. Rico Carty, Alfredo Griffin, George Bell, Tony Fernandez, and Manny Lee are sons of San Pedro de Macoris who played for the Blue Jays. The population has been estimated to be any-where from 32,000 to 80,000, but George Bell says it is actually much larger when surrounding areas are taken into consideration.

Fernandez has moved to the capital, but Bell still lives there. Bell grew up on the grounds of the Santa Fe Cane Sugar Company, a self-contained company town. His father was a railroad engineer. With his baseball earnings, Bell has given his father and his family a new house in San Pedro de Macoris and has built one for himself, his wife, and two children. Bell's father willingly shows visitors the way, on a moped, wearing a Blue Jay batting helmet and T-shirt and Wellington-style boots. Only blocks away from the dirt-floored dwellings of the extremely poor are modern, comfortable houses. And then there are luxurious houses like Bell's.

As in Santo Domingo, the houses in the old part of the city are close to the sidewalks and the architecture is colonial. It must have been a pretty town at one time. Dodger scout Elvio Jimenez says it used to be referred to as ''Little Paris'' in the 1920s.

Behind the sugar cane factory, enclosed by fences, there is a baseball field on company property. This has been the Los Angeles Dodgers' ''baseball academy.'' The Dodgers are planning to open a new complex about halfway between San Pedro de Macoris and Santo Domingo.

The baseball field used to be part of a golf course, Jimenez said, a digital stopwatch dangling from his hand. He was watching the Dodger young Dominicans play the Astro young Dominicans from a little block enclosure behind home plate. George Bell's brothers, Orlando, Juan, and Jose, signed with the Dodgers and work out there. The golf course was built for the Americans who worked in the factory. Jimenez used to caddy for them every day. ''That helped with my English,'' he said. ''I was familiar with the Americans from caddying.'' When the Ameri-cans left, the golf course turned into a baseball field.

Jimenez and his brother, Manny, were among the first players from

San Pedro de Macoris to be signed by U.S. professional baseball teams. Elvio played one game with the Yankees but spent several years in the minor leagues. Manny played seven seasons with the Kansas City A's and the Chicago White Sox. Now Elvio Jimenez coaches third base for Licey, scouts for the Dodgers, and was overseeing workouts of their Dominican players. He also teaches them English in his backyard.

As the game proceeded, there were constant reminders of both the poverty and the agricultural base of the country – 47 per cent of the labour force is in agriculture and 20 per cent is in industry. Carts pulled by oxen, horses, or ponies passed on a nearby road. A couple of oxen and a bull were eating the grass beneath the small, old stands. The bull grazed his way to the entrance to Jimenez's little fortification behind home plate.

Jimenez and Epy Guerrero respect each other, friendly rivals in a competitive business; they would cheerfully steal a prospect from the other if the opportunity arose. The Dodgers and the Blue Jays are ahead of the other teams, who are beginning to discover the Dominican, Jimenez said, because they work at it. Both have a network of bird dogs to help discover talent. "When one of the other teams sends someone to see a player, they will be told that either the Blue Jays or the Dodgers were there," he said. "You can find Epy working all the time, all year round."

Some of the major-league teams who were left behind in exploring the Dominican have decried the "exploitation." The leagues put a temporary embargo on signing Dominicans late in 1984 until a system was worked out. In 1986 a signing-age minimum of 17 was established. A draft of Dominican players also was held. Jimenez scoffs. Before the teams can draft, he says, they have to know where to find the players. "There's so many guys in the country who can play ball, but you have to find them. It's easy to come here and say, 'Well, how come you got so many guys?' Well, we got so many guys because we go get them. They say they cannot find anybody because we've got everybody. And I'm telling you, we can send twenty guys home today and on Monday we can have twenty-five different guys who are good ballplayers."

The strong power hitters are rare among Dominican players. "It's not too easy to find a Pedro Guerrero or a George Bell; it's easier to find a small kid who can catch the ball," Jimenez said. "In the States, you don't find too many skinny guys who can move that way. Everybody's big. Cal Ripken, maybe, is big and can play shortstop. He's an exception. He's one in a hundred."

IN OCTOBER, 1985, Eduard Manuel Dennis made it to Toronto for a major-league baseball game. He had dreamed of Toronto and Exhibition Stadium since July 2, 1977, the day he was signed by Epy Guerrero for the Blue Jays. It was three months before his eighteenth birthday.

The infielder from La Romana in the Dominican Republic had dreamed of reaching the major leagues as a player, but when he finally reached Exhibition Stadium he was in the seats as a guest of the club. To celebrate reaching the American League playoffs for the first time, the Blue Jays invited all their minor-league personnel to share the moment in Toronto. "I really had a good time there," Dennis said during spring training at the Blue Jays' minor-league complex where he was a coach. "It was one of the best times I had in my entire career."

Dennis was a willing worker who played every position but catcher. He pitched on occasion, using his strong fastball, the one that has earned him the name "The Pitching Machine" as a batting practice pitcher. He played four years with Knoxville in Double A before being dropped to Class A in 1984.

"I guess I wasn't good enough to make it to the big leagues," he said. A simple statement, perhaps, but so difficult for a player to say: Eddie Dennis turned 27 in October, 1986.

Dennis is one of the many Dominicans who do not make the major leagues. But unlike most, he has not been abandoned by the sport he loves. The Blue Jays hired him as a coach in 1985, although he played in seven games in 1985, two at Kinston and five at Knoxville. In 1986 he coached the St. Catharines Blue Jays, which had several Latin players, and in 1987 he would manage at Medicine Hat.

A Spanish-speaking coach was important at St. Catharines. Dennis knew what it was like to start out as a professional in a foreign country having to learn a different language. When Dennis began playing in Dunedin in 1978, as a second baseman/shortstop, he knew no English and the coaches spoke no Spanish. "It would have helped me a lot, but there weren't any Spanish-speaking coaches when I came here," he said.

As a rookie professional, he had difficulty understanding what he was being told and he tried to make himself understood through sign language. "It was kind of hard for me to go to the restaurant and eat because I couldn't ask for food," he said. "I couldn't talk to my teammates, so I started teaching them Spanish and they started helping me with my English. One thing that really helped me was watching TV. I mostly watched the baseball games, some basketball, and other sports. You know, what helped me a lot was watching baseball and when you hear the broadcaster, like Tony Kubek, talking about some players."

Since Juan Marichal and the brothers Alou – Felipe, Jesus, and Matty – burst upon the major leagues in the late fifties and early sixties, Dominican players have become a growing force, and Dennis hoped to be a part of it. Now he knows that if he is to make it there, it will be as a coach. "I never made it as a player, but I hope I can some day as a coach. It would be hard for me to see myself go away from baseball."

Many Dominican youths shine shoes to make money for the family. (Tony Fernandez tried but did not like it, so he sold the peanut butter his mother made.) As they get older, they might graduate to selling postcards, trinkets, or pesos for dollars. It is almost impossible to walk the streets of Santo Domingo without drawing a crowd of earnest salesmen.

"I was one of the lucky guys," Dennis says. "My dad worked as a carpenter with Central Romano, a big sugar cane factory, for thirty-five years. I never worked when I was little. I would just go to school and play baseball. My dad never let me work. Really, one of the main reasons I got into baseball was my dad. I remember the first present he bought me was a baseball bat and a glove. When I was little, he used to take me to see the winter-league games."

Someone noticed Dennis playing and contacted Epy Guerrero. "It was a Sunday," Dennis said. "I was still at the park and he asked me to work out. He hit ground balls and clocked me for 60 yards. I didn't hit that day, just took ground balls."

Dennis's father agreed to let him move into Guerrero's home in Santo Domingo and be put through intensive baseball training. Guerrero has often taken prospects into his home, especially before he had the complex operating. "Tony Fernandez and Damaso Garcia and Domingo Ramos, Jose Uribe of the Giants, all those guys used to live in my home," Guerrero said. Dennis lived with the Guerrero family for more than two years, playing for the Dominican Navy team before signing with the Blue Jays for a $4,000 bonus with additional bonus money for each stage above Class A – $1,000 for Double A, $1,500 for Triple A, and $5,000 for the major leagues.

The big money that some of his successful countrymen have made from baseball has eluded him. "I just make enough money to make a living here," he said. "You've got to be in the major leagues to make money."

228

RICO CARTY SAT in the box seats at Estadio Quisqueya. When the "Big Mon" signed his contract with the Blue Jays in 1979, it was a 42-page document, detailing deferred payments and bonus provisions. At the time it was said to be the longest contract in major-league history, but as contracts have become more complicated since then Carty's Blue Jay record fell to Jim Clancy's 1983 contract, which went more than 70 pages. In both cases, the details of deferred payments had much to do with the length.

In December, 1985, Carty, who was serving a brief tenure as president of the Dominican Republic's players' association, talked about the passion of the Dominican baseball fans. "You see it in the streets, guys arguing about my ballplayer against your ballplayer and pretty soon there's a fight," he said. "People kill each other, I'm not kidding. I've seen people arguing about me in the street. I'm in my car and they're arguing right beside. I just get out of there.

"People look up to ballplayers here. Here all the ballplayers live like kings. This is what it's all about here. Puerto Rico, for instance, that's part of the United States. Venezuela has lots of industry. The Americans went in there and almost built Venezuela. They went into Puerto Rico and they build Puerto Rico. Dominican kids want to be ballplayers, because they cannot get a job. They want to be ballplayers so they can help their families. Lots of people . . . go to school, they get degrees, but they cannot get a job. So people want to get out of here. They want to go to Mexico, to Venezuela, Puerto Rico.

"Sugar is our biggest crop. They're trying to build up tourism but it's going to take time. I think the Americans are going to come in here and build different types of factories and there's going to be more jobs."

Some of the Dominican players have had what could be called public relations problems, Joaquin Andujar and George Bell among them. The problems are often the result of being misunderstood. As Carty explained, "What happens is that sometimes . . . we may say it one way but we mean something else. Lots of times I got myself into trouble because of that. It makes you get frustrated and more mad with yourself and other people because you cannot explain yourself in the way you want to."

Bell has shown that frustration at times. He has refused to talk to reporters for quotes. Yet, on a personal basis he is friendly to many of them. He talked during the 1985 playoff series with Kansas City and got himself in trouble because he suggested there was a conspiracy against the Blue Jays, a Canadian team with four Dominicans. His teammates respect Bell's competitive nature, his willingness to play with a sore knee, and his talent.

Bell likes Canada but does not have good memories of the southern United States, where he played as a minor-leaguer. "Canadians are like Dominicans, they accept all people," he says, but he did notice one difference. "In the Dominican you can turn up the radio loud and have a good time. If you do that in Toronto, they call the police."

During the time when it was well publicized that he was not granting interviews to the press, Bell had a two-game suspension for charging the mound against the Red Sox. He served the suspension in Oakland, and for the first game of his sentence he sat in the press box with the three Toronto reporters. He offered to get coffee once. His conclusion: "Hey, you guys really work up here." But he didn't change his attitude about giving quotes that season.

Carty recalled how he learned how to deal with his own situation. It was by smiling a lot. "That's one thing I have seen in the American people. If you have a smile on your face, they love you."

WINTER BASEBALL is played in Puerto Rico, Venezuela, and Mexico, too. In fact, Mexico was a surprise winner of the 1986 Caribbean World Series. While the Dominican Republic and the Blue Jays have become intertwined, several Blue Jays are Venezuelan or play there in winter. Until his mysterious plummet in 1985, pitcher Luis Leal was the best Venezuelan in the Blue Jay system. He is from Barquisimeto. The home team is the Lara Cardinales, who finished first in the 1986–87 winter season only to lose in the playoffs.

The Venezuelan winter league has fallen on difficult times. Venezuela is South America's largest oil producer, and its third largest debtor. Low oil prices, a huge foreign debt, and the resulting weakened economy have also affected the business of Venezuelan baseball. Once, big-name players played there in the winters, but currency controls and devaluations have resulted in fewer imports – a drop from 11 to seven following the 1983 season – and the pay is lower. Instead of Triple A or major-league players, Double A players are being recruited.

Lara's 1986–87 outfield was talented but short on experience: in centre field was Rob Ducey, and in left, before he was hurt, Glenallen Hill. Both had played Double A at Knoxville during the season and were considered among the brightest Blue Jay prospects. The other outfielder was Kash Beauchamp, who played both at Knoxville and Syracuse in 1986. Hill, however, went home with a fractured hand after charging the pitcher on the mound. (Ducey and Blue Jay Cecil Fielder, who led the Venezuelan league with 19 homers, had hit consecutive home runs. Hill, the next batter, was hit by a pitch, which started the brawl.)

Stan Clarke, who was drafted by Seattle during the winter meetings, Tony Hudson, and Don Gordon, also members of the Blue Jay organization, played for Lara. Infielder Alexis Infante and Luis Leal were among the Venezuelans on the team from the Blue Jay system. A surprise development was Venezuelan shortstop Luis Sojo, who had been signed as an amateur free agent by the Blue Jay organization and was named the season's top rookie.

The experiences of the winter leagues are unique in baseball. Lloyd Moseby's last winter in Venezuela was 1981–82. Around Christmas time they were without water for four days. And at the stadium in Caracas, he recalls the police on guard had dogs as well as machine guns. The fans threw rocks, so Moseby took to wearing a batting helmet in the outfield. Fans would also come onto the field for autographs or grab any ball hit to the outfield.

Five years later, Rob Ducey found his first year in Venezuela also was an education. "They have the guards lined up, and there are fights breaking out in the stands," he said. "They throw rocks at you and bottles. They don't mess with you while the play's on, just while you're waiting.

"I always had trouble at a place called Aragua. There was a little kid about six or seven years old throwing rocks at me – it was a shallow centre field so I wasn't far from the fence. He didn't care whether I saw him or not, so I called time, told him not to do it anymore, but he couldn't understand me. So he started throwing them again and then I started getting into it with his father. Finally we called time and Beauchamp and Hill came running over and we were about to go into the stands. Maybe I'm wrong for doing it, but after a while it gets on your nerves."

In Caracas during the playoffs the crowd was particularly frantic, Ducey said. There was a band there and he would start dancing to the music in the outfield. "We heard the same song over and over and over," Ducey said. "Actually, Caracas fans are pretty good. They call you a few things but I must say they will clap for a good play no matter if you're the home team or the away club. They just want to see good baseball – and they want *their* team to win it.''

WINTER BASEBALL is where managers learn to deal with pressure. There's no better place. Ask Jimy Williams, the Blue Jay manager. When Williams first managed Obregon in Mexico, he was single, managing in the California Angels' minor-league system, and thought the experience would help his career. He was warned before he left that he should not let it bother him if he was fired. ''I said, 'Where am I going? What do you mean get fired?' The first year I was there, we lost the first four or five games and I said, 'I'm fired, man, I'm out of here.' That bothered me, because I didn't want to get fired. We went on a streak where we won eight or 10 in a row and ended up winning more games than anybody. But being involved in a situation where I had to win did me a world of good.''

In 1981, after he became the Blue Jays' third-base coach, he was asked to take over after the Obregon manager had been fired. He figured the job could pay some bills since he was married and raising a family. Williams speaks passable Spanish, but when he went out to remove Fernando Valenzuela from a playoff game, all the crowd could see was an American manager removing a national hero. Valenzuela was the 1981 National League rookie of the year and Cy Young Award winner; his team, the Dodgers, had won the World Series. Besides, he had recently been married.

Valenzuela's hometown team, Navajo, did not make the playoffs, and each playoff team could select two players from teams that were eliminated. As the fourth-place team, Obregon had first pick and took Valenzuela, even though he wasn't in top shape.

''Our park holds 6,000 or 7,000 people; that night, they said there was between 18,000 or 20,000 people,'' Williams said. ''They were hanging from the light towers, literally. They caved in the bullpen hut. I heard this noise and looked out there and there was this big cloud of dust. This thing just caved in.''

Obregon was leading 1–0 in the seventh inning. Valenzuela was labouring. With two out and two on, he walked a batter to load the bases. Williams had already been out to the mound once, so if he went out again the pitcher had to leave. As he started from the dugout, the catcher was waving him back. Williams signalled for relief pitcher Bob Gibson, who would later pitch for the Milwaukee Brewers.

"When they boo you down there, they whistle. This time not only did they whistle, they booed," Williams said.

Gibson came in to face Mario Mendoza, the shortstop who had a career average of .215 in nine major-league seasons. "We've got TV cameras all over," Williams said. "We've got fans in the *dugout*. I can hardly see. People are standing all over. This guy from a TV station in Mexico had been trying to interview me between innings. He's standing on the second and third steps. Sometimes I had to holler, 'Get the hell out of the way!' I couldn't see. It was a zoo."

The first three pitches were balls. One pitch away from walking in the tying run. "Aw shit," Williams said, sitting there. "Aw sh-i-i-i-i-t."

The next pitch was a strike. Then strike two. Then a swing and a miss, strike three. Gibson retired the next six batters to save the win.

"What that allowed me to do was get up the next morning and walk the streets," Williams grinned. "Because, if he hadn't got him out, or we'd lost – they'd have had my ass."

NINTH

SPRING TRAINING –
LAND OF HOPE AND STORY

THE FIRST SPRING TRAINING was at Hot Springs, Arkansas, in 1886. Cap Anson had managed his Chicago Cubs to first place the year before and over the winter he devised a way to get a jump on the other teams – find a place with no snow and start practising in March.

Anson was a playing manager. During 22 years with the Cubs, he played every position, including catcher and pitcher. He had a career batting average of .334. The experiment worked. The Cubs finished first again in 1886, their fifth pennant in eight years.

Other major-league teams looked for warm climates to prepare for a new baseball season. In 1906, John McGraw took his New York Giants to southern California; in 1911, the New York Yankees worked out in Bermuda. In 1914, Branch Rickey took his St. Louis Browns to Florida, where he found weather to suit his clothes and baseball-starved retired folks willing to pay to watch an afternoon exhibition game in the sea breezes.

Today, all 26 teams hold spring training camps, 18 in the Grapefruit League in Florida, the rest in the Cactus League of Arizona, with the California Angels splitting time between Mesa, Arizona, and Palm Springs, California.

No other sport makes such a thing of pre-season training. It is hard to imagine anyone being remotely interested in flying north to Canada to watch the Toronto Maple Leafs rehearse for the approaching hockey season.

The pitchers and catchers report to camp late in February, the rest of the squad a few days later, but no player can be forced to appear in camp more than 33 days before the opening of the season. The players are measured for uniforms. They are lined up like school kids to have pictures taken, head shots for the newspapers. (It's even called Picture Day – actually there are two of them, one to get the pitchers and catchers out of the way and the other one later for the rest of the players and late-arriving batterymen.) They take medicals. They catch up on gossip. They slap high fives and low fives. After a week of limbering up and exuberant profanities and chewing tobacco and working on the 3–1 play and the *clink-boink-crack* of batting practice, the teams play a schedule of games that means absolutely nothing.

The music of spring training is basic C&W "Dropkick Me, Jesus, Through the Goalposts of Life." The tourists wheel their Winnebagos in from Owen Sound and The Soo. Baseball Annies lounge in the sun behind the dugouts in high-cut bikinis, working on a tan or a young, corn-haired shortstop, whichever comes first. The trail of spring training leads along traffic-congested highways inadequate for the state's population explosion (Florida will be the third largest state by 1990). Every so often the procession of fast-food restaurants is broken by a motel – or a bar. Sometimes there is a pretentiously designed franchise restaurant-tavern; in each are a hundred customers who must have been part of the franchise assembly kit. The temper of the territory can be found on the bumper stickers and signs on the backs of pickup trucks: "God, Guns, and Guts Made America. Let's Keep All Three." For the baseball people, the mood is upbeat, optimistic – every team is in the running.

Players on the major-league team are given first-class air fare from their homes, or the cash equivalent; non-roster and minor-league players receive coach fare. Major-league players receive $96.72 a day, for expenses ($24.72), lodging ($30.50), and meal money ($41.50). Staff receives the same meal and expense money, and $61.00 for lodging. It is the one time of year when everyone comes together – players, players' wives, players' children, fans, reporters, broadcasters, scouts, agents, owners, managers, coaches, team executives, trainers, team doctors, batboys, equipment managers, PR people, ticket-sellers, suppliers, and assorted hucksters. The charm of spring training is its accessibility. The stadiums seat only a few thousand and the biggest names in baseball are a handshake away. Red-faced tourists lean over the fences and holler at their favourites as if they were next-door neighbours ("Jesse! Jesse! Over here!") and their favourites stop and smile and chuck little Fauntleroy under the chin for the family scrapbook ("Thanks, Jesse! Have a good year!").

The beat writers arrive even before the pitchers and catchers. They check into spacious condominiums paid for by their newspapers, hook up their word processors, test their modems, then search out the cheapest, friendliest restaurants and bars (preferably ones with Ms. Pacman and Galaga video games). Spring training is like a pre-Broadway run, as much for public relations and free publicity as to prepare players for 162 games of baseball. Film crews arrive with semi-trailers of equipment to do commercials and promotional movies and ten-second clips to run throughout the season. The beat writers barely tolerate newsroom colleagues who wangle a spring training assignment although the rest of the year they write about daycare centres and storm sewers. Each on-air TV reporter seems to have nine assistants who sit on the grass beyond third base with clipboards on their laps.

Spring training at first is euphoric, joyous, but all those exhibition games bring on stultifying ennui like mist from the Everglades. It is time to play ball, for real.

THE BLUE JAYS do their spring training in Dunedin, a pretty little town on the Gulf Coast of Florida. It is an ideal location: the Phillies play in Clearwater, a long walk away. The Reds play in Tampa, just over the causeway. The Cardinals and the Mets play in St. Petersburg, south down the coast, though the Mets are moving. The White Sox play a little farther south, in a grand old wooden stadium in Sarasota. To get there you drive over a long, long bridge from which you can watch dolphins sporting in the blue-green waters of the Gulf of Mexico.

It seemed natural to Cecil P. Englebert that the Toronto Blue Jays should migrate to Dunedin in the spring. Englebert had been involved in Little League baseball in Dunedin for 25 years, and he was vice-mayor of Dunedin when the Blue Jays were hatched and searching for a place to perspire in February and March. Eight per cent of the tourists at that time in the Dunedin/Clearwater area came from Ontario. There were direct flights between Toronto and Tampa, an easy drive from Dunedin. And Dunedin was not new to spring training. The Buffalo Bisons of the International League, old rivals of the Toronto Maple Leafs, had trained there at one time, and the Detroit Tigers had an Instructional League club there for a while. Englebert had pursued the Montreal Expos but could not come up with the facility they wanted, a four-diamond cloverleaf arrangement. City council and the mayor charged Englebert with landing the Blue Jays, and through Peter Bavasi a deal was struck. So the Blue Jays held their first spring training in Dunedin at quaint Grant Field, which needed a rush renovation to be ready for the 1977 spring rites. The final coat of paint was applied the night before the pitchers and catchers were to report. A crowd-control fence and additional stands were completed just before the exhibition schedule began. Over the years the park would receive considerably more work, in the clubhouses, in the stands, and on the playing field. Spring training fields are notoriously bad, and Grant Field's was one of the worst. Managers of opposing teams would usually leave their star players at home when they visited the Blue Jays.

During the winter of 1978, another rush job was done to complete a $207,000 minor-league facility known as the Cecil P. Englebert Recreational Complex, which Englebert cannot bring himself to say. He calls it merely the "complex." It gave the Blue Jays more room in which to do their early workouts before the Grapefruit League season began at Grant Field. When the major-league team moves into Grant Field, the minor-league players begin to arrive at the complex. As the complex was nearing completion on an old orange grove in February, 1978, Englebert was elected mayor of Dunedin, a position he held until 1983. The complex was built for the Blue Jays by the city of Dunedin but it also is used for amateur baseball, including Little League, just as Grant Field is used by high schools and a smaller diamond behind the right-field fence is used for a youngsters' league.

The Blue Jays struck a 10-year deal for the complex with a five-year option; but there was a rocky period. The Englebert Complex was dusty and the fields were not good. At Grant Field the short fence in right, listed at 301 feet, did not give an accurate reading of pitchers and hitters and discouraged young pitchers. The Blue Jays openly scouted for another location but eventually worked things out with the city.

In 1984, $420,000 worth of improvements were made to Grant Field and the minor-league complex. By the next spring training, an additional $2.3 million (U.S.) had been spent to improve both facilities. The Blue Jays paid for 68 per cent of the renovations and the city 32 per cent. Right-centre was pushed back from 340 feet to 365 feet, the left-field line was brought in from 345 feet to 335 feet. At the Englebert Complex new batting and pitching areas were completed under a roof. Both facilities had new clubhouses for the Blue Jays and modern offices and conference rooms. Dusty Englebert became verdant.

"This is first class," said pitcher Dennis Lamp. "Last year, it seemed like Joe's Garage or something."

Englebert says Paul Beeston was instrumental in working out the deal with the city. There had been some hostility toward the Blue Jays in the early 1980s, a sense that the team was trying to get a free ride. But Beeston defused the hostility by his presentations at city hall. Englebert was impressed. He doesn't think it could have been accomplished with Peter Bavasi. "I had no problems with Peter but he was tough to deal with," Englebert said. "He was not the type to give anything away. I don't think he'd have gone the distance that Beeston did."

The new agreement with the city runs until 1994, with two five-year options. Under its terms, the Blue Jays took over maintenance of both fields. And attendance has increased as the team and facilities improved. In 1977 the Blue Jays averaged 1,671 fans at Grant Field for 13 exhibition games. In 1985 they averaged 3,022 for 15 exhibition games. In Dunedin, there's a Blue Jay booster club of 300, Englebert says, 70 per cent of them Torontonians who hold season tickets or buy tickets to Blue Jay games in Toronto.

The Blue Jays spent $1.6 million to run their Florida operation – including major- and minor-league spring training and Instructional League – for 1986; they took in $175,000 from exhibition games.

Englebert conducted a survey in 1983 that showed that the Blue Jays brought in $4 million to the area's economy through restaurants, bars, condominium rentals, hotels, gas, and purchases at stores. At about the same time, a *Wall Street Journal* survey showed the Los Angeles Dodgers meant about $4 million to Vero Beach, Florida, where they train. *Florida Trend* magazine projected that a major-league team brings $3.5 to $4 million to a spring training area. He said that according to a 1987 estimate, the loss of the New York Mets during spring training would cost the city of St. Petersburg $5 million. Clearwater figures that the Philadelphia Phillies mean $5 to $7 million to the economy. Four years after his survey, Englebert thinks that the Blue Jays now bring closer to $5 million to the area each spring; since the team became a contender, the following from both the fans and the press has grown larger.

Although much of the money is not spent in Dunedin but in neighbouring areas in Pinellas County, Englebert says Dunedin still shares in it through taxes raised on sales of cigarettes, gas, and alcohol and distributed per capita. Dunedin had a population of about 30,000 when the Blue Jays arrived; that has increased to 50,000, some of them connected with the Blue Jays. Ernie Whitt and Pat Gillick have had condominiums in Dunedin Beach for years. Gillick bought his condominium from catcher Alan Ashby after he traded him to the Houston Astros in 1979. Among recent residents who have a Blue Jay connection are pitcher Jimmy Key, who lives in nearby Oldsmar, manager Jimy Williams and former trainer Ken Carson, who live in Dunedin, pitcher Dave Stieb, Don Chevrier (who does play-by-play of the Blue Jay games on CTV), and trainer Tommy Craig, who live in Palm Harbor.

Chevrier says he might not have a pool as large as Stieb's, but they share the same pool maintenance firm, Anchor Pool Service. When Chevrier was looking at houses in a certain area in Palm Harbor, Stieb told him, "Don't go in there, the lots are too expensive." Stieb had just signed a contract extension that had potential earnings of $25 million.

ONE OF THE FIXTURES at spring-training camp has been Ken Carson. A small, intense man, he served 10 years as team trainer, seven of them with the added duties of director of travel. He moved to Dunedin in 1984 after years of travelling to Florida every November for Instructional League baseball, home to Toronto for Christmas, back to Florida in February for spring training, then back to Toronto to treat the aches and pains and bruises and arrange the road trips until the end of the season in October.

Every spring-training morning, Carson would lead the players to the outfield grass at Grant Field and put them through stretching exercises. The players lined up in rows, then sprawled on the field, joking and jiving, but they followed Carson's regimen assiduously because they knew it worked and they knew injuries shorten careers and lose games. Carson also prescribed individual off-season exercises for the players. For years the Blue Jays had the fewest days on the disabled list of all major-league teams. That began to change in the mid–1980s, partly because of bad luck, partly because the players were aging. The Blue Jays lost Buck Martinez in the head-on collision at home plate in Seattle in 1985 and they lost pitchers Gary Lavelle and Tom Filer for all of 1986.

Carson joined the Blue Jays in November, 1976, when he was 34. He had been the trainer of the Pittsburgh Penguins of the National Hockey League. The reasons he got the job, he says, were because he was a Canadian, which satisfied the immigration department, and because he was certified by the National Athletic Trainers Association.

His assistant in Toronto was Tommy Craig, an American trainer. The Canadian Trainers Association gave the Blue Jays a five-year grace period to find a Canadian. The replacement could be groomed on one of the Blue Jays' farm teams, in Medicine Hat or St. Catharines. "The big thing is getting the licence," Carson said. "You have to have 1,800 hours working under a certified trainer, and the exam is a bitch. They are held four times a year in different parts of the country."

Carson's training career began when he was 16, as an assistant trainer with his hometown Barrie Flyers of the Ontario Hockey Association Junior A League. He followed the Flyers when they moved to Niagara Falls in 1961, then became head trainer for the Rochester Americans of the American Hockey League. Two years later he was working as head trainer for the Pittsburgh Penguins.

He admits he was a babe in the woods when he came to baseball. On opening day, 1977, he stood in the Blue Jays dugout enjoying the pre-game shenanigans, then settled in to watch the game in the snow. Early on the game was held up momentarily because of a White Sox injury at third base. Reserve catcher Phil Roof told Carson to run out to the mound and give pitcher Bill Singer a hot-water bottle. Carson dutifully ran out to the mound, but was stopped by Nestor Chylak, the homeplate umpire.

"Where are you going?" Chylak shouted at Carson.

"I'm going to give this to the pitcher," Carson explained, holding up the hot-water bottle.

"You get your ass off the field!" Chylak boomed.

Carson trudged back to the dugout to find the entire team bent over laughing.

"Roof was a joker and I didn't know anything in those days," Carson said. "He'd throw these expressions at me in spring training. Like, for a double play he told me to shout, 'Turn 'em over!' I'd wait until someone else said it, then I thought it must be all right. So next time there's a double play, I'd shout, 'Turn 'em over, attaboy!' Then he'd get me in a groove and feed me something that didn't mean a damn thing, like 'Kick it in the fender!' So I'd shout, 'Kick it in the fender!' and everybody'd say, 'What's he talking about?' ''

Carson found a great similarity between hockey goaltenders and baseball pitchers. ''The pitchers are probably the toughest players in baseball, like the goaltenders are in hockey. There's an expression, 'I can't wipe my ass after I pitch.' Well, it's true – literally. Pitchers rarely tell you they have a problem.''

It took Carson time to adjust to the different sorts of injuries in baseball and to learn that a minor injury that would have no impact on a hockey player can seriously interfere with a hitter's swing or a pitcher's delivery. At his first spring training in Dunedin, pitcher Bill Singer took Carson out for special sessions. ''To show why a player can mess up his arm if he's got a sore foot, he'd start by demonstrating pinpoint control – knocking a cigarette out of somebody's mouth – then he would take one shoe off and he couldn't do it. Wouldn't even be close. It was a weird way of showing me how everything had to be. I was pretty naive.''

Even after 10 years, the coaches amaze Carson by detecting subtle misalignments and hitches in a player's movements, usually the result of an injury or ailment.

''A player might be able to hide an injury from me, but not from the coaches,'' Carson said. ''If a guy's not swinging right, Cito Gaston will pick it up, just like that. He'll come and tell me something's wrong with a player. I might say I don't think so, then I'll go and ask the player and, sure enough, he's got this little problem. Al Widmar's the same with pitchers. He can tell if a guy's lost three or four miles off his fastball, or if he's dropping his shoulder, or if he's not following through. I've been around hockey with the Penguins and football with the Steelers, but baseball's the toughest sport to understand. The time and the mechanics it takes for a player to make the big leagues is unbelievable.''

For the 1987 season, Carson was appointed general manager of the Blue Jays' Class A team in Dunedin and director of Florida operations. He would be working with another Blue Jay original, Bob Bailor, who had been named field manager of Dunedin. The promotion meant Carson would be able to live in Dunedin year round. As a major-league head trainer, he belonged to the players' pension fund. Finishing his tenth year in 1986 vested him in the major-league players' pension plan, in which trainers participate. He lives close to his work, in a house with a swimming pool. From his backyard patio he can almost hear the crack of the bats at the Cecil B. Englebert Recreational Complex.

Tommy Craig, who had been Carson's assistant since September, 1984, took his place as head trainer. Craig, who turned 31 in April, 1987, set a goal when he was 16 and in New Hanover High School in Wilmington, North Carolina: he wanted to be a head trainer somewhere in professional sports. New Hanover has a sports tradition; the football quarterbacks Sonny Jurgensen and Roman Gabriel went there and so did Harlem Globetrotter basketball star Meadowlark Lemon. But Craig was not destined to be a great athlete, though he tried hard. He was tall and skinny then and a high-school coach suggested he might explore the possibilities of being an athletic trainer.

Craig obtained a Bachelor of Science degree in health and physicial education at East Carolina University and near the end of his college days he also worked as a trainer for the Cincinnati Reds' team in Shelby, North Carolina. Craig joined the Blue Jay organization in 1980 when he worked for the Class A team at Kinston, was in Knoxville the following year, and in Syracuse the next.

A minor-league trainer does more than tend to sore arms. "There were trainers in the minor leagues who drove the bus," Craig said. "I didn't drive the bus but I had to do laundry on the road. The bus driver and myself would load it up in the morning and take it out to a laundromat, take all the washers and dryers we could get, and do it. We'd bring it back to my room and sort it out."

In Triple A, the trainer is also the travelling secretary and equipment manager. In Providence, Rhode Island, one weekend, the hotel attempted to evict the Syracuse team because the Brown University graduation was being held and the rooms could be sold for the full rate rather than the cheaper baseball rate. Craig and manager Jim Beauchamp argued strongly, and Craig even pulled out the letter of agreement. The next day's game was rained out, which solved the room problem, but Craig had to find a flight to Richmond with 25 seats available. The game was called at noon and Craig had his 25 seats on an Air Florida flight at four.

BOBBY DOERR, one of the all-time greats, is standing outside the Blue Jay offices at Grant Field in Dunedin, waiting for a lift back to the Blue

Jays' minor-league complex. Although he retired as a Blue Jay batting coach after the 1981 season, he is invited to spring training late in March each year to offer advice and encouragement at the minor-league camp. At 68, white-haired and trim, he still does justice to a baseball uniform. He had been voted to the Hall of Fame early in March by the hall's veterans' committee, the dinner to honour the occasion having been held in St. Petersburg.

Those who recognize him say hello, shake his hand; some ask for autographs. He's an unassuming sort and his entrance to the Hall of Fame came 35 years after he finished his remarkable, 14-year career as the best second baseman ever to play for the Boston Red Sox.

One of the charms of spring training is bumping into an all-time great sometimes even a Hall of Famer, in the parking lot – as casual as meeting them on the way to buy a jug of milk. One morning it's hello to Tony Kubek, walking by with a television crew.

"Hey, Tony, how ya doin'?"

Another morning it's hello to Red Schoendienst, visiting Grant Field with the St. Louis Cardinals.

"Hey, Red, how ya doin'?"

Today it's hello to Bobby Doerr. He started with the Red Sox in 1937, when he was 19 years old. The year before, he played in the minors in San Diego for $1,800. When he got called up to Boston he thought he could make some big money, maybe $7,000, $8,000 – maybe $10,000. He signed for $3,300.

"That was as good as I could do," he said. "If you didn't want it you could stay home."

The most he ever made was $32,500 in 1951, his final season.

"That was pretty good money. Some guys were making more than that, but I was satisfied. We had a lot of fun back then and I bought 160 acres in Oregon for $2,250. And the guy only wanted a $500 down payment, that's right. It had four million feet of timber on it. From what I sold off I got $35,000, just for the timber. That timber now would be worth a million dollars, that's right."

When the Blue Jays approached Doerr to work as a hitting instructor in 1976 he did not want the job. Doerr let it be known that he had been out of baseball a long time and wanted to stay out of it. Bavasi later called him and asked if he might change his mind.

"I told him there was a 99 per cent chance I wouldn't, but I don't even know why I said that because I really wasn't interested in getting back into baseball."

Roy Hartsfield, the Blue Jays' first field manager, tried again.

"Is there a one per cent chance you might take it on a part-time basis?" Hartsfield asked.

"God, I don't know," Doerr said. "Let me think about it."

In bed that night, Doerr thought it might be fun to teach hitting again without having to be away from home all summer. He asked his wife; she told him to do what he wanted to.

"I began to think, gosh, I'll go to spring training, then visit Toronto three or four times when the club's in town. Spend ten, twelve days, then catch them on their road trips to the West Coast. So I called and said this is only way I would be interested."

That was good enough for the Blue Jays. Doerr enjoyed the work more than he thought he would, spending time with the major-league team as well as travelling out to some of the minor-league clubs, teaching the fundamentals, the basics of hitting a round ball with a round bat.

Doerr does not believe the best hitters today are any worse than the best hitters of his era. The home runs and batting averages might be down, but the schedule is longer, fielders have far superior gloves, grounders bounce truer on artificial grass – and there is the modern phenomenon of the specialty relief pitcher.

"When we played we could look at starting pitchers four times in a game, maybe five. If you didn't get to him the first couple of times, you had a little more percentage to get to him the last time. Now you see one guy maybe two times, then you see another guy your third time up, the middle man. Then you see some guy better than either one of them your fourth time up. It's probably knocked off five, ten hits a year, and when you're talking ten hits out of 500 times at bat, that's about 20 points off your average. Good pitching controls the game."

The exhibition game had been over for some time now. Grant Field was quiet and the parking lot gradually emptied.

Doerr reflected on his duties with the young Blue Jays. "It was fun," he said. "I've got some pleasant memories of those kids, the Barfields and Upshaws and Mosebys."

Moseby had been a challenge. He was only a teenager when he started in Medicine Hat, but he hit well in his two minor-league seasons, over .300. He struggled in his first three years with the Blue Jays, however, and nobody knew exactly what the problem was. Nobody, that is, but Bobby Doerr. Moseby's problem was a lack of concentration.

"I actually watched him play in Oakland, when he was in high school. Then I saw him up in Medicine Hat. Sometimes, jeez, he'd hit the ball so consistently, then there'd be balls he'd miss and you'd say, 'How in the world did he miss a ball like that?' "

One morning at spring training Doerr stood on the mound, feeding balls into the pitching machine while Moseby took his swings in the batting cage. He studied his stance, his swing, his follow-through. He watched the action of the bat on the ball. He was puzzled.

"Once he must have missed 12 balls. Kept missing or fouling them off. And he was making good swings. Then, God dang it, all of a sudden he'd start making contact and he scared me back behind the screen. He was hitting the balls so hard – *Boom! Boom! Boom!* – I thought they might go through the screen."

Bob Mattick yelled to Doerr from right field, telling him to make Moseby wear a batting helmet. Doerr never fussed much over things like wearing a helmet for batting practice, but Mattick was the boss and it was club policy, so he told Moseby to put one on.

"Awww, I don't want to," Moseby said.

"Look, it's policy, and you're going to have to hit with one on during the season anyway."

Moseby stepped out of the cage, scrounged around for a helmet that fit, then stepped back to the plate and Doerr fed more balls into the pitching machine. Moseby whiffed ten times in a row.

"I thought, well I'll be goldarned – the kid's problem is concentration," Doerr said. "He gets distracted, then can't set up on the ball."

Doerr walked off the mound, found a towel, walked back to the pitching machine, and told Moseby he was going to try to distract him from watching the ball.

"I'm going to show you what concentration means," Doerr announced. "You've got to watch the ball."

He fed more balls into the machine, every so often flapping the towel as Moseby set himself at the plate or started his swing. Soon enough, Moseby learned to find a comfortable stance naturally so he could concentrate on the ball and nothing else.

"Sometimes you have to use a crazy gimmick," Doerr said. "That's right."

IAN DUFF IS IN CHARGE of the visitors' clubhouse at Exhibition Stadium. He is listed as a front-office worker for the Blue Jays, and he is an ardent Blue Jays fan, but it is no cinch to be working in the visitors' clubhouse after the Blue Jays have won a crucial game. The defeated players trudge in, cursing, flinging gloves into lockers, kicking over chairs. The man in charge of the visitors' clubhouse wants to let out a Yahooo! – maybe high five somebody, but he must restrain himself. He even makes sure the clubhouse radio is turned off after the visitors lose, so they don't need to hear the Toronto announcers talk about the triumph. It is like a funeral director who wins the lottery just as the bereaved family enters the church.

The worst/best time for Ian Duff was the Saturday in October, 1985, when the Blue Jays beat the Yankees and clinched first place in the American League East. He watched the game in the Yankees' dressing room and knew he was seeing local history in the making.

"It was probably the toughest decision I ever had to make," Duff said. "Should I stay in the visiting clubhouse and take care of the Yankees, or should I slip over to the Blue Jays' side and enjoy the fun? I hemmed and hawed. Then I decided, hell, I've been here ten years and I'm not going to miss it, even if the Yankees killed me the next day. I went to the Blue Jays' clubhouse and shook hands with the players as they came in. I enjoyed the celebration for about half an hour, then went back to the Yankees. I was smart enough to bring a change of clothes, so when I got back only my hair was wet from the champagne. When the Yankees left, I went back to the Blue Jays' side and carried on into the night."

Duff and Jeff Ross, equipment manager for the Blue Jays, are two more originals from 1976. They are good friends. Ross came to Toronto from Montreal, where he worked with the ground crew for the Expos and as a helper in their clubhouse. Duff's route to the Jays was more circuitous.

He was in his last year of high school in 1976, the year Toronto finally got a major-league baseball team, and he and a friend named John Robulack used to visit the Blue Jays downtown offices. Robulack was in his first year at Ryerson Polytechnical Institute, studying landscape architecture. Duff worked part-time at the airport. They decided to apply for season tickets when there were about 4,000 names on the list. They dropped by two, three times a week, hoping to meet the ticket manager, who might get them good seats. They became friendly with the receptionist, who gave them press releases and introduced them to various Blue Jay officials, including Peter Bavasi.

"It got to the point," Duff said, "that if they had a package to go somewhere and we were headed that way they'd trust us to deliver it. Then one night we helped out with season ticket responses. We all went down to this little trailer by the stadium and worked 'til one in the morning stuffing envelopes.''

In December, when Duff and Robulack were visiting the Blue Jays' office before it closed for Christmas, Bavasi said, ''You guys are always hanging around, why don't you work for us?''

''We gave it a lot of thought, did a lot of soul searching,'' Duff said, ''and two seconds later we said, 'Sure! Yeah!' ''

Robulack worked part-time in the visiting clubhouse for about two years while going to school and eventually left to work as an architect. Duff's first job was assistant to John Silverman, the Blue Jay's equipment manager. Duff quit his airport job so that he could go to Florida for the Blue Jays' first spring training.

Silverman and Ross arrived at Grant Field early in February, before the clubhouse was finished. They had to sleep under the stands, in a small room behind the ticket office. By the time Duff arrived, the clubhouse at Grant Field was finished. Silverman and Ross found more suitable accommodation, but Duff continued to bunk down in the clubhouse.

''I was there 24 hours a day. There was always stuff being delivered and people coming around. A freelance reporter showed up after midnight one night and pounded on the door of the clubhouse. He didn't know how to get to the team hotel. There was no heat in the clubhouse. Some of the players complained that it was too cold but Roy Hartsfield said he liked it that way because the players would want to get out to the field.''

Like Duff, Jeff Ross has been coming to Florida with the Blue Jays since the first spring training camp in 1976. He is trim and athletic, with a neat moustache, and he is an avid golfer who often takes golf clubs on road trips during the summer.

As equipment manager, Ross is responsible for ordering the uniforms, bats, and helmets. Baseballs for the regular season – more than 1,600 dozen – are ordered by the office; Ross orders 250 dozen, at $30 per dozen, for spring training alone. The players provide their own shoes and gloves, usually working out a deal with manufacturers. Ross also either launders or has the uniforms cleaned after each game and workout. Special compounds are needed to remove stains from the grass or turf or from the clay sliding areas. In Dunedin and Toronto, there are laundry facilities in the clubhouse. His budget for a season of equipment and uniforms comes to slightly more than $100,000.

Each player gets two sets of home uniforms and two sets of away uniforms. Players who slide often and hard, like Moseby, Fernandez, and Bell, get a third pair of pants. Ross orders the uniforms from Wilson Sporting Goods Company in the United States; they cost $70 each, top and bottom. During a season, the Blue Jays spend upwards of $26,000 on uniforms. The dark blue warmup tops used during spring training and for in-season batting practice cost another $5,000. The satin team jackets range from $40 for the light model to $55 for the heavyweight model: total cost about $2,500.

"We usually have a good idea by December, when the 40-man roster is made up, who's going to be at spring training," Ross said. "A lot of non-roster players will join us later, but we can get something made up for them or find something in stock. I make arrangements for Wilson to be at spring training. We have to order other things, like sweatshirts, caps, the blue socks, the white socks, sanitary hose [the white socks worn beneath the team socks], and odds 'n' ends like letters, numbers, resin, T-shirts, batting gloves. It's all done at the winter meetings because all the suppliers are there."

Caps, at $75 a dozen, run about $3,000; batting helmets, at $25 each, cost about $1,000 for a season; catcher's gear, $500; bats, $20,000.

At spring training the players are measured for their opening-day uniforms, even though only 24 or 25 players make it of the 40 to 50 measured. The spring-training uniforms are hand-me-downs from the previous season. If there is a trade, Ross telephones the equipment manager on the other team.

"I will call up and ask what's Joe Blow's size, and what's he wearing. Tapered shirt? Tapered pants? Cap size? We have a lot of extra uniforms and I keep extra letters and numbers."

In their first year, the Blue Jays had their uniforms made by two companies, Rawlings Sporting Goods Company and Wilson; Rawlings made the away uniforms, Wilson the home uniforms. To simplify ordering and for consistency they eventually switched entirely to Wilson. One problem was that the Rawlings uniforms were made of doubleknit material, while Wilson uniforms were made of warpknit material. Doubleknit uniforms stretch two ways, sideways and up and down; warpknit uniforms stretch only one way.

"We found with warpknit, because it stretches only one way, it didn't shrink as much and felt more comfortable," Ross said. "Some players like the doubleknit because it feels tight. Most pitchers like the warpknit because it feels more loose. Wilson supplies uniforms for 19 teams, so the warpknit uniform is the most popular in the major leagues."

This may change, however. Rawlings announced in 1986 that it will pay an undisclosed sum of money for the rights to make all major-league uniforms, the money to be divided equally among the 26 teams. This would mean free uniforms for all major-league teams, a savings in these belt-tightening times. Rawlings would have a small logo on every uniform and the right to sell replicas of team uniforms to the public. (The teams would share in the income.) But for now the Blue Jays are one of three teams staying with Wilson. They wonder how good the service could be when suddenly Rawlings does all the major-league teams after doing only a few.

The Blue Jays and Expos would like to use Canadian-made uniforms to eliminate duty costs and to get better, local service. "We looked at a few different companies up here that made uniforms but they just couldn't compete," Ross said. "There's no market for that type of material up here. Amateur teams and softball teams wouldn't use it because it's too expensive to import. We've looked into having jackets made up here, too, but they don't have this kind of satin in Canada. They would have to import loads of it to make a profit."

After the previous season's uniforms are used in spring training, they are recycled to the minor leagues. The Triple A Syracuse Chiefs have their own uniforms, so the hand-me-downs go to the Double A Knoxville Blue Jays, the three Class A teams, and the rookie league Medicine Hat team.

There has been discussion about changing the Blue Jays' uniform, after complaints that the Columbia Blue away uniforms are weak. If a change were made, the league would have to be notified by June or July of the preceding year. One idea is a more traditional baseball uniform, with button-up tops and pants with belts. Another is to use richer blue for the away uniforms, like the dark blue shirts the Blue Jays use in batting practice.

Every spring Ross orders enough bats and helmets to survive the season. Every season at least a dozen helmets are broken when players, angered by a bad call, smash them into the ground or fling them into the concrete dugout. Most players wear helmets with ear flaps as extra protection; ear flaps have been mandatory for players who have come into the major leagues since 1982. Only Cliff Johnson, a 13-year veteran, refused to wear any helmet with an ear flap. Left-handed hitting catcher Ernie Whitt only wears one when facing a left-handed pitcher.

The team supplies the bats, which cost $12 each, but duty and tax add 22 per cent. When the exchange rate on the weaker Canadian dollar is added, each bat ends up costing about $18. Ross writes to the players during the winter asking what bats they would like for spring training. Some players get an autographed Louisville Slugger from Hillerich & Bradsby Co., which gives the players $300 or $400 or a set of golf clubs.

There might be a major breakthrough for the Blue Jays and Expos because Cooper Canada Ltd., a Toronto-based company with a reputation for its hockey sticks, gained major-league approval for its bats. Jim Geary of Cooper brought some of the bats to Exhibition Stadium in 1985. ''Tony Fernandez and Damaso Garcia picked up the bats and were amazed at how hard the wood was,'' Geary said. ''They asked if we could make bats for them. We made up some sample bats and they went over quite well.''

The Cooper bats are made with ash from northern Pennsylvania. Buck Martinez had the first hit with a Cooper bat in a major-league game. He also hit the first major-league home run with a Cooper bat.

Major-leaguers go through about 20,000 Louisville Sluggers alone in a season, an average of about 65 bats a player. Jesse Barfield goes through more bats than anyone on the team, about 240 a season. ''He uses a thin handle and lots of time he gets hit on the handle and he can break three bats in a game,'' Ross said. ''Rance Mulliniks only goes through about 70 bats a season – sometimes he'll use the same bat for two weeks. George Bell can be very hard on bats. In the first series against New York in 1985, he broke seven bats in two games. We had to get him more bats sent down from Toronto.''

In any shipment of bats, some are better than others. About four in a dozen are good enough to be used in games, another four are okay for batting practice, and the remaining four might never be used. The players look for a wide grain, which they feel provides a harder hitting surface. Cito Gaston, the batting coach, says narrow-grained bats used to be called coffee tables ''because they looked so pretty.'' He believes fielders have a more difficult time seeing the ball off the dark bats many players use. "You pick the ball up later," he said. "You don't see the bat go through the strike zone as well."

Both Ross and Duff shave bat handles individually for some players. Then there are players who are not at all fussy about bats. Cliff Johnson used any bat that felt comfortable, his or someone else's. Some players hid their favourite bats from Johnson, who sometimes borrowed bats from opposing teams.

Duff orders food for both clubhouses, which leaves Ross time to worry about his uniforms and equipment. In the visiting clubhouse, Duff provides sunflower seeds, chips, chocolate bars, coffee, fruit, cookies, salads, and meals after the game (he has a deal for the post-game meal with the Exhibition Stadium concessionaires). He pays for the visiting clubhouse supplies personally, about $15,000 for the season. The visiting team members tip about $10 a day, sometimes a little more for special errands. In 1985, as well, Duff was put on the Blue Jay permanent staff – usually baseball's visiting clubhouse men are seasonal employees – with all the benefits.

BIG JOHN MAYBERRY is the roving minor-league batting instructor. He looks even bigger than his six-foot, three-inch frame. Yet, he was always surprisingly agile at first base, like many big men who are light on their feet. He played four years in Houston, six years in Kansas City, nearly five years in Toronto, then half a season with the Yankees in New York. His best year was 1975, in Kansas City, when he hit 31 home runs, batted .291, and drove in 119 runs.

Some teams employed a "Mayberry shift" when he came to the plate, pushing the infield and outfield far over to the right and leaving yawning gaps in left field and down the third-base line. It did not much hurt his home-run production – he hit 30 for the Blue Jays in 1980 – but it chipped away at his batting average, making him a .240 hitter. He is a natural teacher, which is why the Blue Jays like to have him at spring training to work with the young players and then to visit the minor-league teams during the season. When he signed his last Blue Jay playing contract in 1981, there was an understanding that Mayberry would be given a job in the organization when his playing days were done.

Mayberry sits on the bench beside Field No. 1. It's not yet 9 a.m. and the young hopefuls are gradually making their way to the field for another day's workouts. Mayberry looks over the quiet field that soon will be a bustle of activity.

"Remember Doug Passmore?" someone asked.

"Oh yeah," Mayberry said, smiling. "I saw him in the Instructional League. He's retired."

Passmore used to work in the kitchen at Exhibition Stadium. He liked pranks, liked keeping the guys loose.

"Remember the time he put the ball on your head?"

"Oh yeah, ain't that something?" Mayberry said, and laughed.

It was before a game at Exhibition Stadium. It had been raining, there was a delay, and the players waited in the clubhouse. Mayberry was stretching on the floor in front of his locker, preparing himself for the game. He had been in a slump, no home runs in 10 games. Passmore came by pep-talking and giving advice. "This is what ya gotta do," he always told the players in the locker room.

He walked over to Mayberry, lying on the floor doing stretching exercises, and put a baseball on his head.

"This is what ya gotta do," Passmore said.

"Yeah, yeah," Mayberry grunted.

"Ya gotta get your wrists and hold the bat up here," Passmore said, in a hitting stance over Mayberry.

And then he swung, a full swing, and knocked the ball off Mayberry's head.

"I'm talking about no light checked swing," Mayberry said. "Uh, uh, he took a full cut. I felt a breeze goin' over my head. It didn't hit me for about ten seconds what the man did, then my heart started beating – fast! This man is crazy!"

Mayberry was traded to the Yankees early in the 1982 season, so he did not get a chance to enjoy the success of the team as a player. Before he left, he helped groom his replacement, Willie Upshaw, who had been an outfielder. "Bobby Mattick asked me to teach him how to play first base a little bit," Mayberry said, "and I did, because you know you can't play this game forever. I always liked Willie."

New York was not a happy experience for Mayberry. He was out of place with the hectic pace and the media horde. To compound things, Mayberry injured his heel and never overcame it. He never regained the feel around the bag he once had and the heel still pains him sometimes in the cold weather. He hurt it against the Blue Jays in Toronto rounding first base on a double he hit off Luis Leal.

Pat Gillick likes Mayberry and the way he handled himself as a proven veteran major-leaguer with an expansion team. Then there was the time in 1981 when Mayberry signed his four-year $3.2 million contract with the Blue Jays. Lawyer Gord Kirke remembers going out to dinner in Kansas City, where Mayberry lives, with Pat Gillick and Mayberry and some others. When it was over, Mayberry reached out and took the cheque in one of his big hands. A small gesture, one might think from someone who signed such a big contract, but apparently it doesn't happen often with the newly created millionaire athletes.

Much of Mayberry's salary came in deferred payments. "I was always a big believer in that," Mayberry said. "I didn't need all the money right then, just enough to live good. I didn't need no Rolls-Royce or Cadillac. The Royals' owner Mr. Kauffman brought me in to Kansas City after the 1975 season when I thought I should have been MVP. Mr. Kauffman said, 'John, what are you going to do with all that money?' Then he says, 'This is what you ought to do.' So I went into his office, his business, not the ballpark, and he wrote down a lot of numbers. I looked at him in this big office and figured he knew what he was talking about and used his plan. It ended up pretty good."

Mayberry is a pleasant, easy-going man, a Blue Jays' major-leaguer when there were too few of them. His coaching manner is low-keyed, encouraging. He remembers when some of the Blue Jay players were learning as they played in the major leagues. Mayberry recalls the young Dave Stieb, the first star created in the Blue Jay farm system, and his glowers at friend and foe in the heat of a game.

"It was just out of hard competitiveness," Mayberry said. "He wanted to win big. I mean, not only might he give a guy on his team a funny look; he'd give a guy a funny look who got a base hit against him. So you can't just say he was down on the team, because he did it to everybody, including himself."

THE HEAD of the social science department at Santa Teresa High School in San Jose, California, was sitting in an office at the Englebert Recreational Complex.

"Dave Stieb is in my mind a street guy," he said, "a pretty good street guy. When you talk about intensity and enthusiasm for his work – some guys talk about it, and a lot of guys write about these guys – Dave Stieb lives it. It's indelibly tattooed on his persona, his body.

When he takes the mound, he has the ambience of a killer. At that point in time, he doesn't care about his mother, his father, wife, son, me. One thing, that batter exists – and I don't even believe he sees the batter."

The man doing the talking taught Dave Stieb history at Oak Grove High School in San Jose. Stieb also was the punter on the high-school football team he coached. The man is Bob LaMonte, who also happens to be a player agent. Football receiver Mervyn Fernandez, who starred with the B.C. Lions and signed with the L.A. Raiders, is his client. So is Dave Stieb.

Most player representatives make it to spring training. Often agreements have been made, publicized as signings in the newspaper, but the contract has yet to be drawn up and signed. A lot of these formalities are completed at spring training.

"I'm not a big-time agent," said LaMonte, 41. He grew up in New York, moved to San Francisco when he was ten. He teaches U.S. history and has a Master's degree in U.S. diplomatic and labour negotiations. He also has a real estate business. He represents eight athletes, all from the San Jose area.

When LaMonte came to spring training in March, 1985, he was working on something big, the seven-year extension on Stieb's six-year, $6 million contract that was signed before the 1983 season. When Stieb was having agent trouble in 1982 he called up his former teacher, who negotiated the two major contracts for him. The 1985 extension could be worth $25 million, perhaps more; but he was guaranteed the $700,000 signing bonus and a $10 million annuity that the Blue Jays took out for him. All he had to worry about on that was that the Blue Jays stayed in business.

"I fully believe it is one of the great contracts of all time," LaMonte said. "But if it's not, then, I mean, I could live with it."

The Stieb signing was significant, following by a few weeks Bill Caudill's contract, which had a possible value of $7 million over five years. It was negotiated by Scott Boras, a former minor-league player turned lawyer who had played in the minor leagues with Caudill.

The morning that the Stieb contract extension was announced, LaMonte sat alone in an office at the complex. "I am of the opinion that 1985 will be remembered as one of the last years this ever went on. I am not trying to sound like a philosopher, but a contract like Dave Stieb's lifetime contract, it's going to be rare. Most of them are predicated too much on magic. I saw what was going on in the USFL. I saw what was going on in major sports. It got to a point where, quite frankly, the escalation was getting ridiculous. In baseball the owners were paying out about $45 million for players who were out of baseball. And they were paying an additional $35 to $40 million on players who were still in the game but not producing. That stuff can't continue."

LaMonte also sees the end coming for agents. "Half the guys don't need agents, to be honest with you," he said. "They don't need an agent any more than they need a hole in the head.

"Five years ago, when I was in my second year in this business, I said agency won't last, effectively, through 1990. I think by 1990 . . . it won't be cost-efficient to be an agent."

THE WHITE-HAIRED MAN sat in the blazing sun in the left-field stands at Al Lang Field in St. Petersburg before the Blue Jays were to play the New York Mets. The man was recognized by a fan sitting in the row in front of him. "Things sure have changed, eh, from the way they used to be with this team," the Toronto fan said. "It used to take a lot to sit through a long game."

"But those games were a little longer for me than they were for you," answered Roy Hartsfield. He was attending the game in his new job as an advance scout for the Houston Astros.

Roy Hartsfield had no chance as a manager, guiding an expansion team through its first three years. The Hartsfield Blue Jays were 166–318. On September 30, 1979, the Blue Jays ended their season at Yankee Stadium with their 109th loss. After the game Pat Gillick, who was not one of Hartsfield's fans, announced in the press box that he would not be rehired – a move that had been anticipated for some time. Hartsfield was on his way home to Atlanta as the announcement was being made. He had been offered an unspecified job in the organization, but he had told Gillick he would prefer an on-field job. "I knew I wasn't going to be back, before the season was over," Hartsfield said, but he still doesn't want to talk about the way he had to dangle on the end of the rope for so long. "I don't want to get into it. It may or may not have been a mistake but I let it lie for seven years and I don't have anything to gain by jumping into the papers with a bunch of stuff, so I won't do it."

He chatted for a while and, as the game was about ready to begin, moved toward the seats behind home plate where the scouts usually sit. Pat Gillick was sitting with Bobby Doerr behind the Blue Jay dugout. "Would you do me a favour?" Hartsfield asked. "Would you go to Bobby Doerr and tell him I'd like to talk to him? I'll be back here."

SPRING TRAINING can be a time for sadness, particularly near the end when the final, tough cuts are made.

Roy Lee Jackson had done about everything a relief pitcher could for the Blue Jays in four years after being traded in 1981 by the Mets in exchange for Bob Bailor. Long, middle, short relief. The occasional start. He even sang the national anthem. In 1984, he was 7–8 with 10 saves to win the Rolaids Relief Award as the team's top reliever.

Jackson was special to several players on the Blue Jays – among them Tony Fernandez, Jesse Barfield, Lloyd Moseby – for having reintroduced them to Christianity. Jackson had an alcohol problem when he was a minor-leaguer in the Mets organization. Then, through teammate Ray Burris, he became a Christian and changed his ways.

Late in spring training of 1985 he was one of the final cuts, and it probably cost him $300,000. His $340,000 contract was not guaranteed. He was cut at the deadline, April 1. One more day and the Blue Jays would have been responsible for his year's salary. He eventually went to Triple A and caught on for the second half of the season with the San Diego Padres at a reduced salary.

His spring training ERA when the Blue Jays cut him was 1.21.

"I was really hurt because of the way they treated me," Jackson said. "I was never a complainer, never a troublemaker."

He sometimes thinks Christians are given a bad rap. "They have this preconceived idea that as a Christian you are a passive person," he said in 1986, when his new team, the Minnesota Twins, was playing in Toronto. "Just because you don't cuss and rant. I think one reason they might think that is because some guys use it as a copout. When they don't do well, they say it wasn't the Lord's will. That's a lie because God always wants us to do the best that we can possibly do."

Was he bitter? "Even with what happened, I'm grateful to them because they really were the first club to give me a chance to pitch on a consistent basis in the major leagues. I have a lot of friends here and Paul Beeston was good to me."

Later, behind the cage during batting practice, Barfield and Jackson embraced.

ONE THING THAT HAS CHANGED about the Blue Jays' spring training is the increase in television and radio coverage. It used to be that reporters from the three Toronto dailies were the only constant media. Now the Toronto radio stations staff large chunks of spring training. Such has been the hunger for baseball back in Toronto in March that The Sports Network telecasts five Blue Jay and five Montreal Expo games during spring training.

In 1986, Labatt's took over the sponsorship of the Expo games from Carling O'Keefe as well as the promotional rights. Labatt's also has the sponsorship of baseball games televised by Canadian stations, including the All-Star game, playoffs, and World Series. Labatt's invested about $30 million to establish TSN, and after a slow start the pay television station is beginning to do better. In addition to 35 Blue Jay games on CTV, TSN shows 40 games plus another 40 Expo games during the season. When Buck Martinez was told he was not in the Blue Jay plans he took over from Tony Kubek as TSN's colour commentator for Blue Jay games, joining play-by-play announcer Fergie Olver.

The Blue Jay games are all produced by TV Labatt. In effect, John Hudson, who is Labatt's director of media operations, is TV Labatt. Hudson is in charge of anything the brewery does on television except the commercials. The second part of his job is to arrange the Blue Jay baseball telecasts. He says the brewery believes in producing its own telecasts so that it gets the highest standards and a degree of consistency. "Everyone else who works for TV Labatt is on contract," Hudson said. "In other words, we have no other staff. Laurie MacDonald, the production manager, Tom McKee, the producer, Michael Lansbury, the director, and Stephanie Williams, our associate director, are contracted. For games in Canada, we contract television equipment from Glen Warren, which is a subsidiary of CFTO, and in the United States a company called Unitel, a big production company out of Pittsburgh. Again, the reason we do that is continuity."

Hudson thinks that baseball might fare better than other sports with the network cutbacks in TV sports advertising. It's a big issue at this stage because baseball derives so much income from television (a five-year U.S. network deal is worth $1.2 billion and expires in 1989).

"Baseball has the advantage of being played in the summertime, which is the primary beer-selling time," he said. "It's got all the summer things going for it and people are more inclined to buy heavily in the better weather. The interesting thing about baseball is that of all the professional sports it has the highest percentage of women viewers."

AT SPRING TRAINING, fans will sit in the stands even if there is no game, merely to watch workouts. And many of them are women. It might be the sunshine, the leisurely pace. It was not unusual then to see people in the seats at Municipal Stadium in West Palm Beach as pitchers threw batting practice. But it did seem strange to see Bob Cox sitting in those seats in 1986. It was his first spring training out of uniform since he signed with the Dodger organization in 1959. The new general manager of the Atlanta Braves wore a green golf shirt and tan slacks. For four years he had been wearing the Blue Jay uniform as manager and for the four years before that he was manager of the same Braves. The big things about the new job were that he could live at home in Marietta, Georgia, a 20-minute drive from the Atlanta ballpark, and the salary, five years at about $1.75 million.

It was strange seeing Cox not sitting in the dugout, not throwing batting practice with the sweat rolling off him, with a gimpy knee and a flinging arm motion because of an old injury. He has an old-fashioned passion for the game. "I'd rather listen to a ballgame on radio than watch it on TV," he said. "It's more exciting. Maybe the broadcasters do hype it a bit, but they make it exciting."

He grew up in the farming community of Selma, California, just south of Fresno. "My dad worked on ranches," Cox said. "He was in the pump business. Water pumps. Drilling wells, pooling them, putting them in, repairing them. They had a loudspeaker on the back of the truck, where they worked the boom. Anytime there was a broadcast of the game, it was on. My whole family was baseball-oriented. In Selma, where I grew up, there was a baseball game going on each and every day and night."

Hampered by knee and arm injuries, Cox made his way through two big-league seasons with the Yankees – 220 games. In his third year in the Dodger organization, he injured his right arm so badly he couldn't move it, couldn't swing a bat. "I'd had it operated on in my senior year in high school," he said. "My elbow, there were bone chips in there, torn muscles. It got better and then everything got progressively worse. I kept working at it and it came around enough to play. In those days they put you on aspirins – that was the medication."

In the winter that the right arm had hurt him so badly, his career was threatened. He set up a fish net in the attic of the garage at home. He started to throw baseballs into it left-handed, trying to learn to throw using his left arm so that he could become a first baseman. "It didn't work,'' Cox said. "I hurt my left arm. I could hardly move it after a week.''

Cox was trying to instill some of the qualities of the Toronto organization in Atlanta. "Everybody knows where each other is coming from in that organization, which makes it so easy to work,'' he said. "You know exactly where Mr. Hardy is coming from. You know Paul and Pat. There's no secrets and everything is done collectively.''

Although people had their doubts that Cox would adjust to the front office, he maintains that it was an easy transition. The move to Atlanta was not so easy for his three-year-old daughter Skyla. "Where's George Bell?'' she kept asking.

Cox left the Jays a few days after the team had lost the seventh game of the 1985 American League playoffs. Early in 1986, the Jays filed a grievance against the Braves. One of the reasons the Blue Jays proceeded with the grievance, according to lawyer Gord Kirke, was that a directive from the commissioner's office told all major-league clubs that if there was evidence of tampering, it was their duty to bring it to the commissioner's attention.

There was no hearing. It was done by written submissions since it was between two clubs and not between a player and a club. The Blue Jays charged that it was more than coincidence that two reporters in two different cities (Boston and Atlanta) would have similar stories at about the same time saying that the Braves would be interested in Cox at about $500,000 a year. The story was picked up by the Toronto papers. The other point of contention was that Cox was signed by the Braves before the December 31 expiry date of his contract. There was a suspicion that the story about the Braves' interest in Cox was leaked through the television network of Braves' owner Ted Turner. The decision went in the Braves' favour because of a lack of hard proof.

Cox was working on one-year contracts in Toronto, which is a club policy for coaches and managers. But the Blue Jays have developed a severance pay system that is unusual in baseball, to help give them some security in an insecure business. If a major-league coach or manager is not rehired after one season of service, he is paid as severance the equivalent of 25 per cent of his salary. If he has completed two years and is let go, he receives 50 per cent. After four years, his severance pay would be a year's salary. When a new manager is named, he does not necessarily bring his own coaches. The Blue Jays feel that the coaches are part of the organization. Moreover, if the coach isn't dependent on the manager for his job, he can be more objective, not afraid to give his honest opinion.

Though Al Widmar and Jimy Williams were hired by Bob Mattick in 1980, they remained as coaches when Cox took over as manager. John Sullivan and Cito Gaston came with Cox and Billy Smith was brought up from the minor-league system to become a major-league coach in 1984. When Cox left, all the coaches remained when Williams was promoted from third-base coach to manager. It creates continuity.

Williams, his wife Peggy, and their four children moved into a house in Dunedin the same year that he was appointed manager. Williams had sold his home in Salt Lake City the year before and rented in Dunedin. Like Cox, Williams grew up in California steeped in baseball. He was raised on a ranch outside of Arroya Grande, population 2,000, midway between San Francisco and Los Angeles. As a boy he wangled a bat from school but he could not resist hitting stones with it when there was no one to play baseball with. "I'd pretend I was the announcer and throw these rocks up in the air and hit them," Williams said. "In time, you hit enough of them you're going to tear it in half. That's exactly what happened. It looked as if a beaver had chewed it."

In high school Williams lost one of the "m's" in his first name because of the way he signed a test as a prank. He decided that he liked it that way.

Williams is a high-strung, quick-moving person, full of energy. "He's a going concern, he can never sit still going here and there, taking his kids somewhere," said Ken Carson, who lives about a mile away. "He's got energy."

At spring training, Williams flits between practice fields, giving a little instruction here, hitting ground balls to infielders there. He never tires of the game, although a freak accident in the Ford Motor Company plant in St. Louis curtailed his playing career. He'd been drafted by the Montreal Expos from St. Louis in the 1968 expansion draft, was in St. Louis after a season with the Cardinals, fulfilling his military obligation in the Army Reserve over the winter. "This fellow finished a cup of coffee and then threw the Styrofoam cup at me," Williams recalled. "I picked it up and threw it back. There was no weight, no resistance. I felt something go in my shoulder. When I went home, it still hurt."

It turned out to be a rotator cuff injury. He reinjured it in spring training and it never came back, despite surgery and rehabilitation at

Toronto's Orthopaedic and Arthritic Hospital, on Wellesley Street. After a couple of years in the International League, Williams became a partner in a 7-Eleven store in St. Louis with the wife of his friend Ed Yawitz. The more he worked in the store, the more he wanted to return to baseball.

When he was offered a job managing in the California Angel minor-league system, he sold his interest in the store. He was 30. He knew he was in for long hours on buses managing in the Midwest League. "But sometimes there were forty-eight hours in some of the days when I was in that store."

There are plenty of 7-Elevens in Florida to give Williams perspective, no matter how badly things go in Dunedin. And there were plenty of warnings at spring training that 1986 might be a difficult first season for Williams as a big-league manager. Relief pitcher Gary Lavelle, trying to come back from an elbow injury, walked off the mound the first time he tried to throw hard in spring training. His season was over and he needed reconstructive surgery on his elbow. So did pitcher Tom Filer. There was the attempt to use Lloyd Moseby in the lead-off position, dropping Damaso Garcia to ninth or thereabouts in the batting order. Garcia's complaints turned Moseby's enthusiasm into awkwardness about the change. "Next year, they'll have me batting tenth," Garcia yelled at a reporter one afternoon as he walked to the parking lot. In May, Williams would berate and fine Garcia for burning his uniform top and cap in Oakland – out of frustration, not for any disrespect toward the team. But in 1987 it would start all over again. The Blue Jays were being picked by the odds-makers as favourites to win their division. New hope. Renewed faith. It has always been thus at spring training.

T E N T H

THE NAME OF THE GAME
IS HARDBALL

WHILE BASEBALL'S MOVERS AND SHAKERS were convening for the annual winter meetings on the Sunday morning, standing around the lobby of the Diplomat Hotel in Hollywood, Florida, and meeting in suites, about an hour's drive down the freeway at the Hilton Hotel in West Palm Beach, arbitrator George Nicolau sat at the head of a large conference table.

Nicolau would be making his first ruling as a baseball arbitrator. On his right was John Westhoff, the panelist appointed by management's player relations committee. To his left was Don Fehr, executive director and panelist for the players' association.

During the next two days they would hear a grievance against the Toronto Blue Jays filed by pitcher Dennis Lamp through the players' association. Lamp alleged that the Blue Jays had dealt with him in bad faith in 1986 by restricting the number of his appearances to 40. Had he been allowed four more relief appearances or two more starts or two relief appearances and one start, his contract with the Blue Jays would have been automatically guaranteed for 1987 at $600,000. But he had fallen short of the appearance numbers in a disappointing season –

2–6, earned run average of 5.05 – and the Blue Jays released him during the World Series. Under the terms of the contract, Lamp received $100,000 for being released. The Blue Jays made the announcement on the day off in the World Series, before the third game in Boston. Lamp responded from his home in Cohasset, Massachusetts, a reasonable drive from Fenway: the team was more interested in cutting costs than winning; pitching coach Al Widmar had been more detrimental than helpful and he was not sufficiently encouraging to the staff.

Gene Orza, the counsel for the players' association, and Gord Kirke, counsel for the Blue Jays, were seated at the table for the hearing, as were Lamp and his agents, Jim Bronner and Bob Gilhooley. The Blue Jays had Pat Gillick, Paul Beeston, manager Jimy Williams, and Al Widmar at the table. Also present was Tal Smith, who acts as a consultant to clubs on major-league player contracts, with statistical data he had prepared on behalf of the Blue Jays. A court reporter took down all the testimony for purposes of a transcript and each witness was sworn in before giving testimony.

It was an important case. Although two of the panelists are not objective and it is obvious which way they will vote, nevertheless "panel decisions" with three panelists instead of one arbitrator become precedents in future cases. The Blue Jays would cite at least two such cases – involving players Billy Cowan and Tito Fuentes. Arbitration panels ruled in favour of both players when asked to decide whether a club was acting in good faith when it terminated the contracts by releasing the players. However, never before had an arbitration panel been asked to examine the extent of utilization of a player by a club. Nicolau had two days to complete the hearing. While allowing each side to develop its case, he maintained a tight control: there would be no rambling discourses.

Dennis Lamp was the first and only Type A free agent signed by the Blue Jays except for their own players. In many ways, Lamp's plight in 1986 was that of the team: pitching wasn't the strength it had been in 1985. And here was a player struggling through a disappointing season openly criticizing management and his treatment. The bloom of 1985 was off the Blue Jays. They prided themselves for having developed into a class organization, but this case, more than any other, would leave a blemish on that reputation.

The controversy involving Lamp begins with the contract signed in January, 1984. Lamp was to receive one point for each relief appearance and two for each start. The first three years had been guaranteed, but Lamp would need 50 points in the third year of his contract or a combined total of 100 points in 1985 and 1986 to renew it automatically for 1987. After a mediocre 1984, Lamp was 11–0 in 1985 for a total of 54 appearance points from 52 relief outings and one start. He finished 1986 with 42 points from 38 relief appearances and two starts for a 1985–86 total of 96 points. The team still had the option to renew the contract and even before the 1986 season began Lamp's representatives had approached the Jays about it, proposing that they waive the appearance qualifications. (In some contracts, appearances in the first and second years will activate a fourth year; but a guarantee of three years at the most was Jays policy – for everyone.)

Lamp, Gilhooley, and Bronner testified during the first day. They felt they had a solid case: the Blue Jays had moved to within 3½ games of the first-place Red Sox on September 1. On September 6 in Chicago, Beeston and Gillick had met Lamp's representatives and told them that while he did not figure in their plans for 1987, they would amend the contract and add 10 points to the required appearance total, thus removing the chance that Lamp could guarantee his 1987 contract. From the conversation emerged the idea that Lamp would receive $25,000 for this concession. Lamp rejected the offer. He did not appear in a game for 26 days in September, and wasn't asked to warm up for 18 days.

Orza is a good litigation-type lawyer. He uses the scattergun approach, shooting out facts, keeping the other side off balance wondering where he's going to hit next. He argued that Lamp would have been used four more times in 1986 if the clause had not been in his contract. He said the Blue Jays should be liable for Lamp's 1987 salary and should compensate each member of the club because the misuse of Lamp had hurt the team's chances of finishing higher in the standing. (Teams must finish first, second, or third to share in playoff money. The Jays finished fourth by losing a doubleheader on the final day of the season.)

It was argued that Lamp had started the season slowly but had been improving. Before the All-Star break he was 2–5 with an earned run average of 5.90; he was 0–1 with an ERA of 2.70 in 11 games after the All-Star break. During the first half of the season, Lamp had pitched to his career average in number of appearances; after the All-Star break he didn't pitch with the same regularity – only twice after the September 6 meeting in Chicago.

More than two months later Lamp was still sad, bitter, and disappointed, but he was preparing for another chance at spring training with the Cleveland Indians at about $275,000 for the season. It hurt him to talk about it. He didn't want to dwell on it.

"If I had known I was going to play for the Blue Jays two years and five months I wouldn't have signed it," Lamp said. "I mean, my contract was for three years. They just took advantage of me. You've got to consider their point, too. They wanted to act like they knew nothing about it."

Lamp recalled when the decision must have been made. He can remember a game in Seattle when he was not used and left-hander Stan Clarke was left in against right-handed batters. Then in September there was the start given to rookie Duane Ward, who had hardly pitched in September, against the Boston Red Sox. He remembers the times another rookie, Jeff Musselman, was used when he thought he might have been. As the hearing progressed there would be the hurt of hearing his former manager speak negatively about him. It was not pleasant. But Lamp was optimistic that he would win. Many people – management and labour – thought he would win.

Gillick was just beginning his testimony when the hearing was adjourned for the day. The players' association was confident of its case, but the Blue Jays had their chance to reply on Monday. Gord Kirke, tired after staying up until three in the morning putting the finishing touches on his case and drained by the proceedings, knew he was in for a battle.

"After the first day," Kirke said weeks later at the Toronto law firm of Goodman & Goodman, "I think that they [Lamp's counsel and representatives] were extremely confident. I think they perceived that the arbitrator was sending out a message to the club that we'd better settle this thing because it's not going that well for the club."

STRANGE THINGS WERE HAPPENING in the game within the game. Owners who had lined up to sign free agents to exorbitant long-term contracts in other years were talking about financial responsibility. Talented players who had fled their old teams to test the market became wallflowers instead of the belles of the ball. Many of them re-signed with their old teams.

What a change. During the winter of 1976–77, when the Blue Jays were preparing for their first season, 24 free agents went through the re-entry draft; almost all had been snapped up. As the Blue Jays prepared for their eleventh season, another change was taking place. The players were angry and the situation threatened to become nasty.

The owners and commissioner Peter Ueberroth insisted that baseball teams were merely coming to their senses, watching their dollars more closely. The players called it collusion. Restraint was one thing; controlling the market was another. The players felt the owners had agreed there would be no competition. Ueberroth would retort that no force on earth could control such diverse personalities as Ted Turner, the owner of the Atlanta Braves, George Steinbrenner of the New York Yankees, Marge Schott of the Cincinnati Reds, and Ewing Kauffman of the Kansas City Royals. Yet, as the players noted, some of the owners, such as Steinbrenner, must have undergone drastic personality changes.

The first hints of things to come were visible in the off-season of 1985–86. On the January 8 deadline, seeing no interest from any other team, Detroit outfielder Kirk Gibson, who had helped his team win the 1984 World Series, decided to stay with the Tigers. But the winter of 1986–87 season would be the real test. There were several attractive free agents available, including outfielders Andre Dawson and Tim Raines of the Montreal Expos and pitcher Jack Morris and catcher Lance Parrish of the Tigers. No movement. Jack Morris even offered his services to New York Yankee owner George Steinbrenner, suggesting that an arbitrator decide his salary for 1987. Steinbrenner, who once collected free agents like marbles, turned him down. Morris then accepted an arbitration offer from the Tigers, which they were entitled to make in the free-agent process. By accepting, Morris retained the right to become a free agent at the end of 1987 and won his arbitration case when he won a $1.85-million salary.

On the Monday morning of the meetings, Ueberroth addressed the situation as part of his state-of-the-game speech. Defining it as fiscal responsibility, Ueberroth said, ''It also goes by the name of grievances on free agency. I think there has been great progress in 1986 and will continue in 1987. You've got to remember that this game was headed for bankruptcy in 1984.''

According to Ueberroth, there were both a minor reason and a major reason for this change. The minor one was television, but it made an impact. The major networks had informed major-league baseball that there would be substantially less income in the future. ABC and NBC had reached an agreement in 1984 with major-league baseball that resulted in a five-year, $1.2 billion deal to televise regular-season games, the All-Star game, the playoffs, and the World Series. Under the terms of the basic agreement reached in 1985 after a two-day strike, the players share in 18 per cent of the national TV revenue compared with the previous 33 per cent share of earlier and considerably smaller national television deals. The TV deal had become a significant source of income to the major-league teams, helping to give them the means to pay the inflated salaries. The deal expires with the 1989 season.

But the major reason for the new restraint, according to Ueberroth, was the opening of the books of the 26 major league teams during the 1985 labour negotiations.

"When we found out the list of losses to the owners of major-league baseball, there was a silence in the room that was hard to describe," he said. "There was not a person in the room who would have guessed that Oakland . . . was number one in terms of losses. They manage their club differently now and are moving quickly . . . but that was a shocker to us. . . . When we saw 20-some teams were losing money, I think people started to look around the room and were embarrassed. Opening of the books showed they were paying $50 million to players who weren't even playing the game any more . . . $2 million to a player for not playing or $3 million to three players not playing and are still paying a scout only $18,000 a year – and looking to cut the scout, to boot – then something's damned wrong with the game."

There was some applause in the room at this last remark. But later cynics wondered: even if owners did manage their business better and had more to spend, would they give the "$18,000 scout" a raise. Others suggested the owners have used creative bookkeeping to show losses where profits exist.

"Fiscal responsibility means being more careful and running their businesses better," Ueberroth continued. "The ownership, for the most part, are some of the best citizens in this country; but some are not paying attention to this part of their lives. We must . . . have viable franchises so that all baseball can progress together. The teams have been encouraged by me to set up their policies. I don't care what they are, as I have no control over them. If they want to sign a player for 10 years, then fine; 20 years, fine. But set up a policy, be forthright about it, be honest, and change it, if need be. Develop your own budgets, figure out what they are, and live by them. . . ."

It's something the Blue Jays had done since the beginning.

BEESTON, GILLICK, WILLIAMS, AND WIDMAR missed Ueberroth's speech. With Kirke and Tal Smith, they had left at six in the morning in two cars – one driven by Gillick, the other by Beeston – to be in West Palm for the final day of Lamp's hearing. Kirke would say later he began to feel more confident as things unfolded on the second day. Gillick finished his testimony, then Williams testified from the manager's standpoint and Tal Smith made a detailed statistical presentation.

Gillick was able to explain the reason for the September 6 meeting with Gilhooley and Bronner in Chicago. Kirke was glad to get Gillick's explanation, because he felt that the newspaper accounts presented it as a "sneaky or conniving move." In fact, Kirke felt it was probably a "most up-front and honest move and yet it got them in a lot of trouble at least in the press." The coaching staff and management had decided at about mid-season that Lamp did not figure in their plans beyond 1986, based on his pitching ability. After a July 20 game in Anaheim, Lamp completely lost the confidence of Jimy Williams. The Blue Jays had scored four runs in the top of the 10th inning to go ahead 6–2. Mark Eichhorn and Tom Henke had already been used. Lamp started the 10th, got the first out on a fly to the warning track in centre field, gave up a single, then took the count to three balls on each of the next three batters, who grounded out, singled, and walked. Bill Caudill got the game-ending out. In assessing Lamp in 1986, Widmar thought Lamp had lost something off his fastball and wasn't getting his sinker to work – and Lamp is a sinkerball pitcher. Lamp, who had overcome physical problems early in the season, was in a Catch-22 situation. As a sinkerball pitcher, he needed work to improve and was not getting it.

Releasing Lamp during the season had been considered. But Gillick and Beeston went to Chicago to "lay their cards on the table," as Kirke put it. They told Lamp's representatives (Lamp was not there) that he wasn't pitching well, that they didn't think he would be back with the team in 1987. They wanted to come up with a plan whereby Lamp could be used if something happened, such as an injury to another reliever, without risk of guaranteeing the contract for 1987. That's when Gillick suggested the increase to the points needed. Lamp's representatives wondered if there would be anything in return for their client, such as $25,000 Lamp was to receive under his contract for tallying 50 appearance points in a season. Gillick allowed that it was a possibility. (According to Lamp's representative, the suggestion of the $25,000 payment was initiated by the Jays.) By increasing Lamp's point requirement, the Blue Jays reasoned, he could stay with the team for the rest of the season and perhaps have a chance to showcase his talent with no pressure on him so that another team might become interested in him for the following season. A longshot benefit could be that if Lamp showed what the Jays considered a startling revival the team could renew the contract for 1987.

Tal Smith, who once worked with Gillick in Houston and New York and now handles salary negotiations and arbitrations for major-league teams, presented the statistical data. The Blue Jays were winners in only 28 per cent of games in which Lamp appeared – a statistic that showed how he was used as much as how he pitched; among relievers on the team only Mark Eichhorn and Tom Henke had more appearances than Lamp (Bill Caudill also had 40 appearances), he was 61st among the 73 American League relief pitchers who appeared in 20 or more games in earned run average and 60th in hits and walks allowed. Eichhorn ranked first in those categories. Smith showed that the Toronto starters were performing better later in the season; from September on, the starters failed to reach the sixth inning only four times. Lamp was used in two of those situations.

Kirke's key witness was Williams. The lawyer went over situations with Williams, game by game. Kirke was impressed with Williams's recall and analyses, as Williams explained why he had chosen a certain pitcher and admitted that in a few cases, with the benefit of hindsight, he may have made the wrong decision. It became clear that Williams had lost faith in Lamp and that as long as Eichhorn was ready and available he would get the call in middle relief. Orza cross-examined Williams, going over the same games. Kirke sometimes had to interject with clarifications; then Orza would continue. The process made Williams testy, and he fired back strong answers. With Lamp sitting there, he gave very negative evaluations on the pitcher's ability, repeatedly saying, "I go with the guys who I think will bring me a win."

Williams was asked whether Gillick had ever told him how to use players. The manager answered that Gillick had not, but once Gillick had sheepishly asked him if there was any way he could use one player a little more. Williams had said that he didn't think there was.

Among the arguments and points that Kirke brought out were that never had Lamp's representatives alleged or suggested he had had a good year and that the team has been noted for its generosity in honouring the spirit of contracts. If a player was close to reaching incentive clauses, the team was known on occasion to pay him anyway, and

Lamp's representatives agreed. In 1985, Lamp had been paid for an incentive that he had just failed to reach.

When the hearing was finished each side was requested to submit written arguments within a week.

Both sides thought they had presented a solid case. "I feel confident about the way things went," Lamp told *Globe and Mail* reporter Marty York, who called him from Hollywood shortly after the hearing. "Let's face it, they didn't say too many nice things about me on the witness stand, but I'd do it again if I had to. I felt I had to go through with it because they dealt in bad faith."

"I felt good after the second day," Kirke said. "Particularly after Jimy had been so strong on the stand and underscored to such a huge extent his desire to win and that's how he manages. It would have been so wrong to find in favour of the player and, in effect, to second-guess Jimy Williams, whose motivations had been to win as many games as possible. Further, it must remain the discretion of the club as to how and when to utilize a player."

Beeston wrote Orza to compliment him on his presentation.

THE PLAYERS' ASSOCIATION, which had pressed for the early December hearing date – the Blue Jays preferred to wait until after the meetings – was late with its written argument. The decision did not come down until New Year's Eve morning. Each side was notified by telegram that the arbitrator denied Lamp's grievance; reasons would follow. Lamp and Orza reacted bitterly. "I believe Toronto's public posture was not their real posture," Orza said. "I believe they were out to preclude Dennis from collecting because they didn't like the contract they gave him in 1984. I can't believe Jimy Williams doesn't . . . read the newspapers and is completely ignorant about players' contracts."

Managers do not like to know the terms of a player's contract, particularly when it might involve appearances. (And, indeed, there have been instances in the major leagues of players being held back to avoid incentive bonuses.) But player contracts are seldom confidential anymore. Contract details have become as much a part of daily baseball news as box scores. In the Lamp case, there was frequent mention of how many appearances he needed, and his plight generated considerable publicity from late August until the end of the season. Lamp was quoted as saying that he did not think it was Williams's decision whether he was used or not, but if Williams was insulted by such suggestions,

270

he didn't show it publicly. Gillick maintained that he made the players available to his manager but did not tell him how to use them.

"They got away with it," Lamp said when the decision came down. "It's terrible, and it's very sad. You go 26 days without pitching and he says he has no knowledge of what's in your contract. I find that extremely hard to believe. If I had lost a game in 1985, they may not have won the division. They didn't show much appreciation in 1986."

Lamp predicted that players would distrust the organization. "You won't see a family atmosphere anymore. It'll be players against management from now on. And I guarantee you'll see a lot more arbitration cases involving the Jays. . . . You're just a piece of meat if you play in Toronto. Management acts like they're the greatest guys in the world, but they're not. If they could finish first and break even or finish third and make $2 million, they'd rather finish third."

There was irony in Lamp's outburst. He had been a member of the Chicago White Sox when they won 99 games in 1983 to finish first in the American League West by twenty games. But the White Sox were not interested in re-signing Lamp, who became a free agent at the end of the season. The Blue Jays did sign him, but he struggled in 1984 as the short man. He had come to spring training in 1985 lean and determined, and back in middle relief he had been an important factor in the Jays' division win. He arrived at camp in 1986 contented. He talked about the White Sox, who dipped to 74 wins in 1984 for a decline of 25 wins. "I think management kind of messed up their situation," he said. "They wanted to save money and they really tore apart the team."

Lamp talked of the "family atmosphere" among the Blue Jay players during the 1985 season. "When you're struggling there's always someone to pat you on the back and try to push you a little bit, which is good."

He talked of the importance of keeping the team and its winning formula together and the players satisfied. "They've gone out of their way to keep everyone pretty much happy," Lamp had said. Even in the best of families, there have been squabbles over money.

REPRESENTATIVES OF THE COMMISSIONER'S OFFICE and observers of the legal scene in sports have styled the case as one of the most important legal decisions to come down for the industry in a long time. "It is an important decision not just for the Blue Jays but for the sports industry generally," agreed Kirke, who in addition to advising the Blue Jays and other clients in contractual matters is a professor of sports law in the Faculty of Law, University of Toronto.

On a wall of Kirke's office there was a framed picture of a Toronto *Sun* front page with the headline "We Did It" and a photograph of Doyle Alexander and Damaso Garcia embracing after the Jays clinched the American League East.

"You can imagine the consequences if we had lost the case," he said. "If we had lost and you're a player representative and one of your players falls two appearances short of a $100,000 incentive bonus, what do you do? You're going to grieve it. Automatic. And the same with one of these contract extension cases.

"The real significance of this case is that it establishes that the manager has the discretion as to how and when to use players and you're not going to wind up in a court of law or before an arbitrator trying to second-guess what the manager does and attempting to tell the manager how to run the club. I think it's terrific that the sports writers and the fans can second-guess the manager – that's great fun; that's part of baseball. But to bring it into a court of law or an arbitration proceeding . . . it would just be a horror show."

Kirke said many baseball people felt Lamp had a good case but that this was based on little information or on misinformation solely from the one meeting in Chicago, where the contract modification had been suggested. He believed strongly that Lamp's contract required him to *earn* the extension and the $600,000 salary for 1987; there was no duty on the part of the Blue Jays to hand it to Lamp on a silver platter, and Lamp's performance in 1986 cost him the extension, not any action by the Blue Jays. He also wondered why it seemed fair that Lamp's representatives tried to renegotiate the terms, but unfair when the club tried.

Kirke said the Blue Jays "were damned if they didn't and damned if they did. . . . You could release him right at the moment you decide that he no longer figures in your plans," he said. "If you do release him, you face the possibility of a grievance on the basis that you released him to avoid giving him an opportunity to extend the contract.

Kirke, who was with the Blue Jays even before they had a name, puts little credence in arguments that the team doesn't want to win. "From a business point of view, there's no way they can make money unless they at least got into the playoffs, if not the World Series," he said. "And there's nothing more ego-gratifying for all concerned than a winner. They knew for the first few years they weren't going to be a winner. But every effort was directed at winning in the future.

"People say the team can afford not to win because Labatt's still gets product identification. But the truth of the matter is that such product identification is only good, or particularly good, if it is associated with a winner. Labatt's doesn't want its product associated with a loser, the bank doesn't want to be associated with a loser.

"The profit element is fairly remote no matter how many games you win, basically. But you want to be identified with a winning ball club, you want an upbeat thing. In the low days of the Blue Jays . . . they could say they were making a significant contribution to the community, building a contending ball club for the city. But common sense says ownership couldn't be satisfied if the Blue Jays produced a last-place club for the next few years."

THE CIGAR WAS BEING WORKED over with some vigour. "The philosophy has not changed at all," Paul Beeston said. "I think the most important thing is to put a championship team on the field. So you have to use everything that's available to you. You want to tie up your players. You want to make sure that your players are compensated in a manner in which they are not negatively thinking towards the ball club, that we're cheap or anything like that. The philosophy of continuing to put a winning team on the field at competitive prices is still there. I don't think you have seen any type of actions from the Toronto Blue Jays which would indicate that we will not go through with that initial philosophy which was to scout the best guys and sign them. We never were on the free-agent market with the sole exception of Dennis Lamp."

The free-agent market Beeston mentioned was the high-profile re-entry players whose signing meant surrendering draft picks. Beeston says he likes Lamp. He had been one of his boosters when the Blue Jays went out to sign him.

"The grievance hearing was very difficult for me, very difficult for Dennis, very difficult for everybody," he said. "We had to . . . say he wasn't a very good pitcher and you don't ever like to criticize people that you like. But the fact is he had a bad year last season and if he had had a good year, there would have been no problem with executing his contract. But he didn't fit in our plans. The fact of the matter was he did not pitch well. It had nothing to do with money, although the money . . . we are still prepared to pay for performance."

Beeston found nothing good about the Lamp situation, other than the fact that an arbitrator proved them correct. "It was never my understanding with that contract, that we didn't have the right to release him whenever we wanted to for whatever reason."

There was another important aspect: the Blue Jays have a policy of not renegotiating player contracts, although they would work on extending a contract as they did in 1985 with Dave Stieb. Yet, when they went to Chicago and made the offer to Lamp, they were, in effect, renegotiating. "We didn't think it was renegotiation at the time, but it clearly was," Beeston said. "It was badly handled on our part. We rationalized that . . . all we were doing was to give him his last incentive bonus."

Lamp was not the only player to accuse Gillick of calling the shots about who should play, and where. Second baseman Damaso Garcia had told anyone who would listen that Gillick, not Williams, had decided that Garcia would no longer be leadoff man. When the Blue Jays started rookie Duane Ward in Fenway Park in the game in which the Red Sox trounced the Jays to clinch the American League East, it was suggested that it had been a management decision. (In fact, it had been arrived at by Williams and Widmar – Gillick privately had wondered about the move.) The players thought management had given up on the season; they lost five of the six remaining games to end the season with seven losses in eight games.

Beeston dismissed the idea that Gillick pulls the strings for Williams. "If Pat Gillick wants to do that," Beeston said, "he's going to have no one who would manage for him and no one to coach for him and no one would want to play here. If that's the case then the owners are going to say, Gillick, you have to change your ways or, alternatively, you're going to have to change the venue where you operate, and the last thing Pat Gillick is, is stupid, so he isn't going to do it."

If the Blue Jays had shed one free agent, they had the task of retaining two major free agents, original Blue Jays Ernie Whitt and Jim Clancy. They were testing a free-agent market that did not seem to exist. Whitt, acting as his own agent, took a tough stance although he dearly wanted to stay in Toronto. Clancy said all along he would be back in Toronto and sounded quite happy about it. Clancy was represented by Alan and Randy Hendricks of Houston, who also represented George Bell. The Hendrickses had good relations with the Blue Jays in their dealings over a number of years despite some hard negotiations.

"There's probably a lot of compatibility in style, we're similar ages, have similar attitudes toward life," Alan Hendricks says. "Beeston is a unique character among baseball executives. And we're not always on a campaign against management. Some agents go to war over every nitpicking item."

"They are completely professional," Beeston said. "They prepare, they work hard, they articulate well. They don't take a tough negotiating session away from the room – you can negotiate and then go for dinner with them and talk about other things and there's no carryover."

If there were to be any ramifications from the Lamp situation, Beeston said they were not readily apparent in the negotiations with Whitt and Clancy. "Nobody has brought up Dennis Lamp per se, that we were dishonest with him and unfair with him and we're going to treat them that way," Beeston said. "On the contrary, both the Hendrickses and Ernie have said that they trusted us, that we were fair, maybe we didn't want to pay as much money as they wanted, but our integrity was not a question."

To help bridge their differences, Whitt had asked for incentive clauses using appearances, but the Blue Jays refused. "I was trying to find a way to bridge the gap. They didn't want to go for it because of the Lamp situation," Whitt said. "I really don't like what happened to Dennis. I don't think there's any question they were trying to cut back on salaries. There's no question it helped them financially. . . . I'm disappointed in them. To me they didn't live up to their contract. I just feel if they have a contract with a player, if the situation calls for that player to get into the game, he should get into it. I don't think the manager should know about contracts. I don't think there's mistrust. They've always been up front with me. I was just disappointed they took that route."

Under the basic agreement reached in 1985 – there was yet no formal document in place – the teams had until January 8 to re-sign players from their own team who had become free agents. If no agreement was reached the team relinquished bargaining rights to them until May 1, when it was unlikely they would still be available – the regular season would already be more than three weeks old.

Whitt and Clancy, like other free agents, found little or no interest from other clubs. There was talk that the Philadelphia Phillies, managed by former Blue Jay bullpen coach John Felske, might be interested in Clancy. When Jack Morris was offering himself to the Twins, the Yankees, the Phillies, and the Angels, it was thought that the Tigers would be ready to pursue Clancy. But when Morris accepted arbitration with the Tigers, that market closed. Clancy wanted to return to Toronto and hoped for a three-year deal. He agreed to a two-year deal on January 6: $850,000 for the first year and $900,000 for the second, much of it in deferred payments, which alleviate taxes and provide money for the future. There also were awards clauses. The final season of his four-year contract brought him $680,000 ($450,000 of it deferred) with another $10,000 for reaching 200 innings pitched. Clancy fell two-thirds of an inning short of reaching his next award level, 220 innings. The Blue Jays paid him that $15,000 bonus anyway.

Beeston enjoys dealing with player representatives and respects the good ones. It's a matter of growing accustomed to them over a number of years, knowing their styles. Tom Reich, for instance, who acts for Jesse Barfield and who was steering Montreal Expo outfielder Tim Raines through the troubled free-agent waters, is likely to wait until near the deadline before making a deal. Certain players also tend to take it down to the end. Indeed, the Blue Jays themselves had developed a reputation for last-minute agreements: Willie Upshaw in 1984, Bill Caudill in 1985, and George Bell in 1986 were signed as the arbitration deadline loomed or had been extended. Beeston and Gillick do look at contract negotiations as a competition, winning and losing. "You want to be fair," Beeston said, "but there's the competition to convince somebody you're right if you are, in fact, right. With the exception of Doyle Alexander, no one's gone away."

The New Year was five days into its first week when the final negotiations on Clancy were held in New York. On the Monday night, January 5, Gillick and Beeston had dinner with the Hendrickses at Jimmy Weston's restaurant on East 54th Street. (The restaurant did not get a good review from Beeston.) The negotiations moved to Randy Hendricks's suite at the Grand Hyatt Hotel, beside Grand Central Station, where the Blue Jays stay during the season. They went downstairs for dessert at the Grand Hyatt, then went up to Beeston's suite to continue the talks. Three hours later, at 2 a.m., they recessed.

On Tuesday morning, Beeston and Randy Hendricks talked on the telephone. They were $100,000 apart on a two-year deal. "If we don't get this deal done, we should both have our asses kicked," Randy Hendricks told Beeston.

"You're right," Beeston said.

In retrospect, Beeston would say, ''If there was not some creative way to work that out, not some way of giving, then we're not doing our jobs because we're supposed to be negotiators.''

Beeston and Gillick went to the commissioner's office and telephoned Randy Hendricks, who was working in the players' association office. They met him for lunch at a Chinese restaurant and the deal was done in 15 minutes. Clancy, who all the while was at his parents' vacation home in Twin Lakes, Wisconsin, was relieved to have it settled and glad to be returning to Toronto.

The differences with both Clancy and Whitt were in length of contract and amount. Whitt had been asking for $2.7 million over three years, with an option on a fourth year. The Blue Jays stayed with the basic offer they had made in November, but it was up considerably from the $550,000 they had offered Whitt at spring training, when the catcher decided to break off the negotiations until after the season.

Beeston thought that at crunch time it might have impressed Whitt that they had been dealing with him straight from the beginning. They were willing to come up slightly for a two-year guaranteed deal with a third year, not guaranteed and at the club's discretion. But Whitt would have to lower his figures. Through his community work, his accessibility to the media, his generous smile, his loyalty to the team, and his desire to stay in Toronto to finish his career with the Blue Jays, he had become one of the most popular Blue Jay players. Whatever interest Whitt did receive from other teams, he said he did not follow up on them. His only other choice was Detroit and he knew the Tigers had a club policy against signing Type A free agents. Whitt also has a good off-season deal with Labatt's in which he agrees to appear at speaking engagements 15 days a year, which usually works out to seven events, including travel days.

Letters to the editor, calls to phone-in shows – all were in favour of Whitt. Besides, his $325,000 salary (not including his deferred payment package) was low in comparison to the salaries of the day. In 1985, the average major-league catcher was paid $532,771; and in 1986, $694,661. Even including the present value of Whitt's deferred payments – spread over the three years of his just-expired contract – his 1986 salary was about $470,000.

On Wednesday night, on the eve of the deadline, Gillick and Beeston drove to the Whitt home in Mount Clemens, Michigan, near Detroit. Gillick and Beeston arrived about 5 p.m., had dinner – Whitt's wife,

Chris, cooked up pork chops, mashed potatoes, baked beans, zucchini bread, spinach salad, cherry strudel, and pumpkin pie – and joked about how much it might be worth to the Blue Jay executives.

When dinner finished the mood became icy. Gillick and Beeston expected that – and expected their visit to be short. The differences were still great. They went to the living room for coffee and handed Whitt the written offer. Whitt, very calm, sat with his legs crossed and looked at the offer

"Oh," he said.

Beeston detected no tension in Whitt. Disappointment, yes.

"You don't like doing it," he said two days later. "You know in your heart what you're doing is right. You've got to convince the other person that what you've done is right. You've analysed the situation. Everything is presented on a professional basis with reasons and it's not getting through. I mean, it's like my kid – he wanted a lot of things for Christmas that he didn't get."

Whitt, as well, had reached his figure scientifically. He wanted parity with catchers of similar ability. He eliminated the highest and lowest figures among catchers. According to his calculations, he felt a three-year, $2.7 million guaranteed deal that he sought would have put him eighth among catchers, not including Gary Carter of the New York Mets, the highest paid player in baseball with a 1986 salary of $2,160,714. Whitt said that, during the negotiations, Beeston and Gillick did not disagree with his figures but would remind him that it was a new market and the escalation of salaries was ending. Whitt could see their point: the pendulum was beginning to swing back and the owners wanted to keep it there. It did not, however, weaken Whitt's conviction that he was right – and he was being cheered on by the Blue Jay fans. The fans were one reason Whitt was glad to stay in Toronto, although he figured he paid 10 to 12 percent more in taxes than he would if he played in a U.S. city.

After dinner, the meeting ended swiftly. Gillick said he'd call Whitt the next day. At 7:30 p.m. they left. On the way to the car, Beeston told Gillick, "You owe me one. I took one for the club."

"What do you mean?" asked Gillick.

"I don't eat spinach and you know it."

Beeston did, however, like pork chops.

On Thursday, with a midnight deadline looming, Gillick made his first call to Whitt at 5 p.m. Gillick was in Toronto, Beeston in Sarnia, where 10 months earlier he had agreed to speak to the Lambton County Chartered Accountants Association on January 8, not knowing then how significant the day would be. Sixty people showed up for the talk, which took about an hour with questions and answers. "I've committed to it, they've advertised it, you've got to show," Beeston said. "Pat's in Toronto, I'm in Sarnia, and Ernie's at home. It's a tale of three cities."

"Look, this is a fine fix we're in." Whitt told Beeston, who had called from the lobby of the Holiday Inn in Sarnia at 9:10 p.m. after his speaking engagement. Gillick had made his second call to Whitt at 6 p.m., and in the emotion of the moment said something that made Whitt angry.

"Everything is off," Whitt said.

Recalling it later, Whitt said, "I was really bitter. He said something that was unnecessary. That's when I became angry."

After that night, Whitt did not talk to Gillick again until spring training, when he wanted to clear the air about the comment.

Beeston talked to Whitt a few times after that, the last time from a highway service centre on the way home. At about 9:30 p.m., after Beeston had talked about the interest-free loan and it was increased to $350,000, Whitt decided to stay with Toronto but that he would play it out to the end.

At another stop at another service centre on the way home, Beeston had called the players' association in New York to try to clarify a point in the offer.

"It almost became a charade," Beeston said. There was a misunderstanding about the interest-free loan. Gillick's interpretation was that it was pre-paid salary, or an advance, and Whitt was adamant about it being an interest-free loan as written on the offer sheet.

Whitt said there was really no extension given on the midnight deadline. But consideration was given because Beeston was in transit. He was the one who had to give approval. It was decided that if Beeston agreed that the $350,000 was an interest-free loan, then Whitt would be considered signed with the Blue Jays. If it was not an interest-free loan, he would still be a free agent.

Driving along Highway 402 between Sarnia and London, Beeston stopped at Lambeth to phone Gillick. The line was busy. "I said I'll wait another half an hour, so I go down the 401 and all hell had broken loose, and he hasn't signed and they've got extensions and I've got to talk to the players' association to straighten this thing around," Beeston said. "They've got to speak to Ernie. I phone Pat back and say, 'Lookit, it's cold out here – you phone the players' association and let the players' association get to Whitt.' "

The agreement was reached at 1:30 a.m., 90 minutes after the deadline. Beeston reached home at 3 a.m. Whitt had settled for $750,000 guaranteed in 1987 and 1988 with a club option for a third year at $800,000. (The team could decide if Whitt's contract would be renewed for 1989.) There would be no appearance clause to activate the contract. ("What if we were trying to work in a young catcher?" Beeston asked.)

The Blue Jays had re-signed both their free agents. Three other top-ranked catchers – Lance Parrish of the Tigers, Rich Gedman of the Red Sox, and Bob Boone of the Angels – had not signed. In all, 11 free agents decided not to re-sign with their clubs by the deadline.

Whitt said the contract was below what he thought he was worth, compared with contracts of catchers of similar ability, but felt he could not afford to take a chance on "the roll of the dice." He did not want to become a victim of the owners' "game plan" to hold down salaries.

The next day, Beeston was at the office, only slightly later than usual. He was tired, but no less exuberant.

"I think that the people who get credit for signing Ernie Whitt in every way are the owners of the ball club, the staff of the ball club, the fans of Toronto, and the media in Toronto," said Beeston. "He wanted to come back to Toronto. It's in spite of us that he signed. He'll think that we're a couple of assholes, that we're cheap skinflint Scrooges. But in spite of that, he came back. He doesn't really, I don't think, hate us. He might respect us, but I'm not sure about that. In time I think he'll come to respect us. He wanted to come here because the city of Toronto had been so good to him. I didn't realize how good people had been on selling him on the city and playing here. I really think that was the key."

WITH THEIR FREE-AGENT SITUATION resolved, the Blue Jay management braced for the next inning in the Winter Game – arbitration. They had three players eligible to have their contract differences settled by an arbitrator, players with three years' major-league service but fewer than the six years required for free agency. They were Jesse Barfield, who led the major leagues with 40 home runs, George Bell, and Rick

Leach. Leach signed a two-year deal, for $260,000 and $300,000, before it was necessary to file for arbitration. Barfield and Bell filed. When the salary totals were submitted, Bell and Barfield came in with figures $25,000 apart. Barfield filed for $1,350,000 and Bell for $1,325,000. The Blue Jays submitted a figure for Barfield at $1,125,000 and for Bell at $1,000,000. Each had worked from a base salary of $650,000, not including incentives, in 1986. As it turned out, neither had to go to arbitration. They both were scheduled to have their cases heard on February 19, Bell in the morning and Barfield in the afternoon. Barfield signed a one-year deal the night before, worth $1,237,500 with a package of incentives that could add to it. Then, about 10 minutes before the scheduled start of Bell's hearing, an agreement was reached on a one-year deal worth $1,175,000, plus incentives. In both cases, there would be continuing talks on long-term deals.

But there is another aspect to the arbitration. Until 1987, a player with two years' major-league service was eligible for arbitration; but in the 1985 agreement between the owners and players it was decided that three years' major-league service would become necessary. The 1986 arbitration requirement would remain at two years, with the change taking effect for 1987. There was no provision for players already in the major leagues who in 1987 would have more than two years service but fewer than three. (For such purposes, 172 days is considered to be a major-league season.) Blue Jay relief pitcher Tom Henke and shortstop Tony Fernandez, both players of quality, were among those affected. Fernandez missed by eight days, Henke by 113 days. In 1986, both players had their contracts renewed by the Blue Jays, a team's right if no agreement is reached before March 11. Tom Henke, who pitched half the 1985 season for the Blue Jays and was an instant star, pitched in 1986 for $191,000, including $15,000 in incentives. Fernandez, who had played the whole 1985 season, was paid $320,000 in 1986, $100,000 of it in incentives.

Henke was upset when his contract was renewed. So was his representative, New Jersey lawyer Craig Fenech, who claimed he had never had a client renewed before. They were even more upset when the Blue Jays' contract tendered by the December 20 deadline offered 20 per cent less than his 1986 total, but with the same incentive clauses. It was the maximum allowable pay cut, which can be made either on total salary including incentives or on the base salary and the same incentives as the previous year are offered. It was obviously a bargaining ploy, just to beat the deadline. The Blue Jays were trying to reduce incentive clauses: as the salary offer went up, incentive clauses could be removed in exchange for additional base salary.

Fenech, who also represented pitchers Joe Johnson and John Cerutti, was loudly critical of the Blue Jays' approach. A disappointed Henke decided not to participate in the Blue Jay publicity caravan. He had originally agreed to take part in the third week of the caravan, in southern Ontario and Buffalo, New York. Fenech and Gord Ash, who was negotiating Henke's contract, did not make any progress in telephone conversations. Ash had upped the offer to $200,000, which made no impression on Fenech. Henke said all he wanted was what was fair: the two sides had a different definition of what was fair. Fenech and Henke figured that fairness would be about $400,000, near the major-league average.

Fenech is a bright, chatty person with greyish hair and of medium height. He prides himself on having a good friendship with his clients. He charges 5 per cent "for the whole thing including the tax work." His partner is a financial planner who worked for E.F. Hutton. Fenech's own pitching aspirations were gone by the age of 14. He pitched a two-hitter and then a three-hitter but hurt his elbow so that in his next start he couldn't throw the ball to home plate. He was politically active at Notre Dame University and then went to the University of California at Berkeley, where he was president of the student body in 1970–71. He says he was heavily into politics and describes himself as liberal Democrat, but "I wasn't nuts. I wasn't throwing bricks."

But he defended some people who were – he was student advocate at Berkeley before he became president. "Student advocate is like public defender," he said. "I would go into hearings and they'd have colour film with sound of my client leading the charge up the campus. There was a little girl who looked like butter wouldn't melt in her mouth. On the film, she looked like some crazed, wild-eyed looney."

After working in corporate international trade law for IBM, he became a criminal defence lawyer and public defender. Acting as a player agent, he says, is enjoyable. "It's a people business, and I like that."

He took over Henke when the pitcher was with the Texas Rangers. Billy Sample, an outfielder who then had another representative, left a message on Fenech's answering machine that Henke was looking for an agent. Fenech went to Henke's home town of Taos, Missouri, where the pitcher's off-season job was laying bricks. "It's not hard to find if

282

you know exactly where it is," Fenech said. "There's basically one street and I asked for Tom Henke. And I ran into Tom in town."

He met the family and found out that Henke was not the biggest. "Each one was larger than the one before," he said. "He has a brother Greg who is an awesome physical specimen, the weightlifter type."

Fenech says he operates on a handshake basis with his clients. "I almost never lose a client," he said. "I think it's a natural selection process. I don't wear a lot of gold. I don't take guys to Studio 54 when they hit Manhattan. I don't drive them around in limos. And so I get the guys who are not interested in that kind of thing. Almost invariably we develop what I would call a very close friendship. That's certainly true in Tom's case."

Henke has been seen in a commercial for Aqua Velva. "When they approached me about it, I was very interested," Fenech said. "I want Tom to get exposure on television. We're talking to them about some additional kinds of things now and I hope something will come of it. Certainly the money on endorsements is not nearly as much in Canada as it is in the United States because the market isn't anywhere near as large. But the Toronto Blue Jays are so important to Canadian sports fans. The Blue Jays are a national baseball team in Canada and that makes a guy like Henke more viable as an endorser of products."

The commercial took 13 hours to shoot.

"There was some discussion about what the Aqua Velva man image is and how a married player fit that image, but we worked it out okay," Fenech said. "You'll notice in the commercial, a picture of his family in the locker. And you'll also notice the girl is an autograph-seeker and it's not a pickup. . . . Your reputation is very important. We did not want to convey the wrong impression."

But during the winter Fenech was more concerned about what impression the Blue Jays were leaving with his client. "If he were to be renewed two years in a row, it would not create a happy climate at all," Fenech said. After a four-day holdout at spring training, Henke signed for $291,000, with incentives to a maximum of $50,000. Fernandez was also upset with his offer; but, unlike Henke, he did not sign. Fernandez, who refused to participate in spring-training games until his contract was settled, said he wanted to be traded. On March 10, the club exercised its right to renew his contract. Throughout baseball, there were similar situations. The climate was getting ugly, the players militant.

WHILE PAUL BEESTON AND PAT GILLICK are involved in the major signings, the more publicized aspect of the game, Bob Nicholson, the 32-year-old vice-president for finance, has other concerns as the team gears up for a new season. His duties include protecting against the fluctuation of the Canadian dollar against its U.S. counterpart.

He likes to buy most of the U.S. dollars the Blue Jays need in November, December, or January. When to buy can be crucial. For the 1987 fiscal year, which began in November, 1986, the Blue Jays' revenues in U.S. dollars will be $13.7 million less than their U.S. expenses. When U.S. liabilities from 1986 – about $1.6 million – are taken into consideration (they are not part of the operating budget), Nicholson had to buy a total of $15.3 million U.S. dollars for 1987. But when? "It's like the stock market or anything else, it's very tough to pick the top or the bottom," said the slender, dark-haired graduate from the University of Toronto. He sat in his small office with an aerial photograph of the team's Dunedin spring-training home, Grant Field, on the wall. Outside, a wicked mid-January storm was dumping its payload over a city, snarling traffic.

"People have guessed so wrong on the dollar," Nicholson said. "I just saw some strength in the dollar that from what I've read and my own feeling I can't see continuing. I just assumed that things weren't going to get a lot better and I bought my dollars at the beginning of January."

The dollar strengthened in relation to the U.S. dollar late in January, creeping back up to the 74-cent level, its highest in two years. By February it was up to 75 cents. Nicholson bought about $10 million of his needs between 73 and 71 cents in forward contracts covering February through September. He could have taken a chance, waited for it go higher, but Nicholson's job is to guard against drastic drops.

"There are a number of routes to go," he said. "One is a forward contract, which is usually an obligation that you have to take delivery of X number of U.S. dollars. It's a purchase agreement. I agree to purchase, say, $100,000 U.S. dollars for a quoted rate in Canadian dollars. We specify a month, so our arrangement usually is that we can buy any time during the month, but by the end of the month we have to have completed that contract. I've purchased around $10 million in arrangements like that for 1987. What happens is that it costs you more each month you go out. Today I could buy dollars for a spot rate in the market. Once I want to buy dollars two days down the road or three months down the road, they start charging me a premium. That's why . . . once they start tacking on the little premiums all the way out until September – I've basically purchased out until September – those dollars are suddenly costing me [more]. This year is better than last year. It was comparatively good in 1985. I bought my U.S. dollars at $1.32 (Cdn.). Last year, I bought at $1.40. This year I really bought in the $1.36 to $1.38 range.''

Early in 1986, when the dollar briefly dipped below 70 cents and there were fears it might sink to 65 cents, Nicholson bought at an average rate of just more than 70 cents for the season. They had waited a month before buying, thinking the dollar might rebound. That wait cost $500,000. It might have been offset had the Blue Jays waited longer as the dollar recovered slightly. ''My feeling was that it was going to come back, but it was a big risk to take,'' Nicholson said. ''We're not in the business of speculating on foreign currency rates.''

In 1985 they fared well. The Jays bought in at about 75 cents and the dollar averaged about 73 cents for most of the year.

''One other method of doing it is what they call foreign currency options. We are starting to get serious about using them after our experiences this past year,'' says Nicholson. ''An option is really just an agreement that allows you to purchase dollars at a specific rate. So in the event we had an option to buy a dollar at 73 cents, but the Canadian dollar shot up to 76 cents or 78 cents, then all we'd have to do is let our option expire. We could actually buy the dollars at 78 cents. What it does is protect us on the down side but allows us to benefit from any substantial gain the dollar might experience.''

Nicholson figures that if the Canadian dollar drops one cent against the U.S. dollar it costs the Blue Jays $285,000 for a year (if they had to pay that higher rate for a whole year). If the dollar climbs, there is a similar benefit.

One of the main guidelines, Nicholson said, is the estimated rate in the team's operating budget, which is prepared in October for the next fiscal year.

'' We get input from the bank, from our director Larry Greenwood, and on occasion our board of directors. They've really just established a guideline for us: work out what our total liability is and then about 75 to 80 per cent of that so we're not really exposed to foreign currency fluctuations.''

It's expensive to deal so much in U.S. funds. The net cost to the club is $5.7 million, including any gains on the exchange rate from any U.S. funds they might bring in.

THERE ARE TWO BOTTOM LINES in a sports franchise. One is measured in wins and losses – the Blue Jays have not had a losing season since 1982. The other is that of any other business, dollars and cents. By that measure, 1986 was the Blue Jays' worst season ever despite the second largest home attendance in their history. They lost $3 million.

The problem is that the $14 million revenue the Blue Jays took in from the gates of their home games in 1986 was in Canadian money. Paying most of the team's expenses in U.S. dollars while most revenue is in Canadian money makes the difference between a loss and a profit. Adding to the problem is Exhibition Stadium, where a sellout brings the Blue Jays $250,000 (Cdn.). In Yankee Stadium, a sellout can bring in $400,000 (U.S.).

For the Blue Jays, the final score doesn't necessarily indicate how they have played the game. Most teams in baseball say they have been losing money – even those that deal almost exclusively U.S. dollars. The Blue Jays have been playing the business of baseball well.

The loss in 1986 was not a surprise. Budgeting for a 2.25 million attendance at home, they had figured on a loss of $5 million. In 1985 they had budgeted for a loss of $4 million based on a two-million attendance. But they made the American League playoffs and went seven games, losing $130,000, a break-even season. In 1984, when there was no pennant race, the Blue Jays lost about $1 million.

A rally by the Canadian dollar would be as welcome as a ninth-inning grand slam. But that could not be predicted. What can be predicted is that until the new stadium is ready in 1989, the Blue Jays will have limited gate receipts. A ticket increase might help if attendance holds up, yet the rental agreement with Exhibition Stadium, and taxes, and the 20 per cent to the visiting team combined leave barely more than half the gate receipts with the team. Weather and pennant races make attendance difficult to predict. As 1986 proved, it helps if the team still has a chance to be first in September. The Blue Jays moved within 3½ games of the Red Sox entering September; the boost in attendance prevented more drastic losses.

Paul Beeston, sleeves rolled up and the hair a little ruffled, sipped a coffee from a Styrofoam cup as he looked at the balance sheet. He wasn't ready to accept the ready-made excuses.

"This was a substantial loss year for us," Beeston said. "Nineteen eighty-five could have been, but because we made the playoffs we broke even. It can't be taken lightly. I think we'll be a lot tougher. I don't think there's any doubt about it."

The Blue Jays budgeted for a loss of $2.9 million in 1987, based on a home attendance of 2.3 million and expenditures of $42 million (Cdn.). "If we can't do better than that," Beeston says, "I'm going to be pissed off."

One of the problems, he says, is that most people, including the players, think the losses are bearable because Labatt's makes up for it in beer sales. "Labatt's owns 45 per cent of the club. Clearly Howard Webster doesn't get any offspin from the Blue Jays' winning. Quite clearly the bank doesn't get any offshoot from us winning. When we lost in 1979 and 1980, Labatt's market share was around 42 per cent. When we're winning it's around 42 per cent. The big thing was the twistoff cap. No matter how many home runs these guys hit, how many no-hitters they can pitch, the twistoff cap outshone them. Labatt's has a vat full of beer, not a vat full of money.

"We have some responsibility. Our salaries have never gone down. In most industries that's natural. But in most industries, they don't go up to the tune of 30 and 40 per cent a year for the same 24 guys."

Beeston looked down at the totals in Canadian and U.S. funds – there is a foreign exchange adjustment at the bottom of the column. It showed that in 1986 the Blue Jays had revenue of about $37 million. Besides the $14 million from the gate at Exhibition Stadium, which is 38 per cent of the team's income, the Blue Jays took in $2.3 million (U.S.) from road games and $3.6 million from "other income sources," most of which was from exchange on U.S. dollars.

Spring training income was $175,000. The Blue Jays' Canadian radio and television rights brought them $9 million, an area in which the Blue Jays do comparatively well financially. Of that, $850,000 was from radio. From the major league's central fund, the Blue Jays took in $4.5 million (U.S.), mostly from the network television deals, the rest from licensing and promotions done through major-league baseball. Concessions, publications, and promotions earned $2.7 million.

Licensing fees for use of the Blue Jay logo brought in $250,000; but licensing is a time-consuming job. "You have to respond to all requests," says Paul Markle, the club's marketing director. "You really got to discourage many of them because their item isn't a good one. . . . If it is a good item, we'll endeavour to license them with the office of registration in Ottawa. It's an arduous procedure but it's necessary."

If the Blue Jays think an item can sell, they want 7 to 8 per cent of the wholesale price as a royalty, sometimes half up front as a guarantee. "We probably have a couple of hundred items licensed and about 60 companies," Markle says.

It could be lucrative if the Blue Jays made it to the World Series. During the "Drive of '85" – Markle's slogan – when they won the American League East, the guarantees and royalties amounted to about $50,000. "That's over a very short month," Markle says. "I would say that during the playoffs we just scratched the surface. If the Blue Jays . . . got into the World Series it would have just gone crazy."

The operation of the major-league team cost $21.1 million (Cdn.). The major expense was $13.3 million (U.S.) for major-league player salaries. Add in the salaries and benefits of the manager, coaches, and the training staff and the total comes to about $13.9 million (U.S.).

Travel costs about $1.1 million (Cdn.). Supplies, uniforms, medical, and insurance of contracts comes to $520,000. The total foreign exchange on the operation of the major-league team costs the Blue Jays $5,723,000.

Running the Florida operation in Dunedin, which includes the major-league and minor-league spring training, the Instructional League, and maintaining the facility costs nearly $1.6 million. It costs $4.5 million to run the minor-league system – player salaries, managers, coaches, office staff, trainers, supplies, uniforms, and money paid the teams. Of that total $1.1 million is for U.S. exchange.

Scouting costs another $2.1 million: $800,000 in salaries, $600,000 in expenses, and $100,000 for the scouting bureau. Foreign exchange costs $528,000.

Operating Exhibition Stadium costs the Blue Jays $3.65 million, which includes the ground crew, game staff, medical staff for games, security police. The big cost is the rent – $1,148,000. But as Beeston points out, "That doesn't include the 25-cent head tax, nor does it include the 10 per cent we pay on concessions, so our total rent last year would have been in excess of $3 million."

Cleaning the stadium costs $570,000. "This may be the cleanest stadium you'll ever be in," Beeston said.

Utilities, including lights, cost $145,000.

The ticket operation – tickets, sellers, mail-order plans, mailing the season tickets, the gifts that are given to subscribers – costs $1.1 million. For the four previous seasons the Blue Jays sent their subscribers a ball autographed by one player. "We sent out an autographed colour picture this time."

The players are paid $3 for each picture or baseball they autograph. They might each do 150 such autographs.

The marketing budget is $1.3 million. Television and newspaper advertising is about $400,000. Giveaway days cost $400,000, but the fee charged the sponsors of these days assures they break even. (In fact, the Jays made about $43,000 on giveaway days in 1986.) It costs in excess of $100,000 to send out the season-ticket brochures, which for 1987 included a collection of action photographs from Blue Jay games, suitable for framing. "We don't need to send out a season ticket brochure," Beeston said. "All we have to do is to send out a renewal form. But that's not the way the Blue Jay style was set up in 1977. There are certain good things about it that have to be maintained."

The public relations budget of $231,000 covers salaries, the media guide, photographs, office supplies, and transportation.

General administrative expenses are $2.5 million. They include executive salaries, accounting and office staff, and executive travel, about $300,000. Another $327,000 is spent on legal and auditing expenses and interest. From October until money starts coming in from season tickets in February, the team runs on a line of credit from the bank. The total cost of baseball operations is $29.2 million. Business operating expenses, stadium operation, tickets, marketing, and public relations come to about $8.6 million.

The cost of amateur bonuses came to $548,000 (U.S.) and the cost of acquiring player contracts was $26,000 (U.S.). With foreign exchange that comes to about $800,000 (Cdn.). That produces a net loss of $1.9 million. Amortization was $619,000 and depreciation was $500,000.

Total loss: $3 million.

"It's not the intent of this office, or this ball club, or this management team to ever see one bigger than that," Beeston said. "Our goal this year is to get it down to under a million-dollar loss. Hopefully in 1988 we can get into a profit of $1. That's where we would like to be."

A break-even year, even a profit, before the team has moved to the new stadium? Beeston hunched forward in his chair, set the balance sheet on his cluttered desk. The cigar had become a misshapen butt by now. "It's going to be difficult. We're going to have to be creative.

We have to watch our expenses. Our revenue is going up, there's no doubt about that. It's not likely that we can do it, but it's possible. I think we are starting to get a handle on it.''

THE ONE WAY TO MAKE IT POSSIBLE is a World Series in Toronto in the funny little stadium that in January looks more like a venue for an event at the Winter Olympics: cold and silvery. Beeston tossed the empty coffee cup into the wastepaper basket just below the Oscar sign. He took the wrapper off a cigar. A World Series in Toronto? He seemed delighted at the prospect. The clap of laughter reverberated through the office, wound its way out into the corridors, and landed somewhere in Section 51.